PUBLIS___

MW01223778

Construction Delay Claims
Third Edition

by Barry B. Bramble and Michael T. Callahan

Construction Delay Claims, Third Edition, provides thorough coverage of delay and impact claims. The authors explain different types of delay, how delays occur, and the defects of delay. Practical information is provided on what to do when delays occur and how to process claims for delay. Information on using the schedule to prove delay and establishing liability for delay is also included. Construction Delay Claims discusses how damages are calculated; what types of clauses to include in the construction contract concerning scheduling, delays, and impacts; and how project delays arise under the various project delivery methods. In addition, a number of chapters are devoted to impact claims disruption, lost labor productivity, and acceleration. Construction Delay Claims is a significant resource for those involved in the management and measurement of time, containing at-a-glance charts and checklists as well as over 1,500 cases.

Highlights of the 2004 Cumulative Supplement

The following developments and issues are included in the 2004 Cumulative Supplement:

- When contract does not include a start date, parole evidence of the party's agreement to a project state date is considered.

- A third type of differing site conditions claim — unanticipated and unknown hazardous material encountered at the project site.

- Granting a time extension subsequent to a contractor delay also waives the owner's right to use the delay to justify terminating the contractor for failing to progress.

- An owner need not perform a delay analysis in order to collect additional time costs to complete after a default termination.

- New York case law continues to hold that contractors are not liable to subcontractors in the event that delays arise from circumstances outside the contractor's control, including the acts of the owner.

- The contractor is responsible for the time needed to develop plans that comply with a performance contract's terms.

- Release of lien in payment application does not bar a delay and acceleration claim.

- A contractor that does not credit the portion of project delay for which it is responsible was not entitled to recover damages on its claim of lost productivity and extended home office overhead.

- If the contractor continues to progress the work in any substantial manner, there has been no standby sufficient to support home office overhead claims.

The Table of Cases is also updated to reflect all changes to the text.

10/03

For questions concerning this shipment, billing, or other customer service matters, call our Customer Service Department at 1-800-234-1660.

For toll-free ordering, please call 1-800-638-8437.

A WoltersKluwer Company

CONSTRUCTION DELAY CLAIMS

2004 Cumulative Supplement

This supplement supersedes all previous supplements.

CONSTRUCTION DELAY CLAIMS

Third Edition

2004 Cumulative Supplement

BARRY B. BRAMBLE

MICHAEL T. CALLAHAN

1185 Avenue of the Americas, New York, NY 10036
www.aspenpublishers.com

This publication is designed to provide accurate and authoritative information in regard to the subject matter covered. It is sold with the understanding that the publisher is not engaged in rendering legal, accounting, or other professional services. If legal advice or other professional advice is required, the services of a competent professional person should be sought.

—From a *Declaration of Principles* jointly adopted
by a Committee of the American Bar Association
and a Committee of Publishers and Associations

Printed in the United States of America

1 2 3 4 5 6 7 8 9 0

ISBN 0-7355-0548-9
ISBN 0-7355-4230-9 (supplement)

About Aspen Publishers

Aspen Publishers, headquartered in New York City, is a leading information provider for attorneys, business professionals, and law students. Written by preeminent authorities, our products consist of analytical and practical information covering both U.S. and international topics. We publish in the full range of formats, including updated manuals, books, periodicals, CDs, and online products.

Our proprietary content is complemented by 2,500 legal databases, containing over 11 million documents, available through our Loislaw division. Aspen Publishers also offers a wide range of topical legal and business databases linked to Loislaw's primary material. Our mission is to provide accurate, timely, and authoritative content in easily accessible formats, supported by unmatched customer care.

To order any Aspen Publishers title, go to *www.aspenpublishers.com* or call 1-800-638-8437.

To reinstate your manual update service, call 1-800-638-8437.

For more information on Loislaw products, go to *www.loislaw.com* or call 1-800-364-2512.

For Customer Care issues, e-mail CustomerCare@aspenpublishers.com; call 1-800-234-1660; or fax 1-800-901-9075.

Aspen Publishers
A Wolters Kluwer Company

SUBSCRIPTION NOTICE

This Aspen Publishers product is updated on a periodic basis with supplements to reflect important changes in the subject matter. If you purchased this product directly from Aspen Publishers, we have already recorded your subscription for the update service.

If, however, you purchased this product from a bookstore and wish to receive future updates and revised or related volumes billed separately with a 30-day examination review, please contact our Customer Service Department at 1-800-234-1660, or send your name, company name (if applicable), address, and the title of the product to:

ASPEN PUBLISHERS
7201 McKinney Circle
Frederick, MD 21704

CONTENTS

PREFACE

This 2004 supplement is the most comprehensive update we have so far prepared in the three editions of *Construction Delay Claims*. Included herein is a detailed evaluation of state law concerning a contractor's pass-through of subcontractor claims to an owner in *Interstate Contracting Corp. v. City of Dallas, Texas*. *Interstate* also reproduced part of a liquidation agreement that may be useful for a practitioner's future reference. Also included is a detailed explanation of when a contractor is on standby by the Federal Circuit in *P.J. Dick, Inc. v. Principi*.

The *P.J. Dick* decision also reminds all the players that delay is to be calculated by the method required in the contract, regardless of any party-agreement to use a different, perhaps more economical, method to do so. One has to wonder how much risks on remand the parties undertake that they will collect nothing for using a more convenient method to measure delay, just like those who refuse to make any delay evaluation. This was again illustrated in *Net Construction v. C&C Rehab and Construction, Inc.*, which is also in this year's supplement.

Overall this year's supplement adds some 35 new case citations that both tweak and detail case law on delay and the resulting additional performance costs. No doubt our courts and boards will provide us more opportunity for the next supplement as well.

September 2003

BARRY B. BRAMBLE
Cherry Hill, New Jersey
barry.bramble@jrknowles.com

MICHAEL T. CALLAHAN
Overland Park, Kansas
cclcc@ix.netcom.com

CONSTRUCTION DELAY CLAIMS

2004 Cumulative Supplement

CHAPTER 1
DELAY

§ 1.01   WHAT IS DELAY?

[A]   Excusable and Nonexcusable Delays

Page 1-6, add after note 33 in carryover paragraph:

In some instances, however, a supplier's delays may be excusable for the prime contractor when the owner is found to have assumed a risk of the manufacturing process. For example, in *Carter Steel & Fabricating Co. v. Ohio Department of Transportation,* 721 N.E.2d 1115 (Ohio Ct. Cl. 1999), the owner specified that a domestic supplier be the source of the structural steel. Only one domestic supplier was capable of complying with the specifications. During the course of performance, the steel components made by the supplier were rejected by the erection subcontractor for defects in fabrication, and late delivery of conforming steel was the cause of 46 calendar days of delay to project completion. The owner assessed liquidated damages of $600 a day to the prime contractor for delay. In considering the matter, the Ohio Court of Claims reasoned that because of the restrictive specifications, there was no opportunity to use another manufacturer to fabricate the steel. The supplier's fabrication delays were deemed beyond the control and without the fault of the prime contractor and its erection subcontractor, and the assessment of liquidated damages was held to be improper.

Page 1-8, add after note 43 in first full paragraph:

Whether a particular delay is excusable or nonexcusable may depend upon whether the contractor assumes the risk of delay by taking actions, even though the actions are permissible under the contract. For example, in *Appeal of D&L Construction Co.,* AGBCA No. 97-205 00-2 B.C.A. (CCH) ¶ 31,001 (2000), the government designated three sources of aggregate in the contract documents for the required road work, and provided for a seven-day approval of the contractor's pit development plan. In tendering its bid, the contractor planned to obtain the aggregate from a nondesignated area. The government rejected the contractor's borrow pit, and the government and contractor negotiated the approval of another source. However, this took longer than seven days, and the contractor claimed that it caused delays in performance. The Board ruled that because the contractor proposed a source different from the borrow pit areas designated in the contract documents, it assumed the risk of the delay in approval.

1

[B] Compensable and Noncompensable Delays

Page 1-10, add to note 70:

However, when determining a subcontractor's recovery under a Miller Act bond, a contractor and its payment bond surety may be obligated for another party's delays as long as the contractor was the primary cause of the project's delay. *See* Consol. Elec. & Mech., Inc. v. Biggs Gen. Contracting, Inc., 167 F.3d 432 (1999); see also **§ 15.02**.

[C] Critical and Noncritical Delays

Page 1-14, add after carryover paragraph:

In *Morrison Knudsen Corp. v. Fireman's Fund Insurance Co.,* 175 F.3d 1221 (10th Cir. 1999), Morrison Knudsen Corporation (MK), a federal contractor, terminated its subcontractor, Ground Improvement Techniques (GIT), for an alleged default and sued GIT for damages. GIT counterclaimed for wrongful termination. A jury found the termination wrongful and awarded GIT roughly half the damages claimed.

The United States Department of Energy hired MK in 1983 to manage its Uranium Mill Tailing Remedial Action (UMTA) project, a cleanup of radioactive mill tailings at sites around the country. MK subcontracted with GIT in March 1995 to clean up the Slick Rock, Colorado site. GIT hired several lower-tier subcontractors. The MK-GIT subcontract obligated GIT to complete the project by December 1996. The contractor's default-termination clause incorporated essentially verbatim the standard federal Default clause for fixed-price construction contracts. The Clause allowed MK to terminate GIT if the work had been delayed, not for excusable reasons, but by GIT's lack of diligence. The contract price was roughly $9.3 million. The project did not go well. GIT and its subs encountered delays, difficulties, and increased costs. GIT attributed these to MK's defective specifications, failure to secure permits in a timely fashion, rigid interpretations of specifications and safety requirements, and propensity to reject proposed work plans. During the contractor's performance, GIT requested extra compensation and extensions of time because of delays to, changes in, and increased costs of the work which GIT attributed to MK. GIT's central theory was that its plan to complete the project before the deadline displeased MK, which could not then earn the maximum possible fees from DOE. MK, in GIT's view, thus sought to hinder and delay the work. MK, on the other hand, attributed the delays and increased costs to errors, omissions, and delinquencies by GIT and its subcontractors.

In September 1995, MK terminated GIT for default. The contract allowed MK to do so if GIT was not diligently prosecuting the work to ensure its timely completion. At the same time, MK sued GIT for damages caused by its alleged default. In challenging the termination, GIT claimed that it had been entitled to extensions of time for various "excusable delays" under the subcontract.

MK asserted that the court erred in denying a proposed jury instruction. The proposed instruction specified that, in order to prove a delay "excusable" under the contract, GIT had to show both that something beyond its control delayed part of its work, and that the problem would delay completion of the entire project. The court's instruction #18, "Contractual Excuse of Delays," told the jury that for each claim of excusable delay, GIT had the burden to prove that it met the subcontract requirements for excusable delay. The instruction noted that the subcontract requirements for establishing an excusable delay were explained in instruction #22. Instruction #22, in turn, concerned "GIT's Counterclaim for Extra Work, Delays and Acceleration—Essential Elements." That instruction told the jury what GIT had to prove in order to recover damages on its delay claims. It required GIT to show that something beyond its control or fault, and unauthorized by the contract, had delayed its work; that it had notified MK, and that MK had refused to allow GIT the additional time necessary to complete the work.

MK argued that a contractor was not entitled to an excusable delay unless it proved both that the delay was on the project's critical path and that it would delay completion of the entire project. MK thus asserted that the court erred in refusing to instruct the jury on the element of criticality. GIT responded that MK had not identified any part of the contract or any cases using the terms "critical path" or "criticality" or mandating jury instructions on those terms. Alternatively, GIT claimed that the instructions as a whole were sufficient. MK did not claim that the contract expressly referred to the critical path or required that excusable delays affect the project's overall completion. It argued instead that the latter requirement was a well-established rule of federal-contracting law.

The appellate court found MK's description of federal-contracting law correct. The court referred to a leading treatise that explained that "a contractor is not entitled to relief upon the mere occurrence of an event that qualifies as an excusable delay. The contractor must show that the event caused delay to the overall completion of the contract." A subsection of that treatise entitled "Delay of Overall Completion Required" discussed the case law establishing that a contractor "is not entitled to an excusable delay unless it can prove that the time lost delayed the completion of the job. It is not sufficient to establish that some work was prevented; the work prevented must be work that will delay the overall completion of the job."

MK's proposed instruction comprehensibly conveyed the requirement that a contractor must prove that a delay affected not just an isolated part of a project, but its overall completion, by explaining that GIT had to prove that:

> the delay was a "critical delay." A critical delay is one which would delay not just the particular activity at issue, but the overall completion date of the work. Many activities may be performed on a project at any time without any effect on the completion of the project. A delay in such non-critical activities will not delay the project overall and cannot constitute an excusable delay. Only delays to activities on the critical path—activities with no leeway in the schedule—may give rise to excusable delay.

The appellate court concluded that MK's proposed instruction accurately stated an applicable rule of law which the trial court's instructions did not expressly state.

GIT argued that any error in defining "excusable delay" was irrelevant, as it was not behind schedule at all. At trial, MK neither argued that GIT's "excusable delays" did not cause overall delay, nor asserted that it did. MK never asserted a link between the legal argument and the outcome in the dispute, stating that any error in omitting the issue from the instruction was purely technical. After carefully comparing the court's instructions, taken as a whole, with MK's proposed instruction, the appellate court concluded that the district court's description of the law, while not faultless, was not reversibly erroneous.

[D] Concurrent Delays

Page 1-23, add at end of section:

Another type of concurrent delay has recently been labeled a "pacing delay." Pacing delays occur when one party makes a conscious decision to decelerate or slow down the pace of noncritical activities to keep pace with the critical delays of another party. A more formal definition would be:

> . . . deceleration of the work of the project, by one of the parties to a contract, due to a delay caused by the other party, so as to maintain steady progress with the revised overall project schedule.

Zack, *Pacing Delays—The Practical Effect,* Construction Specifier 47, 48 (Jan. 2000). Any party to the construction process may decide to slow down its performance of noncritical activities to keep pace with the delayed progress. For example, contractors may adjust the pace of their work in light of delays in owner-furnished equipment, delays by other multiple prime contractors, delays in permits, limited access, or differing site conditions. Owners may slow down their response time to requests for information or submittals, or postpone the delivery of owner-furnished equipment, or the processing of change orders. *Id.* at 48.

Concepts similar to pacing delays have been considered by courts, which generally hold that the party not causing the delay has the right to slow down work when faced with delays caused by another party. For example, Boards of Contract Appeals have explicitly stated that "the contractor is not necessarily required to conduct all of his other activities exactly according to his predelay schedule," *John Driggs Co.,* ENG B.C.A. No. 4926, 87-2 B.C.A. (CCH) ¶ 19,833 (1987). Also, "where the government causes delays to the critical path, it is permissible for the contractor to relax its performance of its work to the extent that it does not impact the project completion date." *Utley-James, Inc.,* GSBCA No. 5370, 85-1 B.C.A. (CCH) ¶ 17,816 (1985), *aff'd, Utley-James, Inc. v. United States,* 14 Cl. Ct. 804 (1988).

The party slowing its performance risks that the other party will not suddenly resolve its delay. The slow down will then become a critical delay or a concurrently critical delay. If such a case arises, the decelerating party may become liable for the impact of its decision to slow down the pace of its performance.

§ 1.03 WHAT IS DISRUPTION?

Page 1-25, add before first paragraph:

Disruption is an activity-specific loss of productivity caused by changes in the working conditions under which that activity was performed. Disruption is a material alteration in the performance conditions that were expected at the time of bid, resulting in increased cost of performance. Lost productivity is a classic result of disruption, because in the end more labor and equipment hours will be required to do the same work.

Delay and disruption are different types of damages. Disruption damages can be traced to specific activities; delay damages cannot. Delay damages are caused only by delays either to the overall contract or to project completion; disruption damages are caused by changes in working conditions that can occur regardless of whether the project's completion date changes. The absence of delay does not preclude the finding of disruption, and the absence of delay damage does not preclude the finding of disruption damages.

CHAPTER 2
ADDRESSING DELAY AND DISRUPTION IN THE CONTRACT

§ 2.02   TIME IS OF THE ESSENCE CLAUSE

Page 2-4, add after first paragraph:

Despite the frequent use of "time is of the essence of this contract" in construction contracts, it is not entirely clear what the phrase does or should mean. Corbin indicated that a time is of the essence clause means that "one who does not perform in full the promised performance, within the exact time specified in the contract, cannot maintain any action at law for the enforcement of the return promise." *Corbin on Contracts* § 37.1 (rev. ed. 1999). Without any other clause in the contract indicating otherwise, this means that if a designer or contractor is a day late completing its plans or building, the owner need not pay and can terminate the contract. The existence of a liquidated damages clause may well indicate that time is not of the essence (despite boilerplate to the contrary) and, therefore, that untimely completion will not relieve the owner of its obligations to pay for work done or to be completed. S. Barat & J. Bobotek, *Time Is of the Essence: Be Careful What You Ask For,* 36 Procurement Law. 10, at 10–11 (no. 1, Fall 2000) (hereinafter Barat & Bobotek).

Page 2-4, add after second to last sentence of second full paragraph:

A subcontractor is not required to honor a "time is of the essence" clause in a subcontract that is not included in its bid documents. In *Lichtenberg Construction & Development, Inc. v. Paul W. Wilson, Inc.*, 2001 Ohio App. LEXIS 4372 (2001), Lichtenberg Construction & Development relied on a bid offered by Paul W. Wilson, Inc. when submitting its own bid on a construction project. After Lichtenberg was awarded the general contract, Wilson refused to sign Lichtenberg's proposed subcontract because it contained objectionable terms, including a time is of the essence clause that required completion under a strict time schedule. Wilson claimed that Lichtenberg had refused to negotiate the disputed terms. Lichtenberg eventually hired another subcontractor to complete the work, paying it $22,500 more than Wilson's bid. Lichtenberg sued Wilson for the additional cost it had incurred. Another subcontractor who had been in the business in the Cincinnati area for the past 25 years testified that, although a general time is of the essence clause was standard language in a subcontract, the practice was for a general contractor and a subcontractor to negotiate the time schedule for completion of the work. Further, if a general contractor was adamant that work had to be completed within a strictly limited time, and refused to negotiate, then the subcontractor simply did not sign the contract. Finally, the other subcontractor testified that if a general contractor knew in advance that a strict time schedule was necessary, it would request the subcontractor reserve a specific period of time in its schedule to work on the project. Based on the industry customs in Cincinnati, the trial court determined that the time is of the essence clause was unreasonable and dismissed Lichtenberg's claim with prejudice. The contractor appealed. Lichtenberg argued that there was insufficient evidence to support a finding that the terms of the time is of the essence clause was unreasonable.

Evidence supported the trial court's finding that the time is of the essence clause, which required Wilson to adhere to a strict time schedule for completion of its work, was a term that Wilson would not have reasonably expected to be included in the subcontract. The strict time schedule was not included in the bid specifications that Wilson had reviewed prior to submitting its bid to Lichtenberg, and Wilson had no reason to expect that an inflexible time schedule would be included in the subcontract. If the time schedule for performance of the work had been included in the bidding specifications, Wilson would have been obligated to honor its bid.

Page 2-4, add after second full paragraph:

In *Bucher v. Schmidt,* 2002 Ohio 3933, 2002 Ohio App. LEXIS 4064 (2002), Bucher agreed to lease a section of its building to Schmidt (lessee). As a wholesale grocer, the lessee required the leased space to be dry, secure and heated to store food. The owner drafted the lease. The owner was to make certain repairs before the lessee moved in. The owner intended the improvements to be completed by May 1, 1994, so that the lessee would be able to occupy the building and operate a business. The owner knew that occupying the building on time was important to the lessee, and it was noted in the lease agreement, which stated, "It is understood and agreed between the parties hereto that time is of the essence of this contract and applies to all terms and conditions herein." The owner contracted with Findlay Plumbing and Heating to perform the repairs required under the lease. While the plumber's work progressed, the lessee contacted the owner and the plumber numerous times to express concerns regarding the progress of improvements and asking when it could occupy the building. The lessee was unable to occupy the building because the improvements were not completed and the building had not received an approval for occupancy. On June 9, 1994, the lessee rescinded the lease. The owner filed a complaint alleging breach of the lease agreement and seeking damages. The lessee counterclaimed to recover its security deposit, first month's rent, and additional damages. The trial court dismissed the owner's complaint and ruled in favor of the lessee in the amount of $3,600. On appeal, the owner asserted that the lessee waived the "time is of the essence" clause as it pertained to occupancy by May 1, 1994. The lessee knew the renovations would take time to complete, and it repeatedly telephoned the owner and the plumber expressing its dissatisfaction with the pace of the renovation work. There was no evidence that the lessee waived the time was of the essence clause. The judgment was affirmed.

Page 2-5, add after first sentence in first paragraph:

Exceptions to enforcing a time is of the essence clause seek to ameliorate the effects of the clause, but make its application unpredictable. Some courts, invoking their general equitable powers, will refuse to enforce a time is of the essence clause if it would unjustly penalize one party or result in a forfeiture. Other courts will carefully examine the facts to determine if a party has waived its right to insist on strict adherence to contractual time limits. Barat & Bobotek, at 11.

Page 2-5, add at end of section:

In light of the delays inherent in construction and the uncertainty about how a time is of the essence clause will be enforced, parties should carefully weigh whether to include one that applies equally to all parties' obligations. In a very busy construction market, an owner may not want to arm a contractor with an argument that it can terminate the contract immediately if the owner is late in making a payment or in providing construction documents to the contractor. Similarly, in a slow construction market, the contractor may not want to give an owner the opportunity to terminate the contract if a milestone date is missed by a day. Barat & Bobotek, at 11.

The parties may be better served simply by stating in plain terms what they mean to accomplish. If the parties decide that the contract is terminable upon the owner's failure to pay on a date certain, they should express this concept in the contract. If the parties decide that the contract is terminable if the contractor does not achieve substantial completion by a date certain, they should include a provision governing milestone dates, grace and cure periods, and the remedies for failure to achieve such dates. Such specific language will benefit both parties should a dispute arise over timely performance or payment. Barat & Bobotek, at 11.

§ 2.03   CONTRACT PERFORMANCE PERIOD

Page 2-9, add after note 14 in carryover paragraph:

Once the parties agree that the contract duration is reasonable, only the administrative procedures in the contract may adjust time or cost. Delayed completion is to be addressed by either the time extension clause or the change order clause. A court may review a disputed time extension or a disputed change order, but not a party's earlier agreement that the duration is reasonable absent fraud, duress, and other similar unconscionable situations. For example, in *Fuschino v. Smith,* 2001 Ohio App. LEXIS 21 (2001), Fuschino brought an action against Smith, the contractor, for the contractor's failure to timely complete an outdoor deck. The contract stated that time was of the essence, and that the work was to be substantially completed as certified by the architect. The contract further specified that any change in the contract completion date shall be made only by written change order. The contract also stated that by executing the agreement, the contractor confirmed that the contract time was a reasonable period for performing the work. On the date of the contract's required completion, the deck was not finished and had not been certified as substantially complete by the architect. The contractor did not seek any change order to extend the time for performance. Although the contractor testified that there were a few weather days, there was no testimony that the weather was unusual or that it prevented timely completion of the project.

The trial court found that the failure to timely complete the deck by the deadline did not constitute a material breach of the contract. It further found that the contractor had substantially completed the job, and that the delay in completion was excused by weather, plan changes, and employment disputes. The trial court also found that the completion date specified in the contract was not reasonable. The trial court entered judgment against the owner.

On appeal, the owner contended that the trial court erred when it found that the contractor's failure to complete the project in a timely manner was excusable and did not breach the contract. According to the appellate court, because the parties had agreed that the contract performance period was reasonable, and that the agreement was clear and unambiguous, the trial court had no authority to substitute its judgment regarding whether the time set was reasonable. It appeared reasonably likely that the work could have been timely completed if a sufficient number of competent workers had worked steadily on the job. The appellate court wondered whether the contractor had underbid the job. Employment problems or plan changes that excused the delay could have been dealt with by a change order extending the time for performance. The contractor breached the terms of the contract by failing to substantially complete the work within the time specified. If there were doubts about whether the performance period was reasonable, the best action was either to strike the part of the agreement that stated the duration was reasonable before signing the contract or to avoid either bidding on or negotiating for the project.

[A]   Commencement of Contract Time

[2]   Notice to Proceed

Page 2-13, add after note 36 in first full paragraph:

or repudiation. In *Anderson Excavating & Wrecking Company v. Sanitary Improvement District No. 177*, 265 Neb. 61, 654 N.W.2d 376 (S. Ct. 2002), Sanitary Improvement District No. 177 (SID) sought bids for a seawall construction and dredging project. The project involved erecting seawalls around three islands in a boating lake and dredging the lake to make it more uniform in depth. The plans called for the dredged material to be disposed of on the three islands. After receiving bids, the SID split the project into two contracts and phases of work. Phase I of the project involved the construction of the seawalls and was awarded to Big River Construction. Anderson Excavating & Wrecking Company was awarded Phase II of the project, which involved the dredging of the lake. Anderson was concerned before the contract was signed that the seawalls would not be able to hold the weight of the dredged material. The "Agreement" portion of the contract documents provided:

> The CONTRACTOR for the Seawall Construction shall commence work on the seawall within thirty (30) days after Notice of Award and shall complete the seawall on one island within twenty (20) working days. All seawall construction shall be completed by April 30, 1993. The CONTRACTOR for the lake dredging shall commence operations immediately upon completion of the seawall on the first island and shall complete all dredging and seeding operations on or before May 28, 1993.

The "Supplementary Conditions" portion of the contract documents provided that "the Contract Times will commence to run on the day indicated in the Notice to Proceed. In no event will the Notice to Proceed be issued later than six months after the Bid opening."

There were delays in the progress of Big River Construction's work. A change order modified the contract to read: "The CONTRACTOR for the lake dredging shall commence operation after September 7, 1993, and shall complete all dredging and seeding operations on or before May 1, 1994." A dispute arose between Anderson and the SID about Anderson's ability to place the dredged material on the islands. A meeting was held on August 19, 1993 to discuss the problem. Three options were discussed at the meeting: (1) issuance of a change order to allow additional payment to Anderson, (2) termination of the contract without financial liability to either party, and (3) execution of the work by Anderson according to Anderson's interpretation of the contract.

On August 24, 1993, Anderson wrote:

> To prepare the islands for placement of dredged materials will cost approximately $27,000.00. If the S.I.D. is prepared to issue a Change Order to that effect Anderson will begin as agreed. However, if the S.I.D. is unwilling to issue the Change Order, then there appears to be only two other alternatives.
>
> First, they could rebid the dredging portion of the contract, and include the areas left unaddressed such as the island preparation. In this case Anderson would be willing to relinquish all rights under this contract without any further expense to the S.I.D., provided that the performance and payment bonds are returned . . . .

The second alternative required all parties to prepare for litigation and rely upon the judicial system for determination. Should this become necessary, Anderson was also prepared to exercise this alternative. The SID did not terminate the contract, but behaved as if there was a contract still in place after the August 24, 1993, letter was received. Anderson never commenced work on the dredging project, and SID did not demand that work be commenced. On December 20, 1996, Anderson brought suit against the SID alleging that (1) the SID refused to go forward with the contract or to sign a proposed change order to the contract about the responsibility for the preparation of the islands, (2) the SID abandoned and breached the contract, and (3) Anderson incurred expenses in preparing to begin work on the contract, including costs incurred for insurance and performance bonds. Anderson's petition alleged a cause of action for breach of contract seeking lost profits, and expenses for preparation for work on the project. The SID denied the allegations and alleged that Anderson had breached and abandoned the contract.

The SID moved for summary judgment. The district court granted the motion and dismissed Anderson's petition, and Anderson appealed. The Nebraska Court of Appeals determined that there were genuine issues of material fact preventing summary judgment on the issue of Anderson's reliance on the contract and reversed, and remanded. On remand, the SID moved for partial summary judgment on the breach of contract cause of action, arguing that the Court of Appeals' decision determined that there were issues of fact only on the "detrimental reliance" cause of action. The district court granted the motion. After a bench trial, the court determined that Anderson had repudiated the contract when it sent the August 24, 1993, letter demanding a change order or that the project be rebid and threatening litigation. The court determined that the unilateral repudiation of the contract precluded any equitable claims for recovery or for breach of contract. The court dismissed the petition. Anderson appealed.

Anderson was neither sent a "notice to proceed" nor was it sent a notice that the contract had been terminated. Anderson also provided evidence that a notice to proceed was different from a change order. The SID, however, claimed that the change order fulfilled the notice-to-proceed requirement in the contract because it set a date fixing the date on which work would begin under the contract. The SID failed to generate a notice to proceed for Anderson to begin work. Anderson contended that the district court erred by failing to find that the SID was in breach of the contract by failing to issue a notice to proceed and by delaying Anderson's performance of the contract. When Anderson repudiated the contract, the SID was excused from performing the condition of issuing a notice to proceed and was excused from performing any of its contractual duties. The judgment was affirmed.

Page 2-14, add after first full paragraph:

Although an industry custom, a preconstruction meeting is not a prerequisite to starting work unless required by the contract. In *Program & Construction Management Group, Inc. v. Davis,* 246 F.3d 1363 (Fed. Cir. 2001), the contractor argued that the project was delayed as a result of the owner's late preconstruction meeting. The General Services Administration contracted to upgrade the heating, ventilation, and air conditioning of the cafeteria, kitchen, and other facilities in a government building. The contractor submitted a delay claim to the contracting officer. The contractor argued that the government did not schedule a preconstruction meeting shortly after issuing the notice to proceed, but instead waited 46 days before holding one. It asserted that it could not proceed with the work until the preconstruction meeting was held. Nothing in the contract, however, required a preconstruction meeting. Regardless of whether there was an industry custom to hold a meeting shortly after issuance of the notice to proceed, a preconstruction meeting was not a prerequisite to the start of work. If the contractor believed a preconstruction meeting was necessary, it should have undertaken to initiate the process by contacting the contracting officer. The time between the issuance of the notice to proceed and the convening of a preconstruction conference did not establish compensable delay to the contractor. The General Services Administration was not responsible for the contractor's erroneous impression that a preconstruction meeting was required to be held before the contractor could start work at the site.

Page 2-15, add at end of subsection:

When a contract does not include a start date, the parties may agree to a project start. Consider *Missouri Department of Transportation v. Safeco Insurance Company of America*, 2002 Mo. App. LEXIS 1761 (2002) (opinion withdrawn). Robertson Contractors, Inc. was the general contractor, and PR Developers, Inc. (PRD) was the subcontractor for the base rock and paving for the construction of a bridge, embankments, ramps and roadways at the interchange of an interstate highway for the Missouri Highway and Transportation Commission (MHTC). The contract provided that Robertson would have 130 working days to complete the Project, starting from March 15, 1999. The subcontract stated that time was of the essence, but did not specify a start date. After the subcontract was signed, Robertson told PRD to prepare to begin its work on March 15, 1999. PRD verbally agreed to this starting date, expecting to be done within 80 working days. PRD had indicated that it would like to start work on the west side of the Project. PRD was not able to begin its work until the end of May 1999, and had to begin work on the east side of the Project, a delay of approximately 50 working days. PRD filed suit against Robertson for breach of contract. The jury returned verdicts in favor of PRD on its claims, and awarded damages for delay of $1,581,192.50 against Robertson and $74,810.16 for non-delay damages.

On appeal, Robertson contended that there was not sufficient competent evidence that Robertson made the specific promises to have the job site ready for PRD to proceed by March 15, 1999. PRD repeatedly testified that Robertson wanted PRD ready to start work on the Project on March 15, 1999. After PRD signed the subcontract, PRD was told to begin its work on the Project on March 15. PRD agreed to be ready and acted in reliance upon that agreement. Robertson contended that this testimony violated the parol evidence rule. The subcontract was not a completely integrated document, and that PRD's testimony concerning the agreement to have PRD start work, or be prepared to start work, on March 15, 1999, did not vary or contradict any terms of the subcontract, which was silent as to the start date for PRD. If a written agreement was not completely integrated, the parol evidence rule had no application, and parol evidence was competent to resolve the meaning. PRD and Robertson did not make the agreement prior to or contemporaneous with PRD signing the subcontract. Accordingly, the testimony concerning the agreement did not violate the parol evidence rule.

Robertson also contended that there was no consideration for the start date agreement, and that it therefore failed. PRD testified that by agreeing to be ready to start on March 15, 1999, PRD, a single project company, was unable to bid on any other projects and undertake work while it was committed to working as a subcontractor for Robertson. By agreeing to be ready to start on March 15, PRD effectively committed equipment and labor to the Project, which resulted in those resources being unavailable for other work in March, April, and May 1999. PRD also stated that PRD had estimated that its work would take 80 work days, and had expected to be able to work on other projects beginning in August 1999. PRD could have started work on the Project much later without causing any difficulties to Robertson, which had 130 days to complete the Project for MHTC. The delays that the Project experienced resulted in PRD not being able to allocate its equipment and employees to other projects until late October 1999. PRD's agreement to commit its equipment and personnel to starting on March 15, earlier than it needed to do to perform the subcontract work, was sufficient consideration to support the Agreement.

[B] Contract Completion

Page 2-16, add to note 49:

Lange v. City of Batesville, 832 So. 2d (2002) (When no performance time is stated a reasonable time to complete construction is implied. Panola County developed plans for construction of an arena. The drawings included a five-lane road leading from the project and intersecting with a highway. The Whitakers and the Langes' property and the arena property shared a common boundary. The county agreed to transfer to the owners an 11-acre parcel of property to the east of the road, but only if a road was built on the Whitaker-Lange property. The county later determined that it did not have the financial resources to continue with the project. The county transferred ownership and the completion of the project to the City of Batesville. While the project was proceeding, a new hospital was constructed on property located west of it. The owners executed a deed donating to the city 4.81 acres of property for the proposed road. The Board of Alderman decided to delay determining the layout of the roads. The owners argued that the action of the board was an arbitrary and capricious decision of the city to alter or ignore its obligation to build the main road on the strip of land donated to the city. The circuit court found that the decision of the board was not arbitrary and capricious. The owners appealed. The city asserted that there was no breach of the agreement, just that the owners' road was yet to have been constructed. The record contained no indication that the owners' road would not be built. There was no ambiguous statement by the board that the road would not be built. Until there was a breach, it could not have been determined what obligations the city had as to the specifics of a road. No time limitation was contained within the contract; therefore, a reasonable time for performance was implied.).

Page 2-16, add at end of carryover paragraph:

For example, in *Mies Equipment, Inc. v. NCI Building System, L.P.*, 167 F. Supp. 2d 1077 (D. Minn. 2001), the owner of a pre-engineered metal building sued the supplier of the building for delay for late delivery of the building to the owner's erection contractor. The owner alleged that the supplier said that the building components could be delivered in six to seven weeks. However, the written agreement between the general contractor and the supplier did not stipulate a firm delivery date, and only stated a requested shipping date. Further, the agreement provided that the schedule was approximate and subject to delays beyond the control of the supplier. The court found against the owner's third-party beneficiary claim against the supplier, as there was no firm contractual delivery date commitment.

If there is evidence that the parties intended a particular completion date, a court will accept extrinsic evidence to determine what the date was. For example, in *Custom Residential Paint Contracting, Inc. v. Klein*, 2001 Tex. App. LEXIS 7260 (2001), Klein entered into a written contract with Custom Residential Paint Contracting to paint the interior and other portions of a new house. The contract contained no provision concerning the time of completion. Disputes arose between the Kleins and Custom Residential concerning the scope, quality, and timeliness of Custom Residential's work. Ultimately, the Kleins hired another painter to finish painting the house. Although the Kleins paid the full price of the contract, Custom Residential sued the Kleins, alleging they failed to pay various change orders for extra work. The Kleins counterclaimed for breach of contract. The Kleins alleged Custom Residential failed to perform as represented and failed to complete its work in a timely manner. The jury found in favor of the Kleins and awarded actual damages of $8,000.

Custom Residential contended that it could not be liable for any delay because there is no time of performance in the contract. The Kleins, however, testified the parties orally agreed that Custom Residential was to complete its work in six to eight weeks. Further, the owner of Custom Residential agreed that the Kleins wanted the project completed in a "very fast time frame." Where the written instrument contained no completion time, extrinsic evidence was admissible to show the time of completion. The Kleins' testimony supplemented rather than conflicted with the written contract. It was sufficient to show Custom Residential failed to complete its work within the time agreed.

Extrinsic evidence may also be important to select one among several possible completion dates. In *Anchor, Inc. v. Laguna Enterprises, Inc.*, 2002 Tex. App. LEXIS 1063 (2002), the court held that a subcontractor's completion date may be determined from agreements after the contract is signed. Anchor, Inc. contracted with the Houston Independent School District to construct a parking lot. The contractor subcontracted with Laguna Enterprises for the construction of a chain-link fence. In a letter agreement signed by both the contractor and the subcontractor on August 22, 1995, the contractor accepted the subcontractor's proposal to perform additional work fabricating and installing a wrought-iron fence. The letter further stated that the "project must be ready to be occupied by owner by the 22 of August." However, the "22" was crossed out, "30" was written in above, and the change was initialed by both the subcontractor and the contractor. A letter from the contractor was admitted that indicated that performance by the subcontractor as late as November of 1995 was acceptable. The subcontractor installed the wrought-iron fence in the first week of October 1995, and submitted an invoice for the work. The contractor tendered a check for the contract amount minus liquidated damages. The subcontractor sued the contractor to recover the remaining amount. The trial court rendered judgment in favor of the subcontractor and the contractor appealed.

The contractor argued that the trial court erred in admitting parol evidence regarding discussions on August 22, 1995, between the contractor and the subcontractor that it would take six to eight weeks for the wrought-iron gates to arrive once they were ordered from its supplier. The contractor argued that the admission of this evidence precluded its argument that the subcontractor materially breached its subcontract by not completing construction of the wrought-iron fence by August 30, 1995. Based on the entire record, the trial court could have concluded that the subcontractor did not materially breach its contract by installing the wrought-iron fence in October 1995. The contractor had not shown that the alleged error was reversible error.

§ 2.04   SUBSTANTIAL COMPLETION

[A]   Definition of Substantial Completion

Page 2-18, add at end of second full paragraph:

Federal contracts often contain specific definitions of substantial completion. For example, in *Kinetic Builders, Inc. v. Peters*, 226 F.3d 1307 (Fed. Cir. 2000), the definition of completion for a fire alarm and smoke detection system in a building alteration contract provided:

> After all equipment for this system has been installed and made operational, and at a time directed by the Contracting Officer, the contractor shall conduct tests to demonstrate that the installation and system operation is in accordance with plans and specifications.

The project was late, and the contractor and the government disputed the reasons for delay and the date of substantial completion. The contractor filed suit to recover its delay costs and the return of liquidated damages withheld by the government. The contractor claimed that the system was installed, fully operational, and capable of passing the required system tests on a date the contractor claimed was the date of substantial completion. However the actual testing of the system did not occur until 22 days later. The court ruled that the date of substantial completion required compliance with the specific provisions concerning testing. It was reasonable for the government to expect the system to be tested before it occupied the building and that the successful completion of the required tests was part of the contract definition of substantial completion.

Page 2-19, add after second full paragraph:

In *Kinetic Builders, Inc. v. Secretary of Air Force,* 226 F.3d 1307 (Fed. Cir. 2000), the Air Force awarded Kinetic the contract for alteration of a building. The government took beneficial occupancy of the building on March 1, 1996, 37 days after the scheduled completion date. The Air Force withheld $4,775.70 in liquidated damages for late completion and credit for unperformed work. The contractor submitted multiple claims to the contracting officer (CO) for additional costs incurred as a result of government-caused delays. The CO determined that the contractor should be permitted 20 days of delay due to a sewer backup. The contractor appealed to the Board. The Board determined that the contractor was entitled only to 17 days of excusable delay because of the Air Force's delay in handling the sewer backup, because substantial completion did not occur until February 26. The contractor appealed the Board's decision to the Federal Circuit court.

The contractor argued that testing of the fire alarm system had no bearing on substantial completion of the contract. The contractor contended that it was prepared to begin carpet installation on February 1, and that the only reason this installation was not finished was the Air Force's delay in dealing with the sewage backup. The contractor asserted that if it had not been for the Air Force's delay in dealing with the sewage backup, it could have completed carpet installation and installation of the fire alarm system, which was capable of being successfully tested by February 4. Moreover, because the Air Force took beneficial occupancy on March 1 and the Air Force delayed dealing with the sewage backup for 17 days, the contractor contended that it was entitled to a total time extension on the contract of 26 days. According to the Federal Circuit court, in addition to bargaining for operational installation of the fire alarm system, the Air Force had bargained for testing of that system to demonstrate that the system was operational. Fire alarm testing was an important requirement to the Air Force before the building could be used for its intended purpose. The determination of when the work on the fire alarm system was substantially complete required more than evidence that the fire alarm system was installed, operational, or capable of being successfully tested. The fire alarm testing did not actually occur until February 26, 1996. The Board's finding was not arbitrary, capricious, or unsupported by substantial evidence.

Page 2-20, add to note 76:

Subsequent owner repairs after substantial completion, which constitute only a small portion of the project, will not preclude the builder from recovering on the theory of substantial performance. In Teramo & Co., Inc. v. O'Brien-Sheipe Funeral Homes, Inc., 725 N.Y.S.2d 87 (App. Div. 2001), O'Brien-Sheipe Funeral Homes, Inc., hired Teramo & Co., Inc. to construct an addition to its funeral home. The parties' contract did not specify a date for completion of the proposed work and time was not of the essence. The project was substantially completed and a certificate of completion was issued. Although the owner made periodic payments to the builder during the course of construction, the owner failed to make full payment of the builder's final bill, leaving a balance due of $17,950. The builder commenced an action to recover the outstanding balance. The owner asserted counterclaims for business allegedly lost due to delays in construction, and for the cost of hiring other contractors to correct problems caused by poor workmanship. The trial court dismissed the builder's complaint, finding that the builder's performance was unsatisfactory in both time and skill. The court also awarded the owner damages based on the profits lost due to construction delay. The builder appealed. There was no clause in the parties' contract that made time of the essence, and the owner had continued to make periodic payments to the builder. Some delay in construction was attributable to the owner's request that no work be performed at the premises while funeral services were in progress. Although the evidence presented in support of the owner's counterclaims established that the owner had expended $6,180 to repair certain items that had not been properly completed in a workmanlike manner, this constituted only a small portion of the project, and did not preclude the builder from recovering on the theory of substantial performance. The appellate court found that the builder should be permitted to recover the outstanding balance due on the contract price, but that the recovery should be reduced by $6,180 for the cost of repairing work found to be unacceptable.

§ 2.06   INTERIM MILESTONES

Page 2-26, add at end of section:

In *Safeco Credit v. United States,* 44 Fed. Cl. 406, 1999 U.S. Claims LEXIS 178 (Ct. Cl. July 27, 1999), the parties disagreed about the effect of modifications on the contract completion dates and, in turn, on Safeco's possible liability for failure to complete the project on time. The court found that the plain meaning of the time extension clause entitled the government to assess liquidated damages for delays beyond the date that each phase was specifically extended. The dispute arose from a 1985 contract for berthing improvements to a naval dock. Safeco Credit was the surety to the contractor and succeeded to its responsibilities and interests. The contract was divided into seven construction phases identified as 1A, 1B, 2A, 2B, 3A, 3B, and 3C, and a mobilization phase. The mobilization phase and construction phases 1A, 1B, 2A, and 2B ran consecutively. With the exception of phase 1B, which was to begin before the completion of phase 1A, each phase of 1A, 1B, 2A, and 2B had to be completed before work on the next phase could commence. Phases 3A, 3B, and 3C ran consecutively, but phase 3A began concurrently with phase 1A. Each construction phase was for construction on one berth. The Navy added or changed work on the project with 53 modifications to the contract. Many of the modifications extended the time period for completion of phases 1A, 1B, 2A, and 2B—those phases of the project which (with the exception of phase 1B, which was to begin before the completion of phase 1A) were to run consecutively.

The government calculated damages based on the dates of completion set forth in the contract and the modifications. If a phase of the project was not completed by the date in the contract, the government assessed liquidated damages for each day of delay beyond the contract completion date for that phase of the project. Safeco interpreted the modifications to extend both the project completion and subsequent commencement dates. If a phase of the project was extended, in Safeco's view, that extension altered the commencement date for the subsequent phase so that it would begin after the completion date of the previous phase. Safeco's interpretation would greatly reduce the amount of damages that could be assessed under the contract. In support of its reading of the contract, Safeco argued that the project was not driven by any particular requirement for completion which drove a project deadline.

To determine the correct method for computing liquidated damages, the court looked to the plain language of all of the relevant contract provisions. The contract expressly provided for time extensions:

> Notwithstanding any other provisions of this contract it is mutually understood that the time extensions for changes in the work will depend upon the extent, if any, by which the changes cause delay in the completion of the various elements of construction. The change order granting the time extension may provide that the contract completion date will be extended only for those specific elements so delayed and that the remaining contract completion dates for all other portions of the work will not be altered and may further provide for an equitable readjustment of liquidated damages pursuant to the new completion schedule.

The court found that the plain language of the contract provision was inconsistent with Safeco's interpretation of the contract. A change in the completion dates for one phase of the contract "may provide" for extension of completion dates for only some portions of the contract work without affecting the commencement and completion dates of other portions of the contract work. For a phase to be affected, the language of a contract modification must explicitly state the intent to change the completion date of that phase. The terms of the contract modifications made it clear that a change in the completion date for one phase of the contract did not lengthen the period of time in which a subsequent phase was to be completed.

Each modification in which a change was made had specified the phases affected and the new completion date(s). For example, Modification P00010 described the change order work to be completed and stated that "the contract amount is herefor changed to read from $9,885,812.00 to $9,896,018.00, a net increase of $10,206.00 and the contract completion date is extended three calendar days up to and including 87MAY08 for Phase 1B, 87OCT08 for Phase 2A, and 88MAR10 for Phase 2B." That unambiguous language provided for extended completion dates for each phase specified. The court found that the plain meaning of the contract language was consistent with the government's view that the government was entitled to the assessment of liquidated damages for delays beyond the dates that each phase was specifically extended in accordance with the contract terms. The court denied Safeco's recovery of any of the liquidated damages withheld by the government.

§ 2.08   NOTICE PROVISIONS

Page 2-29, add new footnote after second sentence in first paragraph:

121.1 *See* E.C. Ernst, Inc. v. General Motors Corp., 482 F.2d 1047, 1055 (5th Cir. 1973) ("The purpose of a notice provision in a contract is to alert the other party that the claimant has a grievance against it.").

Page 2-29, add to beginning of second paragraph:

Generally courts will enforce notice requirements for a delay claim, even if the result is that the claimant is unable to recover on its claim. United States v. Centex Constr. Co., Inc., 638 F. Supp. 411 (W.D. Va. 1985); Westates Constr. Co. v. City of Cheyenne, 775 P.2d 502 (Wyo. 1989); County Comm'rs of Caroline County v. J. Roland Dashiell & Sons, Inc., 747 A.2d 600 (Md. 2000); Byron's Constr. Co. v. State Highway Dep't, 448 N.W.2d 630 (N.D. 1989).

[A]   Time of Notice

Page 2-31, add after carryover paragraph:

In *Commissioners of Caroline County v. J. Roland Dashiell & Sons, Inc.,* 358 Md. 83, 747 A.2d 600 (2000), as a first step in the process of renovating and adding to the County's correctional facility, the County entered into a Standard Form of Agreement Between Owner and Architect with Greenhorne, an architect, for improvements to the Caroline County Detention Center. Pursuant to it, Greenhorne was responsible for designing the renovation and for providing supervision and monitoring services during the actual construction of the building addition. The project consisted of an addition to the existing detention center, and renovation of the original facility. The County contracted with Dashiell for construction of the proposed renovation. For a lump sum, the contractor agreed to furnish all labor, equipment, materials, and services, and to perform all of the work necessary to renovate and expand the detention center by a date no later than 425 calendar days after the date of commencement. Section 3.2 of the Dashiell contract specifically provided that liquidated damages of $500 per calendar day would be assessed if Dashiell failed to complete the project within the 425 calendar day period. The parties included American Institute of Architects, General Conditions of the Contract for Construction, Document A201 (1987). If the contractor wished to make a claim for an increase in the contract sum, written notice was required before proceeding to execute the work. If the contractor believed additional cost was involved, claims were to be filed in accordance with the procedure established therein.

Almost immediately after receiving a notice to proceed, the contractor began to encounter construction delays for which it requested an extension. By letter, a 60-day extension of time was granted. No further completion date extensions were granted. Ultimately, construction of the project was not completed by the required date.

The contractor claimed that an additional extension of time, due to delays, was needed. By letter, the contractor's executive vice-president informed the architect that it was working to develop a claim for lost time due to weather. Subsequent letters tendered "formal notice that J. Roland Dashiell & Sons, Inc. will be preparing a claim against Caroline County as provided under the General Conditions of the Contract for Construction." The contractor later submitted a claim in accordance with Section 4.3 to extend the contract completion date by 522 days and to increase the contract price by $1,061,038.00 for delays allegedly due to architectural and engineer design deficiencies, weather delays, and concealed or unknown conditions. The court found that neither of these letters constituted a proper claim in compliance with Section 4.3 of the General Conditions of the Contract for Construction. Instead, these letters merely indicated that the respondent intended to file claims in the future.

Late notice does not bar all claims, but only limits damages to those incurred after notice. For example, in *Associated Mechanical Contractors, Inc. v. Martin K. Eby Construction Co.*, 271 F. 3d 1309 (11th Cir. 2001), Associated and Eby signed a $3,150,000 subcontract under which Associated was to perform the mechanical, heating, ventilation, air-conditioning, and plumbing work at a correctional center. The subcontract specified that Associated's work would begin on or before May 2, 1990, and would be completed by July 19, 1991. The subcontract required that claims for delay damages must be filed in writing with the contractor within 10 days from the commencement of the alleged damage and a full accounting filed within 10 days after the extent of damage was known or be considered void. The subcontract also provided that Associated agreed to make all claims for damages against the prime contractor in the same manner provided in the prime contract for claims by the prime contractor against the owner. That article provided: "No claim of the contractor for damage shall be valid unless written notice thereof shall have been received by the owner by registered mail within 15 days after occurrence of the event on which the claim is based."

From the beginning, the prison project was plagued by delays. The footings for the buildings were not finished on time. Eby acknowledged the delay at project meetings, but announced at an August 7 meeting that it would make up the lost time by revising the construction schedule. By letter of August 11, 1990, Associated complained to Eby that Associated's excavation and backfilling work was being held up improperly. The project fell further behind schedule over the next month, mainly due to problems with the masonry work, which affected Associated's work schedule because Associated's work had to be imbedded in the masonry. By September 5, 1990, Associated wrote Eby complaining that it could not be responsible for making sure the masonry contractor's work was up to specifications. On September 13, 1990, Associated wrote Eby complaining of delay from Eby's failure to transmit Associated's "submittal data" to the project architect or engineer for approval. According to the letter, Associated had just learned of the problem, although it had been going on since April.

Associated sent letters on October 1, 1990 and November 8, 1990, notifying Eby that Associated was suffering delay damage from the project being 29 days behind schedule. At the November 13 project meeting, Eby announced that the masonry subcontractor had defaulted. Associated wrote Eby again on November 26, 1990, saying that without any bricklayers on site, Associated would have to lay off workers on November 30 because there was nothing for them to do. Associated said it would incur expenses from this delay and would expect compensation. Again, on February 15, 1991, Associated wrote Eby complaining that the masonry problem and other changes had delayed its own work, and that Eby's attempt to make up lost time by accelerating the work was going to cost Associated money. From early 1991 until the project was finally finished, a constant stream of correspondence continued between Associated and Eby about the delays and problems on the project. Associated repeatedly described in its letters expenses it incurred from the rescheduling of its work, which sometimes left it with idle hands and sometimes caused it to have to pay overtime or to be short of workers. In November 1992, Associated presented Eby with a Request for Equitable Adjustment, asking for $737,343.96 and a 462-day time extension. When Eby denied Associated's request, Associated brought suit. Eby filed a summary judgment motion, contending that Associated had failed to give timely notice as required by the subcontract and by the section incorporating notice requirements of the prime contract. The trial court held Associated did not provide Eby with notice of an intent to seek damages on account of those delays until August of 1990, at the very earliest — well beyond the 10 day period provided for in the subcontract for notice of delay claims.

Associated admitted that it knew of certain delays as early as May and June 1990. It argued that the delays did not constitute damages because Associated and Eby both hoped that the early schedule slippage might be recouped. Eby responded that it was patently impossible for the damages to be eliminated, because once the equipment had sat idle and the overhead had accrued, damages had commenced. The subcontract required Associated to give notice when it incurred damage, without waiting to see whether mitigation efforts would be successful. But even assuming that Associated failed to give timely notice for the delays suffered from May through July 1990, and that damages for such delays were not recoverable, those damages were a small part of the total damages Associated claimed for delay and disruption. Associated could not have suffered 462 days of delay between May and July 1990. Many of the problems occurred after the May-July 1990 period. The timeliness of claims based not on the postponed mobilization, but on discrete events such as the default of the masonry subcontractor, must be evaluated separately from those based on the late start. Because the district court did not appear to have taken into account the damages that were caused by events after July, remanded for the district court to determine which claims were barred by failure to give timely notice and which were preserved.

[B] Notice Procedures

Page 2-32, add to end of first paragraph:

For example, a prime contractor has a contractual duty to provide timely notice of other prime contractor's delays as required by the contract. *Biemann & Rowell Co. v. Donohoe Cos., Inc.,* 147 N.C. App. 239, 556 S.E.2d 1 (2001). Biemann & Rowell Co. and Donohoe Cos., Inc. entered into separate contracts with the State of North Carolina to build a multi-million dollar neuropsychiatric hospital under multiple-prime contracts. Each separate contractor was directly liable to the state and to the other contractors. Donohoe was assigned the role of project expediter. The contractor was responsible for maintaining the progress schedule, making monthly adjustments, updates, and corrections, as well as keeping all contractors and the architect fully informed. Delays occurred throughout the project and the contractors were frequently forced to complete work out of the anticipated sequence. To accelerate completion of the project, it was the understanding of the contractors, architect, and schedule coordinator that Donohoe would "dry-in" the building by installing a moisture seal. Donohoe never installed the building seal. The architect indicated that Donohoe was failing to complete work according to the project schedule and to fulfill its duties as project expediter. Biemann and Rowell maintained that the contractor's failure to install the building seal, and its failure to supervise and properly schedule its subcontractors, caused delays to Biemann and Rowell's work. The trial court rendered judgment in favor of Donohoe. Biemann and Rowell appealed.

Biemann and Rowell contended that the trial court erred in finding an express contractual obligation to provide notice of Donohoe's delay to the architect, and that Donohoe's actual knowledge of its potential liability to co-prime contractors was sufficient notice. As arbiter of disputes between the prime contractors, it was necessary for the architect to be notified when one contractor caused delay to another. The general conditions of the project contract provided that a contractor who was delayed by another contractor was to request an extension of time in writing to the architect and owner within 20 days following the cause of the delay. Biemann and Rowell had a contractual duty to provide notice of delay caused by Donohoe. Discussions at weekly foreman's meetings and monthly progress meetings with the architect and owner did not constitute sufficient notice. While the meetings may have provided constructive notice, Biemann and Rowell never gave written or verbal notice of potential claims at the meetings, nor did Biemann and Rowell ever give notice that it was suffering economic harm. Failure to provide proper notice was a breach of Biemann and Rowell's duty to mitigate damages, and prejudiced Donohoe by not providing an opportunity to cure. Biemann and Rowell failed to provide Donohoe with timely notice of its claims. Affirmed.

Page 2-32, add after second full paragraph:

The contractor should make an attempt to comply with requirements to provide delay damages shortly after the occurrence of a delay or it may lose its rights to recover on a delay claim. For example, in *Heckler Electric Co., Inc. v. City of New York*, 715 N.Y.S.2d 619, 186 Misc. 77 (2000), the public construction contract contained a two-part notice and documentation requirement. First, the contractor had to provide written notice to the City within 10 days of any act giving rise to a claim. Then before the 15th day of the following month, the contractor had to provide an itemized statement of the delay damages. In response to a suit filed by the contractor alleging delay, the City brought a motion for summary judgment based upon the contractor's failure to comply with the two-part notice requirement. The contractor unsuccessfully argued that it was impossible to itemize the delay costs in the time required because the delay costs were unknown at the time when the second part of the notice was required. The court reasoned that precise quantification was not required but an estimate of the cost would comply with the itemization requirement. Later the contractor would be able to amend its estimate when it determined the actual damages. Other New York courts have also enforced similar requirements for itemized statements of claim damages, especially when the contractor failed to make an attempt to comply. *A.H.A. General Constr., Inc. v. New York City Hous. Auth.,* 92 N.Y.2d 90, 699 N.E.2d 368 (1998); *F. Garofalo Electric Co. v. New York Univ.,* 270 A.D.2d 76, 705 N.Y.S.2d 327 (2000).

[C]   Actual Notice

Page 2-33, add to note 146:

Allgood Electric Co. v. Martin K. Eby Constr. Co., 959 F. Supp. 1573 (M.D. Ga. 1997).

Page 2-33, add to note 147:

See also Metric Constructors, Inc. v. National Aeronautics & Space Admin., 169 F.3d 747 (Fed. Cir. 1999) (court accepted critical path schedule with no activities for replacing lamps as evidence that trade practice did not require contractor to replace all light bulbs when project finally completed).

Page 2-34, add after note 151 in first carryover paragraph:

The written notice requirement may also be met by other project documentation. For example, in *Welding, Inc. v. Bland County Service Authority,* 541 S.E.2d 909 (Va. 2001), the contractor maintained that the project architect's meeting minutes documented the contractor's intention to file a claim. At issue was whether the contractor complied with the statutory requirement that public works contractors submit written notice of their intention to file a claim at the time of its occurrence. Because of the lack of formal written notice from the contractor, the trial court granted summary judgment in favor of the public owner, ruling that the architect's meeting minutes were not sufficient to meet the statutory notice requirement. Reversing the summary judgment, the Supreme Court of Virginia held that as a matter of law, the meeting minutes could not be ruled out as a way to comply with the statutory notice requirement. Whether the contractor complied with the statutory notice requirement from the architect's meeting minutes was a determination to be made at trial.

Page 2-34, replace first sentence in first full paragraph with:

In countering an argument that actual knowledge should satisfy the notice provision, it may be asserted that although the owner may have been aware of the event, the owner did not realize that it would be the basis of a claim for additional costs.

Page 2-34, add after note 152 in first full paragraph:

Similarly, a general contractor may argue that the contractor's actual knowledge of a subcontractor's delay should not excuse the subcontractor from providing written notice of a delay to the general contractor. For example, in *Associated Mechanical Contractors, Inc. v. Martin K. Eby Constr. Co., Inc.*, 271 F.3d 1309 (11th Cir. 2001), the subcontract contained a provision requiring the subcontractor to give written notice of delay within 10 days of its commencement, followed by a "full accounting" of the delay impact and costs "within 10 days after the extent of the damage is known or the cause of damage ceases, whichever is sooner." The contract between the owner and the general contractor also contained written notice requirements for delay, and the subcontract incorporated the provisions of the prime contract.

The subcontractor incurred "stop and start" delays, resequencing requirements by the general contractor and other delays, but did not provide written notice of the delays to the general contractor. The subcontractor argued that the general contractor had actual knowledge of the delays since it ordered the resequencing of the work. The subcontractor further argued that the two aspects of the notice provision (written notice and full accounting) in effect did not require notice to the contractor until it was possible to quantify the delay damages. However, the court held that written notice by the subcontractor was required despite actual knowledge of the delay by the general contractor. The court reasoned that the general contractor's actual knowledge would not enable it to satisfy its own written notice obligation under the contract with the owner. The court opined that the function of the notice provision in the subcontract was to permit the general contractor to include the subcontractor's claims in its notices to the owner.

[F] Waiver

Page 2-36, add to note 162:

Service Steel Erectors Co. v. SCE, Inc., 573 F. Supp. 177 (W.D. Va. 1983); E.C. Ernst, Inc. v. Koppers Co., Inc., 626 F.2d 324 (3d Cir. 1980); Transpower Constructors v. Grand River Dam Auth., 905 F.2d 1413 (10th Cir. 1990).

Page 2-36, add after note 168 in third full paragraph:

In another case, the court held that the construction manager lacked authority to waive the contractual requirement for written notice of claims. New York University retained an agency construction manager for a medical school building construction project. The University held all of the multiple trade contracts. The terms of the electrical trade contract required prompt written notice followed by written itemization and documentation of costs as conditions precedent to recovery of additional compensation. The electrical contractor admitted that it hadn't strictly complied with the notice procedures but asserted that the construction manager was fully aware of the circumstances giving rise to the claim, receiving written reports of associated costs. The University, however, refused to pay the claimed costs, arguing that the construction manager had no authority to waive the written notice requirements on the University's behalf. When the matter reached the appellate court, it noted that neither the electrical prime contract nor the construction management contract gave the construction manager the authority to change or revise the terms of the electrical trade contract. Rather the electrical trade contract stated that modifications could only be made by written amendment signed by the University. *F. Garofalo Electric Co. Inc. v. New York Univ.,* 270 A.D.2d 76, 705 N.Y.S.2d 327 (2000).

§ 2.09   SCHEDULING PROVISIONS

Page 2-37, replace note 172 with:

For a more complete discussion of other scheduling clauses, *see* Callahan & Hohns, Construction Schedules at 47–86 (2d ed. 1998).

Page 2-38, replace note 175 with:

Callahan & Hohns, Construction Schedules at § 3.3 (2d ed. 1998).

Page 2-38, add to note 179:

A clause requiring the contractor to phase its work with the owner may not give the owner the ability to direct the work in a particular manner. In DRC Corp. v. General Servs. Admin., GSBCA No. 14919-COM, 99-1 B.C.A. (CCH) ¶ 30,649 (1999), the contract for the renovation of portions of two buildings contained a provision that stated "the work shall be closely staged, phased, and coordinated with the Contracting Officer's Technical Representative [COTR] in order to avoid interruption of ongoing Government operations." The contractor allegedly based its bid on a plan dividing the work into two phases to avoid disruption, but the COTR required a three-phase plan that delayed the contractor's timely completion of the contract. When the Board of Contract Appeals decided the merits of the contractor's delay claim, it ruled that the contractor's two-phase plan met the contract requirements, and the government's directive to use a three-phase plan was unreasonable.

Page 2-39, add after carryover paragraph:

Proper scheduling provisions are necessary for the management of construction projects, as well as providing tools and a schedule baseline against which delays and claims can be measured. The schedules developed during construction may be used as proof in court to prove and disprove delays. Construction schedules are often manipulated to justify certain positions, as discussed in **§ 11.06**. Schedules may also be manipulated during the course of construction with the purpose of justifying or refuting time extensions, minimizing the effect of a party's own delays, maximizing the effect of other parties' delays, and increasing recovery for change orders and claims. There are many ways to protect against schedule manipulation. Two examples are contractual defenses written into the scheduling specifications and schedule software tools to identify errors. Zack, *Schedule "Games" People Play, and Some Suggested "Remedies,"* 8 J. Mgmt. Engineering 2, 138 (Apr. 1992). Many owners find it useful to require the contractor to provide "predecessor-successor" reports with all schedule submissions. Other owners require the contractor to use certain scheduling software and to submit all schedules and updates on computer disks, allowing the owner to analyze the schedules.

Scheduling of owner-furnished material or information may also be manipulated in the schedule. For example, the delivery activities for owner-furnished equipment may be inserted into the schedule on or near the critical path to show that if the owner misses the delivery date, the overall completion of the project will be delayed. To deal with this situation, some owners have provided in the contract that the delivery date for owner-furnished equipment should be within a window of "not earlier than" and "not later than" dates.

Another scheduling issue of concern to owners is early completion schedules. See § 11.05[A]. Specifications may require the contractor to indicate its intention for an early completion when submitting its bid, or require the contractor to "escrow" its bid documents reflecting an early completion. Other contracts provide that there will be no time extensions for excusable delays unless the delays drive project completion beyond the contractually required completion date. Another approach is to require a change order or contract amendment for an early project completion.

"Preferential logic" and "sequestering of float" are other scheduling dilemmas that owners may encounter. Preferential logic allows the scheduler to develop schedules that create maximum opportunities for the schedule to reflect owner delays and interferences if events occur, or scheduling sequences are changed that are the owner's responsibility. Sequestering float is similar in that the schedules are created or updated with the intention of allowing little or no float or flexibility for potential delay-causing events. Preferential logic and sequestering of float techniques are difficult to define, hard to detect, and even harder to prevent, generally requiring a thorough review of the schedule. However, there may be ways to limit the scheduler's ability to employ preferential logic, by requiring that the activities be resource-loaded with labor crews and equipment, that the subcontractors accept the schedule, and that the contractor submit the schedule for the owner's review and comment.

§ 2.11   CHANGES CLAUSE

Page 2-45, add after note 219 in first carryover paragraph:

The legal theory of constructive changes is not universally accepted by all jurisdictions, although another legal theory may achieve the same results. For example, in *Sentinel Industrial Contracting Corp. v. Kimmins Industrial Service Corp.*, 743 So. 2d 954 (Miss. 1999), the subcontractor-claimant was able to recover for its costs in performing extra work without a written change order under an estoppel-type theory, as the jurisdiction did not accept the theory of constructive changes. The general contractor awarded the subcontractor a subcontract to disable a portion of an ammonia refinery. The subcontract provided that written change orders were required for any adjustments to the terms or price. The general contract was incorporated by reference into the subcontract, and contained a provision requiring the contractor to comply with directives and instructions even without a written change order. The general contractor directed changes to the sequence and schedule of the subcontract work as well as requiring performance of work not in the subcontract scope. The subcontractor performed as directed and submitted change order requests to the general contractor who refused to approve them.

The subcontractor sued the general contractor to recover for the extra work costs and at trial was awarded $966,375. On appeal, the general contractor argued the lack of written change orders prevented any recovery by the subcontractor. The subcontractor argued that it had to comply with the general contractor's directives or face a possible default termination or breach of contract. Although the legal concept of constructive changes was not recognized under Mississippi law, its highest court allowed recovery for extra work without a written change order under the theory that one may not impose extra-contractual work while denying change order requests.

§ 2.12   DIFFERING SITE CONDITIONS CLAUSE

Page 2-47, add at end of second full paragraph:

In *Ronald Adams Contractor, Inc. v. Mississippi Transportation Commission*, 770 So. 2d 649 (Miss. 2000), the contractor was awarded a state contract to place the base for a highway. The scope required the contractor to cut and fill to a specified elevation. During the performance the state's on-site engineer directed the contractor to undercut below grade and backfill with borrow material. The contractor alleged that the directive had a disruptive effect on its labor productivity and costs of performance. However, the only additional compensation given to the contractor for the cut and fill work directed by the state's on-site engineer was payment for unclassified excavation at the contract unit price rates. Although the contractor failed to give prompt written notice as required by the contract, it submitted a differing site condition claim. The claim was rejected by the state for various reasons, one being the failure to comply with the notice provisions of the differing site conditions clause. Summary judgment was granted to the state. In reviewing the notice issue, the Supreme Court of Mississippi held that the failure to provide written notice would not bar the claim because the state's on-site engineer had actual knowledge of the soil conditions, investigated the conditions and directed the undercutting work. Under these circumstances, written notice by the contractor would have been a "vain and useless act."

Actual knowledge alone may not be satisfactory to meet the notice requirement of a differing site conditions clause. *Ronald Adam Contracting* involved a directive by the owner's agent who had actual knowledge of the conditions and also investigated the conditions, serving some of the purposes of the notice requirements. Mere knowledge of the condition may not be satisfactory to overcome the written notice requirements. For example, in *Dan Nelson Construction, Inc. v. Noland & Dickson*, 608 N.W.2d 267 (N.D. 2000), the claimant argued that the public owner either waived or would be estopped from asserting the failure to comply with the written notice requirement because of the actual knowledge of its on-site representatives. The court rejected this argument, reasoning that the actual knowledge of a potential differing site condition claim would not estop a public owner from raising the notice defense absent a showing that the failure to provide written notice was induced by the actions of the public owner's representatives.

Page 2-48, add after carryover paragraph:

Some industry commentators have indicated that there may be a third type of differing site conditions claim—unanticipated and unknown hazardous material encountered at the project site. The contractual basis for this special category of differing site conditions claim is found in clauses that assign the risk of encountering hazardous material. For example, the American Institute of Architects general conditions provide that if the contractor discovers hazardous material at the project site during construction, it is to stop work in the area and notify the owner of the presence of suspected hazardous material. The owner is then to retain a licensed laboratory to determine whether a hazardous material is present, abate the material, and verify that it has been rendered harmless. The contractor may then submit a request for an adjustment of the contract time and cost. AIA Document A201-1997, and ¶ 10.3.

Even without such a provision, a contractor encountering hazardous material at the project site during the course of construction may be able to recover under the differing site conditions clause, if it can establish the elements of recovery for a Type I or Type II condition. The hazardous material may be shown to be unanticipated, concealed and not readily discovered during a pre-bid site visit because the hazardous environmental conditions were present in limited areas. However, it may be difficult for a contractor to recover on a Type II differing site conditions claim for hazardous material involving the rehabilitation of an old building, a project located on the site of a former service station, of PCBs in the vicinity of an old transformer because these types of conditions may not be "unusual" in the context of the type of the project site. Beard, *Contractor Claims Based on Encountering Unanticipated Hazardous Materials on Site*, 20 Con. Law. 24, 26 (July 2000).

[C] Site Inspection

Page 2-52, add after carryover sentence of carryover paragraph:

Nor is a site inspection clause an absolute disclaimer of responsibility if the actual conditions differ from those represented by the information provided to the bidders in the contract documents. For example, in SMC Corporation v. New Jersey Water Supply Authority, 334 N.J. Super. 429, 759 A.2d 1223 (App. Div. 2000), the contract documents contained a site investigation clause whereby the contractor acknowledged that it investigated the site and became familiar with "reasonably ascertainable" conditions and all other matters upon which information was "reasonably obtainable." The contractor was performing the reconstruction of a culvert using cofferdams that required dewatering. The contractor encountered a "scour hole" in the dewatering area not indicated on the contract drawings that allegedly increased its dewatering costs. The contractor properly submitted notices and a differing site conditions claim, and when it was rejected, filed suit. Upon motion of the owner, the trial court granted summary judgment based upon its understanding that the site investigation clause placed the risk of unforeseen site conditions upon the contractor. On appeal, the court found that the clauses were not an absolute disclaimer, but required a fact finding as to whether the scour hole was reasonably ascertainable from a reasonable pre-bid site investigation.

Page 2-53, add at end of carryover paragraph:

Restrictions on pre-bid inspections in essence requires the bidders to rely upon the subsurface and other information on existing conditions provided by the owner. This increases the risk of delay claims for the owner and reduces the likelihood of them enforcing other owner remedies such as default termination when it involves the restrictions on the pre-bid site investigation. For example, in *Marshall Associated Contractors, Inc.* and *Columbia Excavating, Inc., A Joint Venture*, IBCA No. 1901, 3433-3435, 01-1 B.C.A. (CCH) ¶ 31,248 (2001), the Bureau of Reclamation awarded a contract to the joint venture to produce sand and course aggregate to be used in the construction of a dam. The material for the contract was to be obtained from a government-owned borrow site. The Bureau did not allow the bidders to perform any pre-bid inspections of the borrow site. The bidders were provided geological information, but the Bureau did not provide a particular test pit analysis that was done. In performing the contract, the joint venture found it to be more difficult, time consuming and costly than it anticipated to produce sand that would meet the specifications, and fell behind schedule. The Bureau terminated the contract for default due to the joint venture's inability to produce the required quantity of sand by the completion date. Allegedly if the joint venture had been able to perform a pre-bid site inspection, it would have been able to determine the actual conditions and would have bid differently, but it was prevented from doing so, and was not given the particular test pit analysis that would have indicated some of the problems encountered. The termination for default was set aside by the Board and converted to a termination for convenience.

[F]   Disclaimers

Page 2-54, add to note 299:

Morris, Inc. v. South Dakota Dep't of Transp., 598 N.W.2d 520 (S.D. 1999). The disclaimer clause provided that "the information covering the pit for the project is given to you for informational purposes only. The Department of Transportation does not guarantee the quality or quantity of the material listed in the above information. Interested contractors should investigate the area before considering it for bidding purposes." Unknown to the contractor, the test boring logs were over 10 years old, and dealt with an area where the aggregate was removed by others. Further, the Department had not even visited the pit location in over 10 years, but included the test borings in the bidding documents. In submitting its bid, the contractor relied on the test boring logs in the state-leased pit, and during the course of performance discovered the pit could not produce the required aggregate for the highway project. The contractor filed suit to recover its delay costs. The state supreme court reasoned that the Department understood that bidder would likely rely on the test borings, and had an affirmative obligation to provide more accurate information. Further, the court reasoned that the test borings were included in the bid documents to avoid the cost of borings and to obtain lower bids. It deemed the borings to be a material misrepresentation of the conditions, making the disclaimer unenforceable.

Page 2-56, add after third full paragraph:

Characterizing all subsurface excavation material as "unclassified" may also assist the owner in avoiding liability for delay claims involving differing site conditions. In *Basin Paving Co. v. Mike M. Johnson, Inc.*, 27 P.3d 609 (Wash. App. 2001), the contract for the construction of water and wastewater lines contained three provisions that the court found to be relevant in denying a contractor's differing site conditions claim. The first provision stated that all excavation was to be "unclassified and payment for rock excavation is not authorized." The court found this to be important because the owner made no representations concerning the proportion of rock and other material that might be encountered. Rock would not be a differing site condition as all subsurface conditions were labeled as unclassified. Second, the contract advised the bidders that subsurface rock conditions would be encountered, and further placed the burden of predicting its presence on the contractor. Third, the owner disclaimed responsibility for the test boring logs that later proved to be inaccurate. The contract stated that the information was provided without any owner responsibility for its accuracy or "for any conclusions that the Contractor might draw therefrom." Even though the contract contained a differing site conditions clause, the court held that the contractor was not entitled to additional compensation.

§ 2.13   SUSPENSION OF WORK CLAUSE

[A]   Owner's Responsibility for Suspension

Page 2-59, add at end of second full paragraph:

The contract may contain provisions requiring the contractor to suspend work at the owner's direction due to environmental conditions. In *Housatonic Valley Construction Co., Inc.*, AGBC No. 1999-181-1, 00-1 B.C.A. (CCH) ¶ 30,869 (2000), the U.S. Forest Service awarded a contract to install a sand filter sewage system in a national forest in Oregon. The contract contained provisions requiring the work to comply with the regulations of the Oregon Department of Environmental Quality, allowing the government to suspend work under the standard Suspensions Clause, and allowing the government to suspend work for environmental protection or the contractor's failure to comply with the specifications. The last provision did not allow the contractor to receive a price adjustment for suspensions under its terms. The government ordered the contractor to stop work on the installation of the leach field, and later denied the contractor's claim for remobilization costs and unabsorbed overhead for the period of suspension. Even though the stop work order did not specifically refer to the suspensions clause for environmental protection, the Board of Contract Appeals did not allow the contractor to recover its suspension-related costs because the installation in high groundwater would violate the state environmental regulations.

§ 2.14   TERMINATION CLAUSES

[A]   Termination for Default

Page 2-62, add after note 358:

There is a difference between termination for failure to make progress and termination for failure to achieve timely completion under federal contracts. If the termination is based on failure to make progress, the government must give the contractor a 10-day cure notice and an opportunity to cure. Further, the government must be able to demonstrate that there is no reasonable likelihood that the contractor can complete the work by the required contract completion date. If a valid completion date has already passed, grounds for termination are more properly based upon the failure to achieve timely completion. *Abcon Associates, Inc. v. United States*, 44 Fed. Cl. 625 (1999).

Page 2-62, add after note 360:

The claimant may also allege that the original completion date was waived by additional work and other delays, that no attempt to enforce the original completion deadline was made, and that he was encouraged to continue working. *Quinn Bros., Inc. v. Whitehouse*, 737 A.2d 1127 (N.H. 1999).

Page 2-63, add after note 367 in first full paragraph:

For example, in *AFV Enterprises*, PSBCA No. 2691, 2001 PSBCA LEXIS 8, 01-1 B.C.A. (CCH) ¶ 31, 388 (2001), the U.S. Postal Service (USPS) awarded a contract to AFV to construct a building and lease the facility back to the USPS. AFV was unable to get a building permit, but kept pursuing the matter with the local building officials. Thirty days after the required contract completion, AFV still did not have the building permit, and the USPS notified AFV that the contract was being terminated for default. AFV appealed the default termination, alleging that the USPS had waived the completion date by not acting until 30 days after the required contract completion date. In examining the actions and communications between the parties, the board found that AFV did not continue to pursue contract performance, and the 30-day period was not unreasonably long so as to lead AFV to believe the USPS would not enforce the contract deadline.

Page 2-64, add after note 371:

Granting a time extension subsequent to a contract delay also waives the owner's right to use the delay to justify terminating the contract for failing to progress. Consider *R.W. Granger & Sons Inc. v. City School District of Albany*, 296 A.D.2d 636, 744 N.Y.S.2d 567 (2002). The City School District awarded R.W. Granger & Sons the prime contract for a renovation and addition project at the Albany School of Humanities. The contract encompassed three phases. Phase II dealt primarily with the construction of an addition to the school and was to be completed by February 7, 1995. However, numerous delays extended the scheduled date of completion and, in May 1995, the parties agreed that Phase II was to be substantially completed by June 23, 1995, with total completion by September 5, 1995. While Phase II was completed on June 23, 1995, defendant nevertheless terminated the contract on June 28, 1995 because of plaintiff's failure to timely progress its work. As a consequence, plaintiff commenced its action alleging that it was wrongfully terminated. Following a nonjury trial, the Supreme Court determined that plaintiff's termination was without cause and awarded plaintiff $1,412,745 in stipulated damages, plus interest. Defendant appealed.

Granger's expert engineer testified that based upon a "critical path" analysis, the project was delayed for a total of 133 days. Of the 133 days, the expert attributed all but 15 days to defendant and its agents by reason of their failure to coordinate the work of the various prime contractors and to prepare adequate construction schedules. These failures, in turn, resulted in the mechanical, electrical and plumbing work interfering with plaintiff's work, thereby causing the complained-of delay. The expert attributed only 15 days of the delay to plaintiff, which, in his opinion, was neither substantial nor material to completion of the project. There was contrary testimony on the part of defendant's expert that the trial court resolved. With regard to the 15 days of delay attributable to plaintiff, defendant urged that such was sufficient to justify termination of the contract, which provided that plaintiff's "failure to comply with any of the terms" of the contract would constitute a basis for termination. The 15-day delay attributable to plaintiff was from December 13, 1994 to January 10, 1995. Subsequent to the contractor's delay, the parties mutually agreed to an extension of the completion date of the contract and plaintiff continued working thereon. Under the circumstances, defendant waived any complaint as to that 15-day delay. Moreover, to permit such an insignificant delay to constitute a basis for termination would amount to a forfeiture, which the courts in New York were loath to enforce. The judgment was affirmed.

Page 2-64, add after note 372:

and for abandonment indicated by the removal of equipment from the project site, (Great Western Constr. Co. v. Martin Corp., 13 P.3d 1016 (Or. App. 2000)).

Page 2-65, add at end of carryover paragraph:

The owner's representative responsible for making the decision to terminate the contract for default should be careful in assessing the facts involved, not totally relying upon the information and assessment provided by its own staff. For example, in *The Ryan Company*, ASBCA No. 48151, 00-2 B.C.A. (CCH) ¶ 31,094 (2000), the owner's representative responsible for making the decision whether to terminate the contract for default (the contracting officer), relied upon the project engineer's assessment of the situation. When reporting to the contracting officer, the project engineer withheld information and misrepresented the severity of the contractor's performance problems. Relying upon the project engineer's information without performing an independent fact investigation, the contracting officer terminated the contract for the replacement of electrical substation switchgear. When the default termination was appealed to the Armed Sevices Board of Contract Appeals, the Board ruled that the termination was an abuse of the contracting officer's discretion. It found that the contracting officer owed the contractor an assessment of all of the relevant circumstances.

The level of care that owners may have to use in terminating a contract for default is further illustrated by *CJP Contractors v. United States,* 45 Fed. Cl. 343 (Fed. Claim. 1999). In *CJP Contractors,* the General Services Administration (GSA) awarded a contract to CJP to replace the heating system in a storage depot. A two-phase performance period was required—170 days to install new gas piping and 310 days to replace the existing oil-fired heaters and replace them with gas-fired heaters. The contracting officer issued a stop-work order to CJP to prevent it from removing the existing oil heaters until the new gas-fired units were delivered to the site. Even after the stop-work order was lifted 47 days later when the new units were delivered, GSA was concerned whether CJP's work force would be adequate to complete the installation of the new gas-fired heaters prior to the start of the heating season. GSA representatives prepared a rough estimate of the required labor hours to complete the work. Based upon this rough estimate and the time left to complete the work, the GSA contracting officer concluded that there was no reasonable likelihood that CJP would complete the installation in a timely manner. Therefore, CJP's contract was terminated for default.

In considering the termination on appeal, the U.S. Court of Federal Claims critically examined the actions of the contracting officer. The contract did not require CJP to have the new heating units on site before removing the old heaters. Thus, the court did not find merit in the stop-work order, and granted CJP a 47-day time extension. When the contracting officer evaluated CJP's performance and work force, CJP was measured against the original contract duration without the time extension to which it was entitled and granted by the court. Further, the completion estimate prepared by the GSA representatives was also found to be flawed in that the estimate was prepared in only a few minutes, based solely upon the limited experience of the GSA representatives in such work, and without reference to other sources, such as estimating guides or other corroboration. The contracting officer relied upon the flawed estimate without question or critical examination. The court determined that the contracting officer demonstrated "unreasonably poor judgment" and based its decision on "materially erroneous information."

Page 2-65, add at end of first full paragraph:

To supplement the evaluation, the owner may retain the services of an independent scheduling expert to assess the status of the project, analyze the schedule with all owner-caused delays and other excusable delays, and determine whether the contractor would be able to finish in a timely manner after extending the schedule for all excusable delays. *Thomas & Sons, Inc.,* ASBCA No. 51874, 00-2 B.C.A. (CCH) ¶ 31,166 (2000).

Page 2-65, add after first sentence of second full paragraph:

Under federal contract law, a contractor's failure to make satisfactory progress gives the government the basis to request assurance that the contract work will be completed in a timely manner and corrective measures will be taken to "cure" the default, even though the circumstances at the time may not justify termination for default. The contractor's failure or refusal to provide such assurances to the government may be grounds to terminate the contract for default. *Danzig v. AEC Corp.*, 224 F.3d 1333 (Fed. Cir. 2000).

Page 2-66, add after note 387 in carryover paragraph:

Under the American Institute of Architect's contracts, an architect's certification of default must cite a material breach by the contractor related to the contractual grounds for default. In *Ingrassia Construction Co., Inc. v. Vernon Township Board of Education*, 345 N.J. Super. 130, 784 A.2d 73 (App. Div. 2001), the owner awarded a contract to Ingrassia for renovations and expansion of a high school building. The contract documents included the AIA General Conditions, Document A201, requiring an architect's certification that there exists grounds for default termination before the owner could terminate the contract for default. The contract schedule contained several milestones that were not met. The owner requested that the architect certify that the contractor failed to achieve the progress to meet the schedule milestones due to its failure to provide an adequate labor force. The architect was reluctant to do so stating that it did not have an on-site representative present on a daily basis, and could not make the requested certification from its own independent observations. However, the architect prepared a certification that stated that the contractor failed to achieve the schedule milestones. Based upon this certification, the owner terminated the contract for cause. The contractor filed suit claiming wrongful termination. Upon the contractor's motion for summary, the trial court found that although the architect's certification reflected that the milestones were missed, it did not indicate that the contractor was at fault. The certification was deficient in this respect, and the contractor was entitled to recover damages for wrongful termination. Upon appeal, it was held that although the certification was defective, this did not automatically establish that the termination was unjustified. The owner still could prove at trial that the contract was in default. Reliance upon the designer's certificate of default may not be sufficient for the owner to base its defense against a claim of wrongful termination. For example, in *Driver Pipeline Co., Inc. v. Mustang Pipeline Co., Inc.*, 69 S.W.3d 779 (Tex. App. 2002), the owner (Mustang) awarded a contract to Driver to construct a 100-mile section of gas pipeline by a stated completion date. Heavy rains occurred in the area, and Mustang granted a time extension to a contractor installing an adjoining section of pipeline, but did not grant a time extension to Driver. Further, Mustang's consulting engineer later issued a certificate of default stating that Driver was not staffing the project with an adequate work force or with adequate equipment for the contract work, and that adequate grounds for default termination existed. Relying upon the engineer's certificate, Mustang terminated Driver's contract for default, and Driver brought suit for wrongful termination. Upon consideration by the Texas Court of Appeals, it was decided that Mustang's reliance upon the engineer's certificate of default was not justified. The court noted that the engineer never visited the site, never observed the construction work, did not have accurate information as to the number of workers that Driver had on the project, and did not know what type of equipment was required for Driver's contract work.

Page 2-67, add after note 391 in carryover paragraph:

An important procedural requirement on terminating a contract for default is the owner's notice to the contractor. The notice should provide specifics as to the deficiencies in the contractor's performance. Generalized statements, such as the contractor is "jeopardizing" its contract, may be held to be inadequate notice because of the contractor's inability to cure its alleged default. *Blaine Economic Development Authority v. Royal Electric Co., Inc.,* 520 N.W.2d 473 (Minn. App. 1994). In some situations, the owner's inadequate vague notice of default can be clarified by subsequent discussions that specify the deficiencies. *Danrenke Corp.,* VABCA No. 3601, 93-1 B.C.A. (CCH) ¶ 25,365 (1992). The key is to provide the contractor with enough specific information so it can exercise its right to cure the default. Also, the reasons given on the notice of default should be consistent with the reasons given in the actual default termination. For example, in *Allstate Contractors, Inc. v. Marriott Corp.,* 273 Ill. App. 3d 960, 652 N.E.2d 1113 (1995), the notice of default dealt with noncompliant concrete placement at a specific location, whereas the default termination was based upon deficient concrete placement in a different location. The court found this to be the basis for liability for wrongful termination.

Page 2-67, add at end of subsection:

An owner need not perform a delay analysis in order to collect additional time costs to complete after a default termination. Consider *In Re Stone & Webster, Inc.,* 279 B.R. 748 (Dist. Del. 2002). Maine Yankee Atomic Power Company hired Stone & Webster Engineering Corporation (SWEC) to decommission Maine Yankee's Wiscasset nuclear power generating facility. The Maine Yankee project involved licensing, engineering, health, physics, and radioactive waste clean-up. Pursuant to the Decommissioning Agreement, Maine Yankee issued a notice to SWEC stating that it was terminating the Decommissioning Agreement based upon SWEC's insolvency and because SWEC had not adequately performed under the contract. Soon thereafter, SWEC filed voluntary petitions for bankruptcy relief. Maine Yankee filed proofs of claim in the bankruptcy cases against SWEC. The Debtors objected to Maine Yankee's claims, arguing that Maine Yankee did not properly terminate the Decommissioning Agreement for either insolvency or failure to perform and did not have a right to damages for terminating the agreement on account of SWEC's insolvency.

Debtors argued that Maine Yankee failed to do a proper "delay analysis" of the cause of the six-month delay from the completion date reflected in the Decommissioning Agreement to Maine Yankee's current projected completion date of October 2004. Debtors contended that Maine Yankee could not recover damages associated with delays unless they proved that those delays were chargeable to SWEC and would not have been avoided by SWEC. Debtors argued that because Maine Yankee failed to prove that the delay was chargeable to SWEC, Maine Yankee's damages must be reduced by at least $2.17 million, which was the cost for supervisory labor associated with the six-month delay. The court found that Maine Yankee mitigated its damages by weighing other contractors' bids against its own self-performance bid. Maine Yankee was owed damages based on the cost of completion for the SWEC scope of work. The fact that Maine Yankee now projected that it would not complete that scope of work until six months after the date of completion in the Decommissioning Agreement did not mean that any "delay" costs adjustments were properly compensable to SWEC. So long as the damages that Maine Yankee were recovering were based on Maine Yankee's cost to complete the SWEC scope of work, it was proper for Maine Yankee to recover that entire amount.

After default termination of a contract, the owner may have liability to the subcontractors of the defaulted contractor if it requests them to continue to deliver or install materials after the effective date of the termination. This is particularly true if the owner takes possession of the project site and all materials and equipment on site in order to complete the work. In sorting out the owner's responsibility to the subcontractors and suppliers, courts may find the owner liable to them under informal written agreements, oral agreements or theories of unjust enrichment. *Encore Constr. Corp. v. S.C. Bodner Constr., Inc.*, 765 N.E.2d 223 (Ind. App. 2002).

[B] Termination for Convenience

Page 2-68, add after note 402 in first full paragraph:

In a situation where a termination for default is converted to a termination for the convenience of the owner, a contractor may not recover damages for home office overhead for the period between the default termination and the resumption of the work as a subcontractor to the takeover surety. *Walsky Constr. Co.*, ASBCA No. 52772, 01-2 B.C.A. (CCH) ¶ 31,557 (2001).

Page 2-68, add after first full paragraph:

Also, if the contract is terminated for the convenience of the owner because the work is impossible to perform, the contractor may be able to recover performance costs in excess of the contract price, even if the contractor was in a loss position at the time of termination. Although this may not be the case otherwise, the impossibility of performance results in a situation where the usual limitations on the amount and type of damages may not apply. *D.E.W., Inc. and D.E. Wurzbach, a Joint Venture*, ASBCA No. 50796, 00-2 B.C.A. (CCH) ¶ 31,104 (2000).

Page 2-69, add after note 409:

If the federal government elects to terminate the contract for convenience, the contractor has one year to submit a termination for convenience settlement proposal. If it fails to do so, the contracting officer may make a unilateral determination, and the contractor may waive its right to appeal the matter. *Earth Burners, Inc. v. United States,* 43 Fed. Cl. 481 (1999).

§ 2.15   LIQUIDATED DAMAGES

Page 2-70, add after note 417 in carryover paragraph:

To determine the validity of liquidated damages, courts may consider whether the delay damages would be difficult to prove *at the time the parties entered into the contract,* not at the time of the breach. *Phillips v. B.M. Hogan Co.,* 54 S.W.2d 39 (Ark. Ct. App. 1980). The *prospective* perspective is important in allowing an owner to pre-establish liquidated damages, not a *retrospective* perspective.

Page 2-71, add after note 421 in carryover paragraph:

Liquidated damages determined by the architect without explanation for their computation are an unenforceable penalty. In *Fuschino v. Smith,* 2001 Ohio App. LEXIS 21 (2001), the contract contained a liquidated damage clause requiring the contractor to pay $50 for each day after the completion date that a deck was not completed. The construction was not completed and the owner terminated the contract, completed the deck, and then sued the contractor. The contractor counter-claimed for extras. At a bench trial, judgment was entered for the contractor. The trial court found that the liquidated damage clause constituted a penalty because it bore no reasonable relationship to the actual damages suffered by the owner, and was therefore unenforceable.

The owner appealed and argued that the liquidated damages clause was cre-ated to compensate for the loss of use and enjoyment of the deck for each day that its construction exceeded the assigned completion date. It was clear that the owner wanted to use the deck during the summer months, and had even planned a large party for which extra space was needed that the deck would have provided. Dam-ages for missing these activities would ordinarily be difficult to determine. How-ever, the reviewing court found that the amount of the liquidated damages clause had been set by the architect without evidence to explain the basis for the amount. The only testimony regarding the amount of liquidated damages was provided by the contractor's son and indicated that the normal amount provided for liquidated damages for similar projects was less than one-half of the amount provided for in the contract. The owner's claim for liquidated damages bore no reasonable rela-tionship to the actual damages. At most, the damages from the loss of use of the deck were nominal. The trial court did not err by deeming the liquidated damages provision to be unenforceable.

[A]   Apportioning Delay

Page 2-73, add at end of first paragraph:

The liquidated damage clause may prevent the apportionment of delay. For exam-ple, in *Brashear v. Richardson Construction, Inc.,* 10 P.3d 115 (Wyo. 2000), the court held that the subcontractor could not have delayed completing the project "by April 7, 1998" as stated in the liquidated damage clause, if it did not begin its work until April 13, 1998. The subcontractor and the general contractor in *Brashear* contracted for remodeling of a church. The contract provided:

> In addition to Contractor's other remedies set forth herein, in the event that contractor is delayed in completing the project by April 7, 1998 due to actions or inactions of Subcontractor, Subcontractor shall be liable to Contractor for Liquidated Damages of Three Hundred Twenty[-]Five Dollars ($325.00) per calendar day of such delay.

Initially, the subcontractor was scheduled to begin work on February 1, 1998. The start date was delayed by weather and change orders unrelated to the subcontractor. The subcontractor did not begin work until April 13, 1998. At that time, sheetrockers were still not finished with their work, and they and other trades limited the subcontractor's efforts. In late June, the architect noticed certain problems with the subcontractor's installation of the sisal wall covering. The owner gave written notice of rejection of the sisal installation and a demand to cure. The subcontractor demanded payment for the work completed, but the general contractor withheld payment pending correction of the noted problems with the sisal installation. The subcontractor wanted to try to correct the problems without removing the sisal, but the architect insisted that removal and reinstallation consistent with the manufacturer's instructions were required. After the end of June, the subcontractor performed no significant work. On August 10, 1998, the general contractor terminated the contract and removed and reinstalled the sisal. The project was accepted by the owner as complete on October 1, 1998. The owner assessed liquidated damages to the general contractor pursuant to the general contract for more than 118 days of delay in the project completion. The general contractor allocated 54 days of delay to this subcontractor based upon what the general contractor considered to be a "reasonable" basis, with the remaining days of delay being allocated to the general contractor and other subcontractors. The record contained no evidence concerning the basis for that allocation. No request for extension of time was made by the subcontractor or the general contractor of one another. The record reflected no change order or orders effecting an extension of the April 7, 1998, deadline that triggered liquidated damages in the contract between the general contractor and the subcontractor.

The contract provided for liquidated damages only if the subcontractor delayed completion of the project beyond April 7, 1998. The record contained no evidence that the project was delayed past April 7, 1998, by the actions of the subcontractor. The district court erred when it awarded liquidated damages beyond those contemplated in the contract. If the general contractor had wanted a liquidated damages provision that would apply after the date specified in the contract, it could have provided one, because it drafted the contract. The contract provided for change orders and extensions of time. However, neither party used those remedies to alter the explicit terms of the contract when the April 7, 1998, date passed. Consequently, only the explicit terms of the written contract applied.

The general contractor argued that the subcontractor's testimony showed that the subcontractor understood the contract applied even though work was commenced later than contemplated and that liquidated damages applied whenever a delay was caused. However, the subcontractor's testimony in no way undermined the conclusion that the express terms of the contract did not authorize liquidated damages when the project was delayed long after April 7, 1998, by persons other than the subcontractor. The general contractor argued that, by commencing work after the April 7, 1998, date, the subcontractor had waived its right to claim that liquidated damages would apply only pursuant to the terms of the contract. In fact, the opposite was true. The general contractor waived its right to rely on the liquidated damages provision when it allowed the subcontractor to commence work after April 7, 1998—the contractually specified liquidated damages date—without requiring a change order or amendment to the contract. The award of liquidated damages was based upon the allocation of all the days of delay after the contract was terminated until the project was accepted as complete by the owner. No provision in the contract provided for such an allocation of damages. The district court inappropriately developed its own formula to calculate liquidated damages to be assessed against the subcontractor. The court reversed that portion of the district court's judgment that awarded the general contractor liquidated damages in the amount of $17,550, and remanded.

[B] Termination and Abandonment

Page 2-76, add after note 450 in first paragraph:

In *Fuschino v. Smith,* 2001 Ohio App. LEXIS 21 (2001), the owner contracted for the construction of a deck. The contract provided that "time is of the essence" and specified a completion date. It contained a liquidated damage and termination clause. The construction was not completed and the owner terminated the contract. The owner completed the project with the contractor's labor, then sued for both liquidated damages and the cost to complete. At a bench trial, judgment was entered in the contractor's favor. The trial court found that the owner "legally may not collect" both liquidated damages for delay and additional cost to complete the work.

The owner was entitled to damages for the cost of completion of the deck in accordance with Article 20.2 of the contract, which stated that the measure of damages was the difference between additional costs and the unpaid balance of the contract price. The appellate court thought that the trial court's finding ignored the fact that the owner had stated two separate claims for damages. The first claim, for actual damages, arose from the owner's having had to hire another to finish the project. The second claim, for liquidated damages, was based upon the loss of use and enjoyment of the deck during the interval between the time that it was supposed to have been completed and the time when it was actually completed. The owner was not barred from seeking both actual and liquidated damages, because the two are based upon separate losses.

Page 2-76, add to note 452:

Another case indicates that unless the owner actually reprocures the completion of the work, it may not be able to assess and collect liquidated damages after the contract was terminated for default. In Standard Coating Service, Inc., ASBCA No. 49201, 48611, 00-1 B.C.A. (CCH) ¶ 30,725 (2000), the contractor was awarded a fixed-price contract to paint four different sections of fuel piping and the structural steel trestles that supported the piping. After completing three sections of the piping and trestles, a dispute arose between the government and the contractor concerning time extensions and additional compensation. The contractor demobilized from the project site without performing any of the work on the fourth section, and its contract was terminated for default. Although the government issued a solicitation for the reprocurement of the painting of the fourth section, the solicitation was cancelled. Nevertheless, the government assessed liquidated damages against the defaulted contractor for the period from the time of termination to the estimated completion date of the work that was to be reprocured. The contractor appealed the assessment of liquidated damages for this time period. The Board ruled that liquidated damages could not be recovered for the period of the attempted but cancelled reprocurement. The government could not collect liquidated damages for work that it decided that it did not want.

[C]   Assessment of Liquidated Damages

Page 2-77, add to note 457:

However, in the event of default termination of the contract, unless the owner actually reprocures the completion of the work, it may not be able to assess and collect liquidated damages from a contractor after the contract was terminated for default. Standard Coating Service, Inc., ASBCA No. 49201, 48611, 00-1 B.C.A. (CCH) ¶ 30,725 (2000).

Page 2-78, replace note 467 with:

195 W. Va. 714, 466 S.E.2d 782 (1995).

Page 2-78, add after first full paragraph:

In *Casson Construction Co.,* GSBCA 4884, 78-1 B.C.A. (CCH) ¶ 13,032 (1978), the contractor, though finishing on time, failed to complete a phase of its work that delayed a follow-on contractor. The follow-on contractor was ordered to accelerate. It did so by using overtime and double shifts for several weeks. Casson claimed that its liability was limited to the liquidated damage amount of $240 a day contained in its contract; the real cost of acceleration was $644 a day. The Board pointed to another provision in the contract which stated that the contractor would indemnify the public agency for acceleration payments made to other contractors. The court held that the latter clause controlled and that the same breach could invoke different clauses. The Board would not apply the liquidated damages clause to milestone date delays, only to delay in completing the entire contract performance. The Board noted that the standard language used in the contract was adopted long before the advent of fast-track construction. In *M. Eisenberg & Bros., Inc. v. White Plains Housing Authority,* 55 A.D.2d 599, 389 N.Y.S.2d 390 (1976), the court held that the liquidated damage award did not preclude recovery of additional damages under indemnification provisions in the contract. However, in *Burns v. Hanover Insurance Co.,* 454 A.2d 325 (D.C. 1982), the court held that damages in addition to those provided for under the liquidated damage clause were not recoverable, even though the clause expressly stated that the liquidated sums were for "packing and storing of furnishings'" and "temporary accommodations." The court concluded that to recover more than liquidated damages, the contract must state expressly that the clause is limited to specified types of damages and that other damages are recoverable.

In *Northern Petrochemical Co. v. Thorsen & Thorshov,* 297 Minn. 118, 211 N.W.2d 159 (1973), the court declined to enforce a liquidated damage clause for unanticipated, unreasonable delay. In *Northern Petrochemical Co.,* after completion, serious structural defects were discovered for which large-scale redesign and reconstruction were required. Correction of the defects took eight months. The court affirmed an award based on lost profits because of delayed occupancy and excess operating costs while awaiting occupancy. The court rejected application of the liquidated damages clause, noting that it was intended to apply to normal delay, not to an extraordinary eight-month delay due to redesign and reconstruction. The court's conclusion would limit liquidation to normal, expected delays.

Page 2-79, add after note 477 in third full paragraph:

However, the contract must be clear that the liquidated damages provisions apply to the distinct phasing requirements or milestones. For example, in *Abcon Assocs., Inc. v. United States,* 49 Fed. Cl. 678 (2001), the contract for additions to a mail distribution center provided for three different phases of completion, and required the overall project completion in 510 calendar days. Another provision of the contract set liquidated damages of $750 per day "if the contractor fails to complete the work . . . within the time specified in this contract. . . ." The government withheld liquidated damages based upon the missed milestone date rather than the overall completion date. Subsequently, the contract was terminated for default for failure to make progress. The contractor appealed the default termination arguing that the government wrongfully withheld liquidated damages based upon the failure to meet the milestone associated with the phase, rather than assessing liquidated damages for the overall completion. The U.S. Court of Federal Claims held that the liquidated damages were improperly assessed because the liquidated damages clause was not explicitly tied to the interim phase milestones, only the overall completion date.

[D] Waiver of Liquidated Damages

Page 2-81, add at end of first paragraph:

For example, in *Textor Construction, Inc. v. Forsyth R-III School District*, 60 S.W. 3d 692 (Mo. App. 2001), it was determined that the owner had waived liquidated damages based upon assurances to the contractor from the owner's superintendent, the architect and the architect's representative that liquidated damages would not be assessed.

Page 2-82, add to note 487:

Brashear v. Richardson Constr., Inc., 10 P.3d 1115 (Wyo. 2000) (general contractor waived the right to collect liquidated damages when it allowed the subcontractor to commence work after the contractually specified liquidated damages date without establishing a new completion date, or requiring a change order or amendment to the subcontract).

[E] Establishing Amount and Terms

Page 2-83, add after note 490 in carryover paragraph:

For example, in *Brinich v. Jencka,* 2000 Pa. Super. 209, 757 A.2d 388 (2000), the Jenckas, the homeowners, signed an agreement with Brinich, the contractor, which provided for the work to be "substantially completed" by December 31; that date was subsequently changed to 270 days from the date of their construction loan agreement. Despite the revised completion date, the homeowners contended that Brinich had assured them that the house would be completed by December 31, 1993. Brinich encountered numerous problems that impeded timely construction. First, the excavator encountered an underground spring that continually filled the foundation with water. To correct the problem, Brinich had to extend the foundation and install a sump pump. In the meantime, the blocklayer with whom Brinich had subcontracted for the job began work on another project; therefore, Brinich was forced to find a replacement at a higher price. In January 1994, construction was delayed by extremely cold weather. In addition to these problems, Brinich testified that the Jenckas continually requested additions and/or modifications that not only involved additional costs, but also delayed construction. Construction continued into the spring of 1994.

The parties realized that the house would not be completed on time and executed an agreement extending the time for completion of the home until July 21, 1994. Attached to the agreement was a list of uncompleted work. The agreement also contained a liquidated damages clause in the event that construction was not completed by the extension deadline. The homeowners later refused to allow Brinich on the property after they obtained an occupancy permit and moved into the house in early October. In addition, the Jenckas refused to authorize disbursement of the final draw.

Brinich commenced suit against the Jenckas, alleging breach of written and oral contracts, unjust enrichment, tortious interference with contractual relations, and defamation. The jury returned a verdict in favor of Brinich for $87,635.21 for breach of written and oral contract.

The Jenckas contended that the trial court erred in failing to grant JNOV or a new trial on their counterclaim for liquidated damages. Because it was undisputed that Brinich failed to complete construction prior to the Jenckas' moving in, the Jenckas argued that Brinich was responsible for liquidated damages. The Jenckas provided very little evidence of any actual costs they incurred due to the delay in the construction of their home. Mr. Jencka testified that the liquidated damages provision was suggested by others to "put some teeth" in the agreement, and to encourage Brinich to finish the project on time. He claimed that the amount represented "costs that we were experiencing out of pocket." However, testimony concerning these out-of-pocket expenses was not limited to the delay period. The only expenses relevant to determining the legitimacy of the liquidated damages clause were storage and living expenses of approximately $550 per month, or less than $20 per day. Even if Jenckas' mileage expenses were included, the total still accounted for less than $30 per day. Because the Jenckas failed to present sufficient evidence justifying the $250-per-day liquidated damages figure, the court concluded that it was a penalty and thus unenforceable. The judgment was affirmed.

Page 2-83, add at end of carryover paragraph:

Liquidated damages of $5,000 a week were found not to be a penalty for prolonged inconvenience, discomfort, invasion of privacy, and forced renegotiation with another contractor to complete the job. *The Gables, Gables/Kovens, Inc. v. Choate,* 792 So. 2d 520 (Fla. Dist. Ct. App. 3d Dist. 2001). Choate signed a purchase and sale agreement with The Gables, a developer for a luxury condominium unit. The contract provided that the unit would be completed by May 1, 1996, and that if the unit was not completed on time, the owner would receive a credit of $5,000 per month until closing. By December 1996, the unit was still incomplete and the developer was in bad financial straits. An improvement contract was incorporated into the closing agreement, providing that if the unit was not finished within 30 days the developer would pay the owner $5,000 per week should completion of all the work be delayed beyond 30 days. The interior contractor also agreed to pay the owner $5,000 for each seven-day period of such delay. The contract also provided that if the owner failed to close, he would forfeit his entire $175,000 deposit. The owner moved into the unfinished unit on January 20, 1997. An independently retained contractor testified that the work was incomplete and had been done in a slipshod, unworkmanlike manner. The developer walked off the job and the owner hired another contractor to finish the job. The owner sued. The trial court determined that the owner was entitled to summary judgment on the issue of enforceability of the liquidated damage clause of the closing agreement. The developer appealed.

The developer argued that the liquidated damages at issue were a penalty disproportionate to the owners' actual damages. The parties in the case negotiated for the purchase and sale of a luxury residence. Both sides were sophisticated and were represented by counsel. The appellate court agreed with the owner that the liquidated damage provision had been included because actual damages could not be determined at the time of closing and the owner would suffer significant inconveniences in the event the dwelling was not completed in a timely and workmanlike manner. For the eight to nine months that followed the closing, the owner was forced to live in a construction zone rather than a luxury apartment. Six months after closing, the developer abandoned the premises and the owner was forced to contract another construction company to finish the job. The prolonged inconvenience, discomfort, invasion of privacy, and renegotiation with another contractor to complete the job were exactly the things the parties considered when they agreed to the liquidated damage provision. The appeals court affirmed.

§ 2.16   NO DAMAGES FOR DELAY CLAUSE

[A]   Enforceability

Page 2-90, add after first full paragraph:

For example, in *Landis & Gyr Powers, Inc. v. Berley Industries, Inc.*, 298 A.D.2d 435, 750 N.Y.S.2d 82 (2002), Berley Industries, Inc. contracted with the Dormitory Authority of the State of New York for heating, ventilation, and air conditioning work at a renovation project at Queens College. Berley subcontracted the automatic temperature control work to the plaintiff, Landis & Gyr. Due to delays allegedly caused by Berley's mismanagement of the project and failure to compel another subcontractor, General Sheet Metal, Inc., to timely and properly perform work upon which the plaintiff's work depended, the plaintiff's work was not completed until approximately 418 days after the original contract completion date. Alleging that it was damaged by the delay, the plaintiff commenced its action against Berley seeking to recover the increased cost of the work occasioned by the delay and other damages under theories of breach of contract, tort, and quantum meruit. The subcontract between Berley and the plaintiff contained a clause providing that the plaintiff was not entitled to compensation for delay caused by Berley. On its motion for summary judgment, Berley argued that the plaintiff's cause of action, which sought to recover for extra expenses as a result of delays allegedly caused by Berley, was barred by the no-damage-for-delay provision of the subcontract. The plaintiff failed to raise any factual issue that the delays were not contemplated by the parties, or that Berley's conduct was intentional, willful, or grossly negligent, thus, summary judgment dismissing the cause of action was properly granted.

Page 2-91, replace note 533 with:

221 Ga. App. 543, 472 S.E.2d 88 (1996), *rev'd*, 482 S.E. 279 (1997).

[B] Exception for Delay Not Within the Terms

Page 2-92, add after carryover sentence:

In *Triple R Paving, Inc. v. Broward County,* 774 So. 2d 50 (Fla. Dist. Ct. App. 2000), the standard form contract used by the owner contained a no damages for delay clause that permitted recovery only for hindrances or delays due to fraud, bad faith, or active interference on the part of the county or its agents. Triple R Paving successfully bid on a road construction contract, which included widening a bridge that spanned a canal. During construction, delays resulted from a horizontal sight distance design flaw, a Florida Power & Light (FP&L) utility relocation, and detention pond elevation problems. Triple R filed suit against the owner for delay damages, including lost home office overhead and lost efficiency. The owner, in turn, filed a third-party complaint against the designer for indemnification.

Triple R discovered that the plans did not meet horizontal sight distance standards. The owner then refused to allow the bridge to open. Triple R advised the designer that it would move its manpower and equipment off the job until a solution to the horizontal sight distance problem was discovered; however, it was directed not to do so. While a solution was being worked out, Triple R worked on a portion of the project north of the bridge, but the inability to open the bridge and switch traffic to the other lane impeded its ability to proceed efficiently with its work.

A second delay occurred when FP&L did not show up to remove the power lines because of maintenance problems with its equipment. The third delay resulted from problems involving the detention pond that was to drain into a canal. The canal elevation was higher than depicted in the design and higher than the pond; however, no proof was elicited to show that either the owner or the designer was aware of this design flaw prior to actual construction. Had the construction proceeded as designed, a backward flow would have resulted.

The entire project was finished within the extension period granted for the delays, but not within the original contract period. The work was never completely suspended on the project. According to Triple R, it was never able to become more efficient in performing the remainder of the work. Triple R claimed that during the delays and extended performance period, the company obtained no substitute work to compensate it for lost overhead. The designer moved for directed verdict at the close of Triple R's case, claiming that Triple R had failed to prove that the construction delays were the result of fraud, bad faith, or active interference. The jury returned a verdict that awarded damages to Triple R for loss of efficiency in the amount of $112,929.31, but nothing for home office overhead. The designer claimed that the trial court erred in denying its motion for directed verdict. The court agreed with the designer with respect to the delays occasioned by the FP&L

utility relocation and the detention pond elevation. However, the court found that the delay resulting from the horizontal sight distance design flaw was sufficient to allow a jury to decide the question of fraud, bad faith, or active interference. According to the reviewing court, evidence of the designer's knowledge of the design flaw and the subsequent failure to apprise Triple R of the problem were sufficient to constitute "willful concealment of foreseeable circumstances which impact timely performance," such that the no damages for delay clause may be overcome. However, in view of the owner's and designer's lack of control over FP&L and the lack of proof of knowledge as to the detention pond flaw, the appellate court found the evidence insufficient to show fraud, bad faith, or active interference, and so reversed in favor of the owner and the designer on those damage claims.

There are other arguments that may be raised to avoid the application of no damages for delay clauses. For example, in *PYCA Industries, Inc. v. Harrison County Waste Water Management District,* 177 F.3d 351 (5th Cir. 1999), the claimant argued that the no damages for delay clause was superseded by federal contract provisions that authorized increases in contract time and price for changes in the work. The project was a waste water treatment facility that was partially funded by the U.S. Environmental Protection Agency (EPA). The EPA special conditions were incorporated by reference into the contract documents. They provided for time extensions and the recovery of time-related costs, and further provided that the special conditions would supersede other conflicting contract provisions. A no damages for delay clause was included in the contract documents. In dealing with the issue, the court reasoned that the EPA special conditions were minimum requirements that EPA grantees must include in the contract documents, but the grantees were expressly authorized to impose more stringent terms. The no damages for delay clause was an additional requirement, not a conflicting provision, and the court enforced the no damages for delay clause to preclude the claimant from recovering its delay costs.

The contract clause preventing recovery for delays caused by a utility does not bar contractor claims based on an owner's own performance problems. In *Scoccolo Construction Co. v. City of Renton,* 9 P.3d 886 (Wash. Ct. App. 2000), Scoccolo Construction, Inc. was awarded a contract with the City of Renton to widen Park Avenue. The contract provided that the relocation of utilities would be effected by the relevant utility companies, not the contractor, although the contractor was required to coordinate relocation efforts with the utility companies. The contract further provided that no additional compensation would be made for delay caused by actions of any utility company. A franchise agreement between the city and the utility gave the city the authority to compel the utility to relocate utilities at the utility company's cost and expense. The contractor claimed that the utility did not complete its obligations under the contract with the city in a timely manner, which delayed the contractor's work on Park Avenue. The contractor filed suit against the city to recover damages due to delays in the contract, and the city moved for partial summary judgment in light of the contract language providing that the contractor would not receive additional compensation for delays caused by the actions of any utility company. The trial court granted the city's motion for summary judgement. The parties appealed.

The contractor argued, among other things, that summary judgment was inappropriate because: (1) the city knew that the utility was delaying the contractor's work, but did not exercise its right to direct the utility to complete the work or to have others complete the work if the utility failed to perform; (2) the city breached its implied duty to cooperate with the contractor and facilitate completion of the project; and (3) the contractual language precluding additional compensation for delays caused by the actions of utility companies was invalid under a statute. The city argued that the statutory prohibition applied only to the actions of the city or its agents and that the utility was not the city's agent. The appellate court noted that the statute was a legislative reaction to state cases upholding the protections afforded by a no damages for delay clause. The court then stated that the contractor's claims were based on the actions of the city and not the utility. The court that indicated claims against the city were not barred by the no damages for delay provision. The fact that the utility companies contributed to delays did not shield the city from potential liability based on its own contractual breaches. The statute by its plain language voided a particular type of construction contract clause that purported to prevent delay damage claims. The appellate court noted that even if the statute invalidated the language in the contract, the contractor could not necessarily recover for delays related to the conduct of the utilities. However, summary judgment was inappropriate because it was based solely upon the existence of the no damages for delay clause in the agreement. The trial court's summary judgment order was reversed.

[C] Exception for Delay Not Contemplated by the Parties

Page 2-93, add after note 548 in first carryover paragraph:

In *Clifford R. Gray Inc. v. City School District,* 277 A.D.2d 843, 716 N.Y.S.2d 795 (2000), an electrical contractor had a contract to renovate and expand a school. The parties' contract included a no damages for delay clause. The contractor filed suit for money damages for delays. The trial court concluded that the clause did not preclude the contractor's suit and awarded money damages. Both parties appealed.

The construction schedule contemplated three phases. Phase II (the construction of a new addition to the school) was to continue for 10 months and be finished in February 1995. However, it was not substantially completed until September 1995. Similarly, although phase III (renovation of an existing building) was anticipated to take six months, with completion in August 1995, the work was not concluded until July 1996. Among the various causes of the delays were the owner's failure to timely obtain easements for electrical and drain sewer installations; the failure of the owner's construction manager to adequately supervise and coordinate the work of the various contractors, including the failure to prepare coordinated construction schedules and drawings; the termination of both the construction manager (in December 1994) and the general contractor (in June 1995); and the owner's decision to hire 30 subcontractors in lieu of replacing the general contractor. The appellate court found that the project impediments were wholly unanticipated and of a character and magnitude not ordinarily encountered or anticipated by parties to a contract of this nature. Moreover, the evidence established that the owner's construction management team failed to substantially fulfill the express contractual obligation to schedule and coordinate the work, resulting in extensive work interruptions or delays and inefficient labor deployment. The court saw no basis to disturb the state supreme court's determination that there was a pervasive and ongoing breach of the contract.

Page 2-93, add after note 552 in first carryover paragraph:

and delays resulting from the owner's mismanagement of the multiple trade contractors. *Clifford R. Gray, Inc. v. City Sch. Dist. of Albany,* 277 A.D.2d 843, 716 N.Y.S.2d 795 (2000).

Page 2-93, add after note 553 in first carryover paragraph:

The exception to the no damages for delay clause for unanticipated delays is also found in some statutes (Cal. Pub. Cont. Code § 7102 (1985 & Supp. 1990)), and may be found in the contract provisions as well. *Howard Contracting, Inc. v. G.A. MacDonald Construction Co.,* 83 Cal. Rptr. 2d 590, 71 Cal. App. 4th 38 (1999).

Page 2-94, add after note 558 in first carryover paragraph:

In one contract, the owner expressly advised the contractor of the possibility of unmarked or inaccurately located utility lines. The contract also contained a specific clause disallowing damages for delay due to unanticipated utility interferences. The contractor encountered 26 different unmarked or mislocated utility lines that interfered with its contract work to install three miles of water main, and claimed that they resulted in 18 weeks of delay. The contractor filed suit to recover its delay costs. Although the trial court directed the verdict in favor of the contractor, the appellate court concluded that the contract clearly contemplated this type of delay and the no damages for delay clause was enforceable for this type of delay. *DiGioia Brothers Excavating v. City of Cleveland Dep't of Public Utilities,* 734 N.E.2d 438, 135 Ohio App. 3d 436, *appeal denied,* 727 N.E.2d 134 (2000).

[D] Exception for Unreasonable Delay

Page 2-95, add after note 565 in first carryover paragraph:

For example, where the owner failed to obtain the necessary permits to allow the work to proceed, a four-month delay was held to be unreasonable. *Howard Contracting, Inc. v. G.A. MacDonald Constr. Co., Inc.,* 71 Cal. App. 4th 38, 83 Cal. Rptr. 2d 590 (1999).

[E]   Exception for Active Owner Interference

Page 2-95, add after note 569 in first full paragraph:

or where the owner issued the notice to proceed to the contractor knowing that the required preliminary work had not been completed. *U.S. Steel Corp. v. Missouri Pacific Railroad Co.*, 668 F.2d 435 (8th Cir. 1982).

Page 2-97, add after note 579 in first full paragraph:

or "inexcusable incompetence" (*John E. Gregory & Sons, Inc. v. A. Guenther & Sons, Inc.*, 432 N.W.2d 584 (Wis. 1998)), or "intentional or gross fault" (*Pellerin Constr., Inc. v. Witco Corp.*, 169 F. Supp. 2d 568 (E.D. La. 2001)). The actions of the owner may need to be more than negligent; they may be required to reach the level of gross negligence or intentional misconduct. *Landis & Gyr Powers, Inc. v. Berley Indus., Inc.*, 750 N.Y.S.2d 82 (App. Ct. 2 Dep't 2002).

Page 2-98, add at end of carryover paragraph:

Also the court in *Mississippi Transportation Commission v. SCI*, 717 So. 2d 332 (Miss. 1998), held that the owner's refusal to grant time extensions on a timely basis could be interpreted as active interference or bad faith preventing the application of the no damages for delay clause from barring the contractor's recovery of delay damages.

Chapter 3
RESPONSIBILITY FOR DELAY

§ 3.02   OWNER-CAUSED DELAY

Page 3-5, add after first full paragraph:

New York has developed a line of cases that contractors are not liable to subcontractors in the event delays arise from circumstances outside the contractor's control, including the acts of the owner. In *Triangle Sheet Metal Works, Inc. v. James H. Merritt and Co.*, 79 N.Y.2d 801, 588 N.E.2d 69, 580 N.Y.S.2d 171 (1991), the New York Court of Appeals denied a subcontractor recovery for delay damages, after finding that the delay was not the fault of the general contractor. Triangle, a subcontractor on a construction project for New York City, sought recovery against Merritt, the prime contractor, for performance delays, which were contributed to by the City, other contractors, and weather delays. The trial court dismissed the claim and the appeals court affirmed, holding that:

> This case falls squarely within the general rule that, absent a contractual commitment to the contrary, a prime contractor is not responsible for delays that its subcontractor may incur unless those delays are caused by some agency or circumstance under the prime contractor's direction or control. Contrary to Triangle's contention, there is no basis for concluding that a prime contractor—which oftentimes lacks control over much of the work to be performed at a particular project—has implicitly agreed to assume responsibility for all delays that a subcontractor might experience—no matter what their cause. *Id.* at 802 (citations and quotations omitted) (emphasis added). See also Norcross v. Wills, 198 N.Y. 336, 91 N.E. 803, 805 (1910) (holding that a party to a construction contract will be "answerable for all losses caused by delays, which his control of the work should make him responsible for . . .").

The *Triangle* court concluded that a subcontractor unhappy with this rule "should bargain for the inclusion in its subcontract of a provision" to the contrary. *Id.* at 803.

Similarly, in *Regional Building Systems, Inc. v. Planning Commission of Regional Building System*, 320 F.3d 4821 (4th Cir. 2003), Regional Building Systems (RBS), a manufacturer of modular housing units, contracted with Aspen Knolls Construction Corporation to manufacture, deliver, and install 1,000 housing units on Aspen Knolls' property in Staten Island. RBS subcontracted with Bedford Construction Corporation under which Bedford was responsible for transporting the modular units manufactured by RBS to the Aspen Knolls building site, and then erecting and completing the structures. Aspen Knolls experienced financial difficulties and defaulted on a number of payments to RBS. Without these payments, RBS experienced a severe cash flow problem and was unable to meet its contractual obligation to deliver the requisite number of housing units to Bedford. Consequently, RBS suspended its work under the subcontract. Aspen Knolls later ceased paying RBS altogether, forcing RBS to terminate the Aspen Knolls contract as well as the subcontract with Bedford. RBS filed a voluntary petition for relief under Chapter 11 of the Bankruptcy Code. Bedford filed a claim in the amount of $1,448,226.49. The bankruptcy court determined that Bedford was only entitled to recover an additional $22,067.82. The bankruptcy court denied Bedford's claim for delay damages, holding that New York law prevented such a recovery when the contractor was not responsible for the delays. The district court affirmed the bankruptcy court's decision. Bedford appealed the holding that New York law did not permit a subcontractor to recover delay damages from a general contractor.

Bedford argued that financial difficulty did not excuse performance under a contract and that delay damages were proper. In its opinion, the bankruptcy court concluded that Aspen Knolls' breach of its payment obligations to RBS was the cause of RBS's suspension of work. The court found that RBS acted reasonably, suspending deliveries only after Aspen Knolls had defaulted on several payments and resuming them once payments were again made. RBS terminated the contract only after Aspen Knolls had defaulted on two invoices totaling over $3,000,000.00, which the court determined so severely hampered RBS's cash flow that RBS was justified in suspending work. During this time, RBS kept Bedford fully informed about Aspen Knolls' financial troubles, knowing that Bedford also had direct contracts with Aspen Knolls. Having determined that the delay was caused by Aspen Knolls' failure to pay RBS, not by any wrongdoing of RBS, the bankruptcy court concluded that RBS was not liable to Bedford for delay damages. Bedford could not claim delay damages for circumstances beyond RBS's control. Accordingly, the denial of delay damages to Bedford was affirmed.

Whether the contractor is liable to the subcontractor for acts out of its control or for acts of the owner should depend on what the subcontract states about owner-caused and third-party-caused delay. Without reference to the risks of owner delay in the subcontract, the court's determination that the contractor is, as a matter of law, not at risk for the owner's actions may be appropriate. However, where a contract contains language indicating otherwise, such a contract should be enforced.

[A] The Project Site

Page 3-9, add at end of first full paragraph:

The owner may not be able to limit the contractor's ability to recover for delayed utility relocations by disclaiming liability in the contract. For example, in *Scoccolo Construction, Inc. v. City of Renton,* 9 P.3d 886 (Wash. Ct. App. 2000), the city awarded a contract to Scoccolo to widen a city street. The contract provided that the city would have the utility company relocate their utility lines, and that the contractor would not be compensated for any delays caused by the utility company. A separate agreement between the city and the utility company provided for the relocation of utility lines at the utility company's cost and pursuant to a schedule agreed upon by the city and the utility company. Scoccolo was delayed in its work by the failure to timely relocate the utility lines. Scoccolo sued the city for its delay costs, based upon the city's failure to act to direct the utility company to perform rather than the utility company's delays. The court found the city liable to the contractor for the delay costs incurred for the city's breach of an implied duty to cooperate with Scoccolo and to facilitate the relocation of the utility lines. In ruling in this manner, the court avoided the issue of the enforceability of the no damages for delay clause, as such clauses are not enforceable under Washington state statutes.

[D]   Owner's Responsibility for Design

Page 3-14, add to note 48:

In Alaska Dep't of Natural Res. v. Transamerica Premier Ins. Co., 856 P.2d 766 (Alaska 1993), the court articulated the owner's responsibility as follows:

> Unlike design professionals, project owners owe purely contractual duties to the accuracy of the designs. When providing plans and specifications to a contractor, an owner makes an implied warranty that they will be sufficient for their particular purpose. If the defective specifications cause the contractor to incur extra costs in performing the contract, then the contractor may recover these costs that result from breach of the implied warranty. The implied warranty is part of the bargain between the owner and independent contractor and does not exist outside the contract.

Owners often take a proactive approach in the time period between contract award and the start of construction to hold preconstruction meetings to discuss scheduling, design issues, mobilization, safety plans, special construction requirements, submittals, and coordination of the trades. Delays may often be averted by discussions and problem resolution at preconstruction meetings. Although preconstruction meetings may be good practice for owners and are often the custom in the construction industry, absent a contractual requirement, the owner may not be liable to the contractor for delays for the sole reason of not timely scheduling and holding such meetings. For example, in Program & Constr. Mgmt. Group, Inc., GSBCA No. 14178, 00-1 B.C.A. (CCH) ¶ 30,641 (1999), the contractor requested that the government hold a preconstruction meeting to discuss schedules, safety, submittals, and other issues. There were no contract provisions or other requirements for preconstruction meetings. There was a meeting, but it was not held until nearly seven weeks after contract award. The contractor alleged that it incurred more than a month in front-end delays because of the government's failure to schedule a preconstruction meeting earlier. The board, in ruling in favor of the government, reasoned that without a specific requirement for a preconstruction meeting, it had to reject the contractor's claim and find that there is no implied duty to hold a preconstruction meeting.

Page 3-15, add at end of first full paragraph:

If multiple proprietary products are specified, the owner warrants that each and every specified item is suitable for its intended purpose, and it makes no difference whether the contractor selected the particular product from various alternatively specified items. *Hawaiian Bitumuls & Paving v. United States*, 26 Ct. Cl. 1234 (1992).

[E]   Owner's Contract Administration Responsibilities

Page 3-18, add after note 73 in first full paragraph:

The owner's contract administration duties include providing the contractor with a complete set of plans and specifications. *Overstreet Elec. Co.*, ASBCA No. 51654, 00-1 B.C.A. (CCH) ¶ 30,588 (1999).

§ 3.03   DESIGNER-CAUSED DELAY

Page 3-30, add to note 159:

Cases and jurisdictions allowing the contractor to bring an action directly against the designer include: Gulf Contracting v. Bibb County, 795 F.2d 980 (11th Cir. 1986); Malta Constr. v. Henningson Durham & Richardson, Inc., 694 F. Supp. 902 (D. Ga. 1988); Berkel & Co. Contractors, Inc. v. Providence Hosp., 454 So. 2d 496 (Ala. 1984); State v. Tyonek Timber, Inc., 680 P.2d 1148 (Alaska 1984); Donnelly Constr. Co. v. Oberg/Hunt/Gilliland, 677 P.2d 1292 (Ariz. 1984); Danforth v. Acorn Structures, Inc., 608 A.2d 1194 (Del. 1992); Comtech Int'l, Inc. v. Milan Commerce Park, 711 So. 2d 1255 (Fla. Dist. Ct. App. 1998); NBD Bank v. Krueger Ringier, Inc., 686 N.E.2d 704 (Ill. App. Ct. 1997); Normoyle-Berg & Assocs., Inc. v. Village of Deer Creek, 39 Ill. App. 3d 744, 350 N.E.2d 559 (1976); Koss Constr. v. Caterpillar, Inc., 960 P.2d 255 (Kan. Ct. App. 1998); Gurtler, Hebert & Co. v. Weyland Mach. Shop, Inc., 405 So. 2d 660 (La. Ct. App. 1981); Milton Co. v. Council of Unit Owners of Bentley Place Condos., 708 A.2d 1047 (Md. Ct. Spec. App. 1998); Prichard Bros., Inc. v. Grady Co., 428 N.W.2d 391 (Minn. 1988); Jim's Excavating Serv., Inc. v. HKM Assocs., 878 P.2d 248 (Mont. 1994); Conforti & Eisle, Inc. v. John C. Morris Assocs., 418 A.2d 1290 (N.J. Super. Ct. Law Div. 1980), *aff'd*, 489 A.2d 1233 (N.J. Super. Ct. App. Div. 1985); Davidson & Jones, Inc. v. County of New Hanover, 255 S.E.2d 580 (N.C. Ct. App. 1979); Tommy L. Griffin Plumbing & Heating v. Jordan, Jones & Goulding, Inc., 463 S.E.2d 85 (S.C. 1995); Midwestern Elec., Inc. v. DeWild Grant Reckert & Assocs., Inc., 500 N.W.2d 250 (S.D. 1993); John Martin Co. v. Morse/Diesel, Inc., 819 S.W.2d 428 (Tenn. 1991); Thomson v. Espey Huston & Assocs., 899 S.W.2d 415 (Tex. App.

1995); American Towers Owner's Ass'n v. CCI Mech., 930 P.2d 1182 (Utah 1996); Daanen & Janssen, Inc. v. Cedarapids, Inc., 573 N.W.2d 842 (Wis. 1998).

Cases in which the contractor has not been able to recover directly against the designer for economic losses without being in privity of contract include: Bowling Green Mun. Utils. v. Thomasson Lumber Co., 902 F. Supp. 134 (W.D. Ky. 1995); City Express, Inc. v. Express Partners, 959 P.2d 836 (Haw. 1998); Duffin v. Idaho Crop Improvement Ass'n, 895 P.2d 1195 (Idaho 1995); Fleischer v. Hellmuth, Obata & Kassabaum, 870 S.W.2d 832 (Mo. Ct. App. 1993); Floor Craft Floor Covering, Inc. v. Parma Cmty. Hosp. Ass'n, 54 Ohio St. 3d 1, 560 N.E.2d 206 (1990); Gerald M. Moor & Sons, Inc. v. Drewry, 467 S.E.2d 811 (Va. 1996); Rissler & McMurray Co. v. Sheridan Area Water Supply Joint Powers Bd., 929 P.2d 1228 (Wyo. 1998).

Page 3-30, add to note 162:

Miami Heart Inst. v. Heery Architects & Eng'rs, Inc., 765 F. Supp. 1083 (S.D. Fla. 1991) (owner recovered delay damage paid to contractors and subcontractors as a result of architect's delay to project; in addition, court allowed owner to recover additional architectural/design expenses and out-of-sequence construction costs incurred to modify building due to designer's errors and omissions). *See also* R. Crewdson, *Recovering Delay Damages Against an Architect: An Owner's Approach,* 9 Constr. Law. 24 (Jan. 1989).

Page 3-30, add after note 165 in second full paragraph:

Designers may attempt to limit their liability for delays and other damages resulting from their performance. The most common types of clauses limit the designer's exposure to the available insurance coverage, to a specified amount, or to a duty to reperform the services that caused the problem. The effectiveness of such limitation of liability clauses depends upon a variety of considerations embodied in statutory and judicial law, such as whether the parties negotiated and expressly agreed on liability limitations, whether the clause was an indemnification or a limitation of liability, the sophistication and bargaining powers of the parties, whether the damages were tort or contractual in nature, the reasonableness of the liability cap, the clarity of the language, and the level of negligence or intentional actions by the designer. Zetlin & Chillemi, *Building a Safe Haven: Clauses Imposing Monetary Limits on Designer Liability,* 20 Constr. Law. 5 (Jan. 2000).

[A] Designer Defects

Page 3-32, add to end of subsection:

Design problems like the ones mentioned are often avoidable, especially through methods such as peer reviews, in which an independent multidisciplinary panel is engaged to review the proposed design to obtain the insights and experiences of other architects, engineers, and similar professionals. Not only are errors often discovered and resolved, but additional value can also be obtained for owners, cost savings explored, and a longer-term perspective developed to minimize the obsolescence of the project. *See Owners and Designers Are Airing Experiences Through Peer Review,* 254 Engineering News-Rec. 66 (Nov. 13, 2000), and *Face-to-Face Peer Reviews May Have No Peer in Quality,* 254 Engineering News-Rec. 104 (Nov. 13, 2000).

[C] Tardy Shop Drawing Review

Page 3-34, add to note 191:

The general contractor may also have the duty to coordinate the shop drawings and related information from its own subcontractors, and may be responsible for delays in failing to provide proper coordination. Some of the contract clauses may appear onerous, as in W.M. Schlosser Co. v. United States, 767 F.2d 870 (Fed. Cir. 1985), in which the shop drawing coordination clause was enforced to the detriment of the contractor. The shop drawings were required to include great detail concerning location, layout, and alignment, a higher standard than the contractor believed was the custom and requirement.

[D] Delay Due to Tests and Inspections

Page 3-35, add at end of section:

Architects can delay the release of retention to a contractor by unjustifiably withholding certificates of substantial completion. Architects can take the position that, because the contractor has not achieved substantial completion, the contractor is liable for late completion and liquidated damages. R. Lowe & E. Walthall, *When Architects Withhold Certificates of Substantial Completion, and Other Problems,* 19 Constr. Law. 5 (No. 4, Oct. 1999).

In case law, the terms and doctrines of substantial completion and substantial performance are used interchangeably. Substantial completion is a term of art used in the construction industry to measure the time commitment of the contract. The definition of substantial completion used by the parties, however, is similar to the definition of substantial performance used by the courts. Like the doctrine of substantial completion, the doctrine of substantial performance provides for performance of a contract that, although possibly not full performance, is so close to contract terms that it would be unreasonable to deny the promisee the full contract price—subject however, to the promisor's right to recover damages that result from the failure to render full performance. Lowe & Walthall, at 5.

Although a contractor may be substantially complete in terms of work on the project, defects in the work may prevent the owner from using the project for its intended purpose and thus, prevent a finding of substantial completion. Lowe & Walthall, at 8.

The court in *Utley James of Louisiana, Inc. v. Louisiana Division of Administration,* 671 So. 2d 473 (La. Ct. App. 1995), held that a prison construction project was not substantially complete because of a 48-page punch list that included aesthetic issues, an inoperable fire alarm system, an inoperable sewage lift system, and coordination problems with subcontractors. The contract defined substantial completion as the date the architect issued certification of substantial completion. The court affirmed the trial court's holding that substantial completion did not occur until the architect issued the certificate. Lowe & Walthall, at 8.

Once substantial completion has been attained, the architect is under a legal duty to issue a certificate. This principle was reflected in *Haugen v. Raupach,* 260 P.2d 340 (Wash. 1953), in which the court held that the contractor was entitled to the balance under the contract, without having to obtain a certificate of substantial completion. Although the architect felt that there was substantial performance, he yielded to the owner's insistence that work was not done properly. The court held that:

> [I]f the architect is satisfied that there has been a substantial performance of the contract, it then becomes his duty to issue the certificate of completion, and if he does not do so, his conduct is regarded as arbitrary and capricious. If the architect is in collusion with his principal, or yields to his opposition to the issuance of the certification when such opposition is not justified, then in such cases the contract has a legal excuse for not obtaining the certificate as a condition precedent to recovering on his contract.

The *Haugen* decision, instead of resolving the problem, created two more complicated and unanswered questions: (1) whether the "arbitrary and capricious" standard applies even when the architect has not yet determined whether substantial completion has been obtained; and (2) whether a contractor has a cause of action against an architect who acts arbitrarily and capriciously by withholding a certificate of substantial completion. Lowe & Walthall, at 8-9.

Although it appears that liquidated damages cannot be assessed against the contractor, several courts have interpreted contractual provisions to allow them, even if the contractor obtains substantial completion. In *Ledbetter Bros., Inc. v. North Carolina Department of Transportation,* 314 So. 2d 761 (N.C. Ct. App. 1984), the North Carolina Court of Appeals held that, under terms of the contract, liquidated damages could be assessed for the time period between substantial performance and final completion. In *Ledbetter,* the liquidated damages provision expressly recognized that failure to complete the work would result in increased inspection and administrative costs to DOT including the inspection costs arising between substantial performance and final acceptance. The contract provisions stated that no part of the project would be accepted until final acceptance. Lowe & Walthall, at 9.

The Pennsylvania Supreme Court, in *Sutter Corp. v. Tri-Boro Municipal Authority,* 487 A.2d 933 (Pa. 1985), issued a similar holding. The court held that the authority was entitled to liquidated damages for each day past the agreed completion date, despite the fact that it was able to begin using the sewage treatment plant, because the contract stated that liquidated damages accrued for any work that should remain uncompleted beyond that time. In *Vrgora v. Los Angeles Unified School District,* 200 Cal. Rptr. 130 (Ct. App. 1984), the California Court of Appeals relied on prior case law in holding that use and occupancy of a building by the owner did not prevent the assessment of liquidated damages until the contract was fully performed. Lowe & Walthall, at 9.

Although substantial completion entitles a contractor to the balance of the contract price (less any damages caused by the contractor's breach), AIA contracts modify this approach. Under A201-1997, the contractor is not entitled to the balance until the architect issues the final payment certificate. In theory, the owner could withhold the entire retainage, but in practice courts interpreting the AIA document would apply the substantial completion doctrine to determine whether the amount was reasonable. Lowe & Walthall, at 10.

§ 3.04   CONTRACTOR-CAUSED DELAY

[B]   Contractor Management Problems

Page 3-38, add to note 219:

Cape Romain Contractors, Inc., ASBCA No. 50557, 00-1 B.C.A. (CCH) ¶ 30,697 (1999).

Page 3-38, add after fourth full paragraph:

The contractor is responsible for the time needed to develop plans that comply with a performance contract's terms. *P.R. Burke Corp. v. United States,* 277 F.3d 1346 (Cal. Fed. Cir. 2002). Burke's contract to repair and improve a sewage treatment plant required that it keep the plant in operation during the entire construction period. Portions of the trickling filter pump station and chlorine contact tank that Burke was required to construct appeared in the same location as the existing trickling filter. Burke's draft demolition plan entailed demolishing the trickling filter at the beginning of construction to make way for the new structures that were to be built in its place. The government, however, indicated that this would cause "operational" problems and provided a suggested alternate sequence of tasks. Burke submitted a new demolition plan, but asserted that adapting its plans to conform to the government's suggested sequence would cost Burke approximately $400,000 and would extend the estimated completion date approximately nine months. The government approved Burke's demolition and construction plan but rejected Burke's adjusted performance schedule and sued the government.

Burke contended it incurred delay damages for the period the government kept requesting contract-compliant demolition plans. Burke, in addition, argued that the government's suggestions about the demolition and construction sequence were binding changes to the contract's design specifications and that Burke therefore had no choice but to follow them. The contract showed that the contractor, not the government, had to design the trickling filter. The time needed to develop plans that complied with contract terms was chargeable to the contractor, especially when the contract expressly required submission of design plans and work schedules for approval. Therefore, because it was Burke's responsibility to determine how to perform the demolition and construction and because the contract could be performed as written, Burke did not require a change order to be able to perform its obligations under the contract. The government's subsequent actions did not convert the agreement from a performance contract to a design contract. None of the asserted actions indicated that Burke had to abide by the government's suggested sequence. The government never actually did anything to prevent Burke from immediately submitting its own contract-compliant demolition and construction plan. In addition, nothing suggested Burke had no discretion to deviate from the suggested demolition and construction sequence.

Burke was contractually required to prepare a demolition plan, submit it to the government and obtain the government's approval. The government had a right to review this demolition plan and ensure that it conformed to the contract requirements. On October 31, the government received Burke's first demolition plan. The government had no contract obligation to issue change orders, modifications, or suggestions on sequencing or do anything else before October 31. When it submitted this plan, Burke was aware that the government would almost certainly reject the request. Ten days after receipt, as expected, the government returned the demolition plan to Burke for correction, because the plan included taking the trickling filter off-line for the duration of the contract, a sequence that conflicted with the "remain in operation" term. As a matter of law, the ten-day period could not be attributable solely to the government because it was caused by Burke's failure to comply with the contract. The government was merely exercising its right under the contract to receive, review, and approve a plan that conformed to the contract. Burke could not recover damages for the ten-day period after October 31.

Page 3-41, add after note 242 in first full paragraph:

In one case, the general contractor was found not to be responsible to a subcontractor for its alleged failure to coordinate the work of the other subcontractors. In *United States ex rel. Virginia Beach Mechanical Services v. SAMCO Construction Co.,* 39 F. Supp. 3d 661 (E.D. Va. 1999), the mechanical subcontractor sued the general contractor building a warehouse for the Navy in Virginia Beach, Virginia. The project initially was delayed by the late delivery of a prefabricated building by another subcontractor. The mechanical subcontractor demobilized from the project site without completing its work and filed suit claiming that the general contractor failed to make timely payments and to coordinate the work of the subcontractors. The general contractor filed a counterclaim that included a request for a portion of the liquidated damages assessed against the general contractor by the Navy for late completion. The court found that the failure of the mechanical subcontractor to complete its work was a material breach of the subcontract, excusing the payment obligation of the general contractor. The court also addressed the issue of the responsibility of the general contractor to coordinate the work of the subcontractors:

> In a project involving multiple contractors, however, the duty to coordinate work and thereby avoid hindrances does not necessarily fall on the general contractor. Instead, the terms of the various contracts involved will determine who assumed that obligation. . . . While [the general contractor] may have, in fact, inherited this duty by virtue of its status as general contractor, the Court will not make that assumption absent evidence proving such. *Id.* at 674–75.

The finding of the court may have been the result of its consideration of the proof on the matter rather than a general statement of the duties of a general contractor.

§ 3.06   DELAY NOT CAUSED BY PARTIES TO THE DESIGN AND CONSTRUCTION PROCESS

Page 3-50, add to first full paragraph:

For example, in *Brown v. Olin Chemical Corp.,* 231 F.3d 197 (5th Cir. 2000), the owner bore the cost of excusable delay that resulted from a third party's air pollution, because the owner failed to prove that the delay was due to the unreasonable acts of others. Intervenor Horseshoe Entertainment (owner) procured an unfinished vessel to replace an old casino. A number of contractors and subcontractors were hired to finish the vessel. During the course of the finishing work on the riverboat, the construction workers fell ill. This forced the owner to shut down the finishing project until the workers could recover and monitoring and safety systems could be put in place. The workers' illnesses were apparently caused by exposure to sulphur dioxide and sulfuric acid. The owner alleged that emissions from the manufacturer's plant were the cause of the chemical exposure, and sued the manufacturer for the increase in the cost of the construction of the riverboat caused by the delays and lost profits for delay in placing the riverboat into service as a casino. The manufacturer filed a motion for summary judgement, which the district court granted. The owner appealed.

The owner argued that summary judgment should not have been granted because the manufacturer was responsible for the emissions and thus should be liable for the damages incurred because of the construction delay. The appellate court stated that the evidence did not show that the manufacturer exceeded acceptable emissions limits at any of the times at issue, nor that the manufacturer had exercised anything less than reasonable care in the operation of its plant. The owner argued that proof of negligence was not necessary because strict liability pursuant to a statute applied. The owner also argued that the doctrine of *res ipsa loquitur* applied, relieving the need to prove the manufacturer's negligence. The appellate court pointed out that amendments to the statute required a showing of negligence. The appellate court also stated that the workers' illness was not the type of injury that did not ordinarily occur in the absence of negligence. The owner had not shown that the workers fell ill as a result of chemical exposure or that they could not have fallen ill from chemical exposure when the nearby chemical plants were operated with the exercise of reasonable care. The owner had also failed to negate the possibility that the chemical exposure could have been caused by another source. There are several other chemical plants in the vicinity, and any one of these plants could conceivably have been the source of the exposure. The appellate court affirmed the district court's grant of summary judgment.

[A] Weather

Page 3-53, add after note 358 in second full paragraph:

In *Pete Vicari, General Contractor, Inc. v. United States,* 47 Fed. Cl. 353 (2000), Pete Vicari, General Contractor, Inc., entered into a firm fixed-price contract with the United States Coast Guard (USCG). During the course of performance, adverse weather conditions at the site delayed project completion. Consequently, Vicari submitted a series of requests for equitable adjustment to the contract, all of which were granted. The contractor submitted additional requests for three-day, nine-day, one-day, and four-day extensions of time due to weather delays. The contracting officer denied all requested modifications except for the four-day extension.

Count I of the complaint requested compensation for weather delays through August 31, 1998, constituting 58 days at $378.56 per day, for a total of $86,564.42 in damages. Count III sought reimbursement in the amount of $72,961.71 for the cost of obtaining builder's risk/wind insurance, which the plaintiff claimed was necessary for adverse weather conditions at the job site. Vicari sought the cost of maintaining the additional insurance.

Rather than proceed under the clause dealing with adverse weather, Vicari argued that, in order to comply with the safety and health clause of the contract, it had been required to keep workers from the job site when dangerous conditions were present. Vicari maintained that excessive rain presented a danger to the safety of workers on the job site, thereby necessitating exclusion of employees from the project on those days of adverse weather, and that Vicari was therefore entitled to an equitable adjustment to the contract price. Although artful, Vacari's argument ignored general principles of contract interpretation. The plain meaning of the contract established that delays arising from severe weather would be governed by the delay clause, not the safety and health clause. To interpret the contract any other way would render the FAR provision governing severe weather meaningless and superfluous. The sole remedy for severe weather, provided in FAR § 52.249-10, is a time extension for completion of the project. Moreover, severe weather and rain are acts of God and presumptively not within the control of the USCG. The USCG cannot be held responsible absent clear contractual terms allocating liability for acts of God.

Vacari alternatively contended that the contracting officer acted arbitrarily and capriciously in denying certain requests for extensions of time due to weather delays. The defendant responded that the contractor failed to provide the requisite documentation to support these requests and that published meteorological records indicated normal weather conditions during the days in question. Vicari rejoined that the contract did not require requests for additional time extensions to be supported by published records of the National Weather Service. Rather, the contract required the officer to establish a reliable method for determining site conditions and to monitor conditions on a daily basis, which plaintiff charged he failed to do. Vicari kept its own record of weather conditions in a project diary and used this information to document its claims to the contracting officer. The contracting officer ultimately rejected this diary. Even assuming the correctness of Vicari's documentation and the failure of the contracting officer to consider the proffered weather records, monetary recovery was precluded both by FAR § 52.249-10 and the decisional law ascribing delay due to acts of God to a cause other than the USCG.

Page 3-54, add after note 364 in first carryover paragraph:

If a contractor enters into a contract to be performed during a time period when harsh weather conditions are normally incurred, it may have difficulty demonstrating that the conditions it actually encountered could not be anticipated. For example, in *Blue Ribbon Remodeling Co. v. Meistrich,* 709 N.E.2d 1261 (Ohio Mun. Ct. 1999), the contractor was to install concrete piers under the foundation of an existing apartment building in Cincinnati, Ohio. The contract was signed at the end of December and provided that the work was to be completed 30 days later, on January 29. The contract stated that the completion date was subject to "weather conditions or other circumstances beyond the control" of the contractor. The general contractor experienced difficulties in performing the work and its subcontractors refused to work because of the conditions at the project site. The contractor did not complete the work in the time allowed by the contract, and in March left the project without completing the work. The general contractor filed suit to recover payment for the work it performed, alleging that it was unable to meet the completion date because of snow and rain. The court ruled that the weather conditions it encountered could have been anticipated. The work was to be performed during the winter time frame, and the actual weather conditions were typical for the area in the winter months.

Page 3-56, add after note 381 in first full paragraph:

In some contracts, the owner may stipulate a specific number of weather days allowed for time extensions and disclaim any liability for other weather-related delays. Such a provision was used in *Randolph & Co.,* ENG B.C.A. No. 6373 99-2 B.C.A. (CCH) ¶ 30,472 (1999), where the Corps of Engineers awarded a contract for the construction of a dike that provided for up to 36 days of time extensions for inclement weather and disclaimed responsibility for additional weather impact, including time extension. During contract negotiations, the successful bidder attempted to increase the number of excusable weather days, but the Corps refused to agree to an increase. The contractor experienced more than 36 days of weather-related delays and was assessed liquidated damages. The contractor appealed the matter to the Board and the government filed a summary judgement motion on the issue. In denying the motion, the Board relied upon the Federal Acquisition Regulations provision requiring identification and estimates of performance uncertainties. The Board allowed the contractor the right to pursue the appeal further if it could prove that the Corps refused to negotiate in good faith.

CHAPTER 4
EFFECTS OF DELAY

§ 4.02   PREVENTING EARLY COMPLETION

Page 4-5, add after first paragraph:

For example, in *Keeney Construction v. James Talcott Construction Co.*, 309 Mont. 226, 45 P.3d 19 (2002), the University of Montana (UM) awarded a general construction contract to James Talcott Construction Co. The general contract contained an initial completion date of May 31, 1997. Representatives from Keeney Construction and Talcott attended a preconstruction meeting to present a preliminary bar chart schedule that showed a December 1996 finish date. Two days later, Keeney and Talcott entered into a subcontract for the site work. The subcontract stated that Keeney agreed "to complete the work of this Subcontract as required by job progress or within the following time limits: As directed by James Talcott Construction, Inc. Time is of the essence on this project." The project architect stated that the UM did not want an early completion date and requested that Talcott prepare a schedule to reflect the full contract period. The UM and Talcott later entered into a change order which added three additional housing units and extended the completion date to June 30, 1997. Taylor ultimately issued a Certificate of Substantial Completion on October 1, 1997. Keeney filed a complaint against Talcott and the UM for delay claiming that it had an early completion date of October 31, 1996. Talcott filed a motion for partial summary judgment. The district court granted the motion and Keeney appealed.

The subcontract stated that Keeney agreed to work at the direction of Talcott. The subcontract clearly authorized Talcott to set Keeney's completion schedule. In order for an early completion date to apply to Keeney, the parties would have had to modify the subcontract. Keeney argued that the minutes of the preconstruction meeting did just that. During that meeting, the parties discussed an early completion date. Keeney explicitly agreed in the subcontract, however, to complete its work at the direction of Talcott. Because the language of the subcontract was clear, Keeney could not rely on extrinsic evidence to support its contention that the parties intended an early completion date. Alternatively, Keeney argued that the preconstruction meeting minutes, along with various conversations, represented an executed oral agreement, which modified the written contract. The preconstruction meeting, however, took place two days before Talcott and Keeney executed the subcontract. Modifying a contract that the parties have not yet entered into was logically impossible. The district court concluded that Keeney could not recover damages for delay from Talcott because Keeney worked "as directed" by Talcott.

Similarly, *McDaniel v. Ashton-Mardian Co.*, 357 F.2d 511, 516 (9th Cir. 1966) (interpreting a contract, which stated that a subcontractor agreed to complete a project "as directed by the Contractor," to mean that the contractor had the right to direct and control the time of doing the work) involved a subcontractor that worked "as directed" by the general contractor. In concluding that the subcontractor could not receive an award of delay damages, the *McDaniel* court held that the "as directed" language accorded the general contractor the right to direct the time and manner of the subcontractor's work.

§ 4.07   THIRD-PARTY CLAIMS

Page 4-13, add after carryover paragraph:

On the other hand, without a duty, a third-party cannot bring a delay claim against a party. For example, in *Jenne v. Church & Tower, Inc.*, 814 So. 2d 522 (Fla. Dist. Ct. 4th Dist. 2002), the court concluded that a course of dealing could not create third-party beneficiary status. Church & Tower, Inc. contracted with Broward County to design and construct a detention center. The contract provided that the project was to be substantially completed within 548 days of the "project initiation" date. The anticipated completion date was October 4, 1997. Although the county began to occupy the facility in February 1998, a final Certificate of Occupancy was not issued until October 28, 1998. Sheriff Ken Jenne sued the contractor for breach of contract, alleging that the delay in completing the facility caused him to incur labor costs and expenses associated with transporting inmates to other counties, resulting in over $13 million in damages. The sheriff contended that he was the intended third-party beneficiary of the contract between the county and the contractor. The contractor moved to dismiss the complaint, arguing that the sheriff was not an intended third-party beneficiary and that damages were barred by the liquidated damages clause of the contract. The trial court dismissed the complaint with prejudice. The sheriff appealed.

The sheriff alleged that the parties intended that he primarily and directly benefitted from the contract. There was a federal court decree that ordered the sheriff to develop reorganization and jail population management plans for the jail system. The county requested construction proposals, which stated, "It is the intent of the County and the Broward Sheriff's Office that the program and schematic plans comply with the foregoing applicable laws." There was a proposal submitted by the contractor that the sheriff claimed "acknowledges that the contractor needed the sheriff's approval for performance under the contract and acknowledged that it would be working together with the sheriff throughout the project." The sheriff alleged that he purchased furniture for the jail, appointed his office personnel to the selection committee, and made decisions on site location and management. The factors did not confer third-party beneficiary status on the sheriff. Negotiations and dealings between the parties cannot modify a written contract to create the parties' "intent," when the lack of such intent was evident from the contract. The parties to the contract were the county and the contractor, and the contract involved the construction of a public facility funded by the county. The contract was intended to directly and primarily benefit the citizens of the county, not the sheriff. The sheriff received only incidental or consequential benefit from the contract's enforcement, so he was precluded from suing for a breach of it. An article concerning "Defective Work," gave the county, not the sheriff, the right to notify the contractor to make corrections. The liquidated damages clause allowing the county to recover delay damages indicated that the parties to the contract did not intend that the sheriff enforce a separate remedy for the same delay. Affirmed.

§ 4.08   ABANDONMENT AND TERMINATION

Page 4-16, add to first paragraph:

However, in *Fuschino v. Smith,* 2001 Ohio App. LEXIS 21 (2001), an Ohio appellate court concluded that an owner did not waive the completion date when the owner permitted the contractor to continue working on the project, when there was no evidence that the owner acquiesced in the delay. The mere fact that the owner attempted to get the project completed by the contractor did not indicate acquiescence. Instead, the evidence showed that the owner recognized that the delay constituted a breach (in fact, the owner sought the architect's approval for termination), and that the owner's purpose in permitting the contractor to continue working was not to excuse the breach, but instead to pursue the most expedient course to complete the project. The completion date provisions were not waived. The owner was entitled to terminate the contract and to seek damages for the cost of completion of the project.

Page 4-16, add after note 52 in fourth paragraph:

If a contractor does not achieve final completion of a project by a predetermined date, and default is tied to final completion, the owners may terminate the contract. For example, in *Jeffrey M. Brown Assocs., Inc. v. Rockville Center, Inc.,* 2001 U.S. App. LEXIS 5575; 7 Fed. Appx. 197 (4th Cir. April 3, 2001), Jeffrey M. Brown Assocs., Inc., entered into a fast-track contract with Rockville Center, Inc., to design and build a retail pavilion and theater on the owner's land. The contract provided that time was of the essence, because the owners had to meet an occupancy schedule for their incoming tenants. The contractor completed enough work on the theater portion of the project to receive a temporary occupancy permit from the city, while work on the retail portion of the project continued. Disputes arose concerning the quality of the contractor's work and delays in construction. The owner hired consultants to determine the scope of the deficiencies. The consultants prepared a deficiency list, and the contractor agreed to complete its work by a fixed date. A 15-day cure period allowed the contractor to cure any breaches after completion. The owner notified the contractor that it had not achieved substantial completion. This triggered the 15-day cure period. On the completion date, the city's chief inspector wrote a letter to the owners that a final certificate of occupancy would not be issued until a defect in an expansion joint was repaired. The owners deemed the contractor to be in default and terminated the contract. The contractor sued, alleging that the owners breached the agreement by terminating the contractor and by refusing to pay the contractor the escrowed funds. The district court granted the owners' motion to dismiss. The contractor appealed.

To achieve final completion, the contractor was contractually required to obtain a final certificate of occupancy. The contractor admitted that it did not obtain a final certificate of occupancy. The exhibits the contractor attached to its complaint revealed that it was not entitled to an extension of time. The consequence of the contractor's failure to achieve completion was the contractor's default, and the risk that it could be terminated with no notice or opportunity to cure. The owners were free to terminate the contract and take back the escrowed funds when the contractor defaulted. The contractor failed to state a claim for breach of contract.

§ 4.09   OTHER EFFECTS OF DELAY

Page 4-18, add at end of section:

As discussed in the supplement to § 1.01[D], one type of concurrent delay is a pacing delay. For example, a contractor may adjust the pace of its work in light of delays in owner-furnished equipment, delays by other multiple prime contractors, delays in permits, limited site access, or differing site conditions. The party slowing its performance takes the risk that the other party will not quickly resolve its delay and that the slow down will then become a critical delay or become a concurrently critical delay. In such a case, the decelerating party may become liable for the impact of its decision to slow down the pace of its performance.

There are several practical effects of such pacing delays. First, the party slowing down its performance has in one sense caused noncritical delay to certain activities. Second, the party decelerating its work may be unaware that the decelerated activities are actually on the critical path or on a parallel critical path. Third, even if the deceleration only consumes float on noncritical activities, these activities may later become critical. With the float consumed, it now has little flexibility, and may face exposure to delay damages from other parties.

CHAPTER 5

DELAYS, DISRUPTIONS, AND LOST LABOR PRODUCTIVITY

§ 5.04   JUDICIAL RECOGNITION OF LOST
            PRODUCTIVITY CLAIMS

Page 5-6, add at beginning of note 10:

Delay claims are based upon the premise that the project duration has been longer than anticipated; delay damages focus on the cost of extended performance, such as extended site costs, extended or unabsorbed home office expenses, and escalation of labor and material costs. See **Chapter 12**. Lost efficiency relates to additional expenditure of labor, materials, equipment, or other resources made without achieving an increase in productivity. It is possible to experience a loss of productivity without experiencing delay.

Page 5-8, add before last sentence in section:

See *John E. Green Heating & Plumbing v. Turner Construction Co.,* 742 F.2d 965 (6th Cir. 1984); *S.L. Harmonay, Inc. v. Binks Manufacturing Co.,* 597 F. Supp. 1014 (1984); *Clark Concrete Contractors, Inc. v. General Services Administration,* GSBCA No. 14340, 99-1 B.C.A. (CCH) ¶ 30,280 (1999).

§ 5.05   CAUSES OF LOST EFFICIENCY

[D]   Adverse Weather

Page 5-15, add after second paragraph:

    A recent study in the *Journal of Construction Engineering and Management* detailed the impact of material delivery practices and adverse winter weather conditions on structural steel erection activities on three similar projects. The original schedule had called for a four-week erection period in November. Because of delays in the shop drawings, and other factors related to the completion of other buildings at the site, the erection did not begin until the following January. Erection took place in harsh winter conditions. H. Thomas, D. Riley, and V. Sanvido, *Loss of Labor Productivity Due to Delivery Methods and Weather,* 125 J. Constr. Eng'g & Mgmt. 39, at 40 (No. 1, Jan./Feb. 1999).

The most significant factor affecting the construction plan was the complexity of the steel. Considerable time was spent shaking out steel as it arrived. Instead of setting the steel directly from the delivery trucks, all the steel was off-loaded and sorted prior to resuming the erection process. This practice resulted in double-handling of the steel. Thomas, Riley, & Sanvido, at 40. It also appeared that an orderly sequence of the work was not maintained. For instance, while all 579 pieces of steel were erected, only a few pieces were aligned, bolted, and tightened. Also, all 304 joists were in place, but no welding was done. No decking was installed. The absence of joist welding and decking was caused by fabrication errors to some joint connection plates. Access to these joints had to be maintained until the errors were corrected. The completion of several other connections was delayed because pieces of steel were lost in the snow. The remaining work on the connections resulted in a delay to the welding of metal joists and the erection of metal decking. Once these connections were completed, the joists and decking were completed. Thomas, Riley, & Sanvido, at 41.

The daily and baseline productivity showed the best that the contractor could do based on actual performances. Once the effect of repetition dissipated on workday 7, the baseline productivity was about 1.25 wh/pc. In the absence of the disruptions, the contractor should have performed at this baseline rate. The contractor worked at or near this baseline for 11 of the 21 workdays. The baseline was an estimate of the best productivity that a contractor could achieve on a particular project. It was based on actual performance and was the productivity when there were the fewest or no disruptions to the work. Therefore, the baseline was mainly a function of the design complexity. Thomas, Riley, & Sanvido, at 42.

Various numerical schemes have been tried to calculate the baseline productivity. The best approach is to visually fit a curve to the lowest and most consistent daily productivity values. These values need not be consecutive. Thomas, Riley, & Sanvido, at 42.

There were a number of fabrication errors with the steel members. This may have been because the fabricator subcontracted the detailing of the shop drawings, and the quality of these drawings seemed sub-par. As a result, many connections required corrective measures in the field. On some days, these problems simply slowed progress. On other days, considerable time was spent making corrections. The fabrication problems were observed primarily in the latter half of the erection process, after workday 21. Because the steel was delivered while the work was in progress and shakeout was done upon arrival, the steel deliveries interrupted the erection process. Assessing the influence of the factors described earlier is not a straightforward process because of the early effects of improvements from repetition (learning curve) and multiple adverse factors occurring on the same day. The analysis showed that the effects of wind and crane relocations were insignificant, and these factors were deleted from the model. Thomas, Riley, & Sanvido, at 43.

The work was affected by weather events, such as high wind, snow, and cold temperatures. On three weather days, the crew worked less than a full day. Interestingly, on each of these days, productivity was near or better than the baseline.

Overall, weather affected 12 of the 21 workdays. Of these days, the productivity was near or better that the baseline on three days. These are the only days when the crew worked less than a full day. Thomas, Riley, & Sanvido, at 42.

The most significant weather event was snow, which reduced the crew efficiency by 35 percent. This value is less severe than losses reported in an earlier publication of weather events (losses of 65 percent) related to rain. Cold temperatures also had an effect, resulting in a loss of efficiency of about 30 percent. This value was greater than losses estimated by the National Electrical Contractors Association, which estimated that for a relative humidity of 3–5 percent and temperatures of 212° C, the loss of efficiency was in the range of 12–14 percent. The loss of efficiency (about 30 percent) due to temperatures less than 27° C was greater than that stated in other literature sources. The work days on which material deliveries were made showed the largest reduction in efficiency, by almost 40 percent. Thomas, Riley, & Sanvido, at 43–44.

Erecting structural steel directly from the delivery truck was determined to be the most efficient erection method. The double-handling of steel on the Research Building project led to a productivity increase of 0.27 wh/pc, which equates to an additional 108.9 work-hour overrun. Thomas, Riley, & Sanvido, at 46.

To achieve good productivity, projects must experience relatively few disruptions. Projects that experience many disruptions are subject to the ripple effect, where even the best undisrupted days are worse than the baseline, which is based on observations from other comparable projects. To assess the ripple effect, the baseline productivity of the three projects was compared to the baseline of 1.25wh/pc. When compared to the baseline productivity, the Research Laboratory project experienced little or no losses of productivity beyond those attributed to the specific factors discussed before. Thomas, Riley, & Sanvido, at 44.

Multiple regression modeling is essential in productivity analyses because workdays often have multiple events occurring that are of interest. In many instances, the consistent term in the regression model must be defaulted to zero for the model to be valid. Binary variables are frequently used to represent the presence of potentially adverse factors. Thomas, Riley, & Sanvido, at 45–46.

[E] Out-of-Sequence Work

Page 5-17, add to end of first full paragraph:

In *Clark Construction Group, Inc.,* No. VABCA-5674, 00-1 B.C.A. (CCH) ¶ 30,870 (2000), Clark originally planned to construct VAMC West Palm using a "horizontal" construction sequence. The planned sequence involved first constructing the piles, pile caps, and foundation of the hospital. Clark planned to erect the structure by moving horizontally from west to east. Instead of completing the construction of a hospital wing from the basement to the top floor before moving on to complete another wing, Clark intended to complete the structure of each floor of all three wings before constructing the next floor. For example, the third floor of the west wing would be constructed; the construction forces would then proceed to build the third floor of the center wing and immediately move on to the third floor of the East Wing. Clark planned to support this construction sequencing with three tower cranes deployed from west to east. The contract did not specify any particular construction sequence. A critical path method progress schedule was required for the project. A fully developed CPM employing horizontal construction scheduling logic was never approved by the VA. However, Clark developed an "interim" schedule that reflected scheduling logic using a horizontal construction sequence.

As a consequence of a stop work order, Clark re-sequenced the job from the planned horizontal to vertical construction. Consequently, Clark commenced vertical construction of the West Tower where the foundation was complete, while concurrently on a limited basis, continuing East and Center Wing foundation work. The Interim Critical Path Method schedule, still under development at the time a stop work order was issued, was abandoned. The actual CPM schedule approved by the VA incorporated the revised construction sequencing. In accordance with the contract requirements for CPM preparation, this initial CPM reflecting vertical construction did not reflect actual construction times related to the first 15 months of construction.

The change to vertical construction precluded two subcontractors from anticipated efficiencies in crew movement and material distribution. The vertical construction, as simple common sense indicated, and as the evidence showed, presented more difficult material handling, crew supervision, and work area access problems. These problems translated to lower labor productivity. The board found that the subcontractors' explanation of the effect of the changed sequence met the "fundamental triad of proof" to entitle it to recovery for the change in construction sequence.

Out-of-sequence work can also disrupt only one trade's work, causing that work to be performed in different time periods rather than in one continuous period. For example, in *Paliotta v. Department of Transportation,* 750 A.2d 388 (Pa. Commw. Ct. 1999), the contractor was awarded a contract to widen a highway. The scope of the work included constructing concrete curbs. The contractor's planned method of pouring the curbs was to use a slip-form machine in one continuous operation. However, the relocation of utility poles by the power company, under a separate agreement with the department, was performed over a period of time; thus, the contractor was not able to perform the curb work as planned, but rather had to do it in three phases as the utility poles were removed. This made use of the slip-form machine impractical, and the contractor hand-formed the curbs in a more labor-intensive manner with a significantly lower daily production rate. The contractor claimed the additional costs involved, but the department denied the claim. The dispute was taken to court and a ruling was issued in the contractor's favor based upon a finding that the change in the planned sequence as the result of interferences was compensable for the contractor. Expert testimony corroborated the contractor's planned production rates and estimated costs, and the court allowed the contractor to recover its increased performance costs for the curb work over its estimated costs.

[H] Cumulative Impact of Multiple Changes

Page 5-24, add after note 80 in third full paragraph:

However, the mere fact that there are numerous change orders, without further evidence of their affect on the unchanged work, the overall project completion or additional cost may not establish a claim for cumulative impact. In *Coates Industrial Piping, Inc.*, VABCA No. 5412, 99-2 B.C.A. (CCH) ¶ 30,479 (July 26, 1999), the Department of Veterans Affairs (VA) awarded a contract to Coates to upgrade boilers and replace an incinerator at the VA Medical Center in Salt Lake City. Coates claimed both delay and lost labor productivity under a cumulative impact theory due to numerous change orders. At a hearing before the VA Board of Contract Appeals, Coates was able to establish that design deficiencies resulted in over 150 change order proposals and contract modifications. However, Coates offered no evidence of either impact of the changes, cumulative effect, or an explanation of how its costs were affected by the cumulative impact. The numerous changes alone were the basis of its proof of the cumulative impact claim. The Board did not find this to be persuasive.

[1] Defining the Cumulative Effect

Page 5-26, replace note 87 with:

American Institute of Architects, *The Architect's Handbook of Professional Practice* 694 (1994).

Page 5-28, add at end of first full paragraph:

In *Centex Bateson*, VABCA Nos. 4613, 5162, 5165, 99-1 B.C.A. (CCH) ¶ 30,153 (1999), the Board required the contractor to provide a reasonable explanation of how the number of changes or other incidents caused the cost overruns that the contractor sought to recover in the claim. The Board further suggested that to demonstrate causation, the claimant may be required to show that there were no other reasons for the loss of productivity or cost overrun that the contractor is attempting to recover. This may amount to a requirement that the contractor prove a negative: that there were no other causes of the cost overrun. Keating & Burke, *Cumulative Impact Claims: Can They Still Succeed?*, 30 Constr. Law. (Apr. 2000).

[I] Constructive Changes

Page 5-33, add to note 121:

Sentinel Industrial Contracting Corp. v. Kimmins Industrial Serv. Corp., 743 So. 2d 954 (Miss. 1999) (subcontractor-claimant was able to recover for its costs in performing extra work without a written change order under an estoppel theory, as the jurisdiction did not accept the theory of constructive changes). Not all jurisdictions recognize the concept of constructive changes. However, there are legal theories and approaches that may allow a claimant to recover its costs nevertheless. For example, in Sentinel Industrial Contracting Corp. v. Kimmins Industrial Service Corp., 743 So. 2d 954 (Miss. 1999), the subcontractor-claimant was able to recover for its costs in performing extra work without a written change order under an estoppel-type theory, as the jurisdiction did not accept the theory of constructive changes. The subcontractor was awarded a subcontract to disable a portion of an ammonia refinery by the general contractor. The subcontract provided that written change orders were required for any adjustments to the terms or price. The general contract was incorporated by reference into the subcontract, and contained a provision requiring the contractor to comply with directives and instructions even without a written change order. The general contractor directed changes to the sequence and schedule of the subcontract work as well as requiring removal of equipment not in the subcontract scope. The subcontractor performed as directed and submitted change order requests to the general contractor who refused to approve them.

The subcontractor sued the general contractor to recover for the extra work costs and at trial was awarded $966,375. On appeal, the general contractor argued the lack of written change orders prevented any recovery by the subcontractor. The court found the subcontractor's arguments persuasive—that it had to comply with the general contractor's directives or face a possible default termination or breach of contract. Although the legal concept of constructive changes is not recognized under Mississippi law, its highest court allowed recovery for extra work without a written change order under the theory that one may not impose extra-contractual work while denying change order requests.

§ 5.06   PROVING LOST PRODUCTIVITY CLAIMS

Page 5-37, add after third sentence in section:

Quantifying the loss of productivity may also involve examining quantities, establishing units of production, documenting labor hour expenditures and labor costs, calculating productivity, developing a productivity baseline, determining and measuring the causes of productivity losses, and quantifying the economic loss.

[C]   Preserving the Right to Collect Lost Productivity Costs

Page 5-41, revise note 151 to:

1990 GSBCA LEXIS 496

[D] Experts

Page 5-44, add at end of carryover paragraph:

The use of expert witnesses to address "non-scientific" construction issues may come under increasing scrutiny by trial courts. Under recent case law, trial courts have a "gatekeeping" responsibility in allowing expert witness testimony, and may apply various factors before allowing expert witnesses to testify. The factors may include: (1) whether the theory or techniques used by the expert can be tested; (2) whether the theory or technique has been subjected to peer review and publication; (3) whether there is a high known potential rate of error; and (4) whether the theory or technique has general acceptance within the community of experts in the field. *See* Davidson, *Supreme Court Extends Trial Court's Role as "Gatekeeper" of Expert Testimony,* 1 Constr. L. & Bus. 99 (Winter 2000).

Page 5-45, add to note 172:

J.R. Roberts Corp., DOTCAB No. 2499, 98-1 B.C.A. (CCH) ¶ 29,680 (1998). Also, in Hensel-Phelps Constr. Co., ASBCA No. 49,270, 99-2 B.C.A. (CCH) ¶ 30,531 (1999), the Armed Services Board of Contract Appeals noted the fact that the expert testifying on the loss of productivity had not reviewed change orders, daily reports, and other project records. The Board thus did not accept the expert's testimony, because it was not based upon a reliable foundation.

[E] Trade Publications

Page 5-46, add after first paragraph:

In *Clark Construction Group, Inc.,* No. VABCA-5674, 2000 VA B.C.A. LEXIS 4 (Apr. 5, 2000), the board stated that quantification of loss of efficiency or impact claims was a particularly vexing and complex problem. The board recognized that maintaining cost records and identifying and separating inefficiency costs was both impractical and essentially impossible. The board admitted that percentage estimates for lost efficiency may be an appropriate method to quantify such losses.

In *Clark,* the board used the productivity factors from the MCAA Manual as the best method to arrive at the percentage estimates for a subcontractor's undeniable productivity losses. As a foundation to their use in *Clark,* the MCAA Executive Vice President had testified that the productivity factors contained in the MCAA Manual were developed by MCAA's Management Methods Committee, but were not based on any empirical study determining the specific factors or the percentages of loss associated with the individual factors. These factors were intended to be used in conjunction with the experience of the particular contractor seeking to use them because percentage of increased costs could vary from contractor to contractor, crew to crew, and job to job.

The board stated that the MCAA factors were widely used in the industry for estimating and productivity valuation purposes. In assessing productivity loss, the MCAA factors were generally used as a guideline as interpreted by experienced project personnel familiar with the specific circumstances of a particular job and contractor. As contemplated by the MCAA Manual, the board used their reasonable judgment of how the factors applied.

For the change from a horizontal to vertical construction sequence that resulted in reduced productivity because of more difficult internal communication within the building and more difficult control of labor forces arrayed over different floors, the board concluded that the applicable MCAA Factors were "Dilution of Supervision" and "Site Access". Because the sequence change occurred early in the project permitting the subcontractor to adjust to the condition, the board determined the percentage of loss for both conditions as "minor". MCAA attributed a 10 percent loss of efficiency for a minor Dilution of Supervision Condition and a 5 percent loss of efficiency for a minor Site Access problem. Thus, the productivity of the subcontractor's installation labor was adversely impacted by a factor of 15 percent. As the subcontractor acknowledged however, concurrent with the inefficiencies resulting from the change in sequence, were other causes affecting labor productivity not attributable to the VA. These other causes; late stair installation, late building dry-in, lack of CPM coordination or adherence, and man-lift congestion problems, lead the board to adjust the 15 percent inefficiency factors as contemplated in the Manual. When taken together, the non-VA causes of labor inefficiency equaled the impact of the change in sequence. The board adjusted the 15 percent indicated inefficiency factor for the construction sequence change and found that the change to vertical construction impacted the subcontractor's efficiency by 7.5 percent.

[F]   Historical Data

Page 5-46, replace note 180 with:

J. Borcherding & L. Alacon, *Quantitative Effects on Construction Productivity,* 11 Const. Law. 1 (No. 1, Jan. 1991).

[G]   Job-Specific Data

Page 5-53, add after carryover sentence in carryover paragraph:

In *Clark Construction Group, Inc.,* No. VABCA-5674, 2000 VA B.C.A. LEXIS 4 (Apr. 5, 2000), the board stated that contemporary records were required to prove lost labor productivity. In *Clark,* a subcontractor contended that three circumstances, for which the VA was responsible, adversely impacted the productivity of its labor constructing a VA hospital and caused the subcontractor's labor to be overrun by 97,594 man-hours. First, the subcontractor asserted that the change in construction sequence caused by stop work orders resulted in its labor being less productive and required excessive expenditures for preparation of coordination drawings. Second, the subcontractor contended that the site was excessively wet, both outside and inside the building, because of the stop work orders and the VA's improper proprietary roof specification. Finally, the subcontractor claimed that the VA's endemic failure to timely respond to RFIs adversely effected both the subcontractor's coordination drawing effort and the labor productivity of its installations, causing an increase in labor coordination drawing costs. The subcontractor provided various detailed quantum analyses and methodologies in support of its request for a judgment of $1,935,092.

The board found that the subcontractor made little, if any, effort to cite contemporaneous project records in support of the testimony. Given the labor overrun that the subcontractor knew had begun very early in the project, the board found it difficult to believe that the contemporaneous documentation contained in the record would not provide relevant evidence supporting both the fact that an impact on productivity occurred and the extent of that impact. Therefore, the board inferred that the contemporaneous project records did not support the subcontractor's position. The board found that the after-the-fact, conclusory assessments of the project managers or the opinion of its experts were not sufficient substitutes for the subcontractor's underlying obligation to contemporaneously document the severe adverse impact on labor efficiency it claimed resulted from the changes and RFIs. *Citing Centex Bateson,* 99-1 B.C.A. P30,153; *Fru-Con Construction Corp.,* 43 Fed. Cl. 306 (1999); *Triple "A" S.,* 94-3 B.C.A. ¶ 27,194, 135,529-30; Michael R. Finke, *Claims for Construction Productivity Losses,* 26 Pub. Cont. L.J. 326–28 (1997).

§ 5.07   LOST PRODUCTIVITY DAMAGES

Page 5-53, add after note 206 in carryover paragraph:

Both approaches attempt to quantify the differences between what the work would have cost without the disruptive events and what the work actually cost as a result of experiencing the disruptive events.

CHAPTER 6
ACCELERATION

§ 6.02   DIRECTED AND CONSTRUCTIVE ACCELERATION

Page 6-7, add after first full paragraph:

Directed acceleration that is litigated usually involves a problem with the direction to accelerate. For example, consider *K.P. Meiring Construction, Inc. v. La Quinta Inns, Inc.*, 2003 Tex. App. LEXIS 1048 (2003). K.P. Meiring Construction, Inc. contended that the following language in an agreement accelerating the completion date in a construction contract constituted an enforceable agreement, "[i]n either case, La Quinta agrees to negotiate a future project with K.P. Meiring Construction, Inc." La Quinta Inns, Inc. moved for summary judgment on K.P.'s fraud claims on the basis of the economic loss rule and the absence of an enforceable contract. The parties entered into an acceleration agreement as evidenced by La Quinta's letter to K.P. An agreement that did not contain all material terms was not enforceable. The agreement to negotiate a future project was simply an agreement to agree and was not enforceable because it left material terms open for future negotiations, including the amount of K.P.'s profit. If the parties had not entered into a binding agreement, K.P. would not be able to show detrimental reliance, and summary judgment would have been proper as to K.P.'s fraud claims. Although the portion of the acceleration agreement relating to the promise to negotiate a future project was not a separately enforceable agreement, K.P.'s fraud claim addressed the misrepresentations made by La Quinta to induce K.P. to enter into the acceleration agreement, not simply the promise to negotiate a future project. K.P. alleged that by inducing it to enter into the acceleration agreement, K.P.'s principal officer was forced to suspend his bidding activities and supervision of other projects, and K.P. incurred additional expenses in meeting the commitment under the acceleration agreement, including personnel, labor, materials and lost business opportunities. Accordingly, the trial court erred in granting summary judgment as to the fraud claims based on the absence of an enforceable agreement.

§ 6.04   THE OBLIGATION TO ACCELERATE

Page 6-11, add after sixth sentence in second full paragraph:

An owner cannot insist that a surety accelerate to complete at the original contract time if the surety elects to progress and pay liquidated damages. For example, in *St. Paul Fire & Marine Insurance Co. v. City of Green River*, 2001 U.S. App.

LEXIS 6269, 6 Fed. Appx. 828 (10th Cir. 2001), the Wyoming Joint Powers Water Board constructed a 32-million-gallon-per-day water treatment plant. St. Paul Fire and Marine issued a performance bond to guarantee the contractor's performance. The construction agreement required substantial completion of the project by December 1, 1998, and included a time is of the essence clause with a liquidated damages assessment after the stated December 1 completion date. The contractor fell behind in construction of the plant and the board issued a notice of termination for default. This triggered the surety's obligations under the performance bond. The surety had several options in the event of contractor default, and chose to complete the project by September 24, 1999, paying the daily penalty after December 1, 1998. The board, however, informed the surety that it had stepped into the shoes of the contractor for all purposes and thus was bound by the time is of the essence clause and the December 1, 1998, completion date. The board rejected the surety's proposed performance and declared the surety to be in breach. The surety sued to be discharged from further performance obligations on the ground that the board had breached the terms of the performance bond. Both parties sought summary judgment. The trial court granted summary judgment to the city. The surety appealed.

Although the surety essentially stepped into the shoes of the contractor upon the latter's default, it did not follow that the surety was bound by the original completion date. The board would continue to be entitled to $2,500 per day liquidated damages, but the surety under the bond need only proceed with reasonable promptness. The appellate court concluded that because the surety had selected one of the bond options available to it and was ready to proceed to completion, the board's rejection of its proposed performance breached the agreement. The surety's offer to substantially complete the project, by a date that the board conceded would have been acceptable, would have occasioned much greater expense. It was not unreasonable for the surety to seek compensation from the board for the cost of accelerating performance beyond the reasonable promptness standard the bond specified.

§ 6.05 CONSTRUCTIVE ACCELERATION

[A] Excusable Delay

Page 6-23, add after note 75 in first full paragraph:

An examination of contract clauses other than the time extension clause may assist in determining whether a particular delay is excusable. For example, in *Unarco Material Handling,* USPS No. 4100, 00-1 B.C.A. (CCH) ¶ 30,682 (2000), the board considered a contract that allowed the owner to delay the start of the performance period. The U.S. Postal Service (USPS) awarded a contract to Unarco to install an integrated material and storage distribution system at a mail facility then being constructed. The contract allowed the USPS to delay the start of the work by 30 days without additional cost, and provided for a 60-day installation period with liquidated damages of $3,400 for each day that the contractor finished late. Because of delays and union problems affecting the contractor constructing the facility, Unarco's start date was postponed by the USPS for more than three months. Upon receipt of the notice to proceed, Unarco notified the USPS that it could not begin the installation work, because one of its subcontractors had scheduled other work. Because Unarco was unable to begin in a timely manner, it requested additional time for performance, but the request was denied by USPS. Unarco accelerated its performance to avoid liquidated damages, bringing in additional personnel and working overtime. The Postal Board of Contract Appeals examined the contract clause concerning notice to proceed and the facts relating to the claimed delays, and found in favor of Unarco on its acceleration claim. The USPS contract required the contractor to assume the risk of a late start, up to 30 days, but thereafter the risk of delayed notice to proceed was not the contractor's. Even though the contract performance time was adjusted for the duration of the late start, unavailability of the subcontractors to begin work was an excusable delay for Unarco, allowing for an additional time extension beyond the time extension to adjust for the late notice to proceed.

§ 6.07   ACCELERATION COSTS

Page 6-46, add after first sentence of second full paragraph:

In the same way, contractors should record the overtime costs separately from regular time labor costs. Courts may not find it appropriate to use a percentage mark-up of the total labor cost to approximate overtime premiums (*J&K Plumbing and Heating Co., Inc. v. State of New York*, 235 A.D.2d 751, 652 N.Y.S.2d 369 (1997)) or the total cost method of proving overtime by comparing estimated labor costs with actual labor costs (*John F. Harkins Co. v. School Dist.*, 313 Pa. Super. 425, 460 A.2d 260 (1983)) because the actual overtime premium of the labor cost can be easily determined if proper records are kept.

CHAPTER 7

PROJECT DELIVERY METHODS AND DELAY CLAIMS

§ 7.02   DESIGN-BID-BUILD

Page 7-4, add at end of section:

Another variation of design-bid-build contracting is known as Job Order Contracting (JOC). Job Order Contracting generally involves the use of a competitively bid, firm price contract that is awarded for a multiple year period, based upon a comprehensive set of general specifications and a unit price catalog for the various types of work to be performed under the JOC procurement. In essence, JOC provides an umbrella contract for smaller construction, repair and maintenance work. Typically, the types of work are repairs, maintenance items, or components of larger construction projects, like removing a wall, rebuilding interior partition walls, relocating ductwork, rather than constructing an entirely new facility. The catalog of work items may contain as many as 30,000 line items, breaking down the price for the various work activities into labor rates, material and equipment costs, geographical factors, an overall pricing coefficient, a factor for work accomplished for work during other than normal work hours and other adjustment factors. The bidder's pricing coefficient is to include indirect costs, design and engineering costs, general and administrative costs, insurance, wage rate changes, inflation and profit. Individual work orders are issued to the contractor for specific tasks based upon a description of the task, unit of measurement and a unit price.

JOC procurements are not merely minor contract awards but a comprehensive procurement system that results in a master contract for many construction tasks and often spans a year or more. The JOC agreement is a "sole source" contract often designated as an indefinite quantity contract with aliases such as Delivery Order Construction, Simplified Acquisition of Base Engineer Requirements (SABER), Task Order Contracts and Solution Order Concepts. The bounds of the contract amount may be set through a pre-established contract minimum and maximum dollar amount that can be awarded under the contract.

Typically, JOC contracting is used for facilities repair, maintenance, rehabilitation, modernization, tenant fit-out and minor construction tasks by owners with large facilities or several locations, such as municipalities, school districts, colleges and universities, utility companies, public housing authorities and large private owners. At the time of the JOC solicitation, the owner may not be able to give specific information concerning the types of projects or tasks anticipated for the

JOC award, but may be able to provide information on its past JOC assignments or similar work. Precision in the standard or performance specifications and a fairly comprehensive list of work tasks will assist the bidders to understand the nature of the owner's intended procurement. The owner may also allow or encourage the bidders to visit its facilities to examine the conditions of the facilities, the types of work that may be required and the working conditions.

The owner obtains bids and pricing from several bidders during the master JOC solicitation process. Each bidder is requested to provide a work task catalog with pricing for each work element. The bidders are to provide information on its past performance and qualifications. In many JOC procurements, the proposals are evaluated on several qualifications standards: management ability; subcontracting support; experience and capability of the technical staff; and fiscal management plan. The bid evaluation may be weighted between qualification factors and price considerations, often with price weighted less. On other JOC procurements, the bidders must first meet a qualifications threshold and then the pricing aspects become determinative for an award.

Once a JOC contract is awarded, task orders may be given to the JOC contractor based upon pricing in the work task catalog. The process for an individual task order may begin with a meeting where the contractor and owner's representative will review the scope of the individual task order. The scoping process may include an on-site inspection, a proposed written scope of work, the contractor's comments on the proposed scope, and the contractor's pricing proposal using the unit price data in the work task catalog. The details and design elements given to the contractor may vary depending upon the nature of the task, the difficulty of the work, and the owner's access to engineering and design resources. Some owners provide detailed designs, whereas other owners provide only programmatic, schematic or general design criteria. The contractor may be required to submit a schedule and certain technical data with its proposal. The contractor's pricing may be compared to an estimate prepared by the owner, and reviewed for conformance with the scope of work elements and the pricing aspects of the work task catalog. Once the owner is satisfied with the contractor's proposal, a firm fixed price or lump sum work order is given to the contractor as well as a notice to proceed for the individual task order.

Many owners find that there are several advantages of Job Order Contracting. JOC allows the owner to effectively manage numerous minor construction and repair projects through a central control procedure, minimizing the cost and time for administering numerous bids, awards and approvals. Owners find that JOC contractors have an ongoing incentive to perform quality and timely work even though the assignments are small because of the JOC contractor's belief that there may be many more tasks ahead that will make the overall JOC contract profitable. If the owner believes that quality work is not being performed, it does not have to award other task orders. Owners may stop task order awards after the minimum contract amount has been reached or may terminate the JOC contract for lack of performance. Some JOC contracts have partnering provisions to assist in quality and other concerns. Many owners find that using JOC contracting they are able to expeditiously complete small tasks, quickly mobilizing the designated JOC contractor. Because design specifications are not required for each new project, the lead-time for individual projects is also reduced. JOC contracts are reportedly producing responsive and dependable long-term relationships between owners and JOC contractors. Other owners indicate that they are able to maintain cost control and management, and overall the work is performed on a lower cost basis. Delay claims may be minimized due to similar reasons.

In order for a JOC procurement to be successful, there must be a measure of mutual trust. As one owner noted, the JOC process "is somewhat susceptible to being abused." This owner claimed that the JOC contractor fraudulently inflated the contract task order costs by misrepresenting the quantity, quality and types of material used on over 200 projects. While such abuses may exist, overall the JOC process is found by many owners to be an acceptable method of procurement. ("Denying Guilt, Firm Pays Out Settlement to End Fraud Case," *Engineering-News Record*, 14 Feb. 18, 2002; "General Services Agency Purchasing, Job Order Contracting," *www.ventura.org/gnd_jury*; "Job Order Contracting Overview," *www.ic.usa.edu/IC-Overview*).

§ 7.03 THE FAST TRACK

[A] The Potential for Delay on Fast-Track Projects

Page 7-5, add to note 5:

See also Wisch & Vaughan Constr. Co. v. Melrose Properties Corp., 21 S.W.3d 36 (Mo. Ct. App. 2000) ("fast tracked" meant that construction would begin prior to the completion of final architectural plans and specifications. On a "fast tracked" project there was ample opportunity, if not almost a certainty, that disputes will arise between the general nature of the initial documents and the final architectural plans and specifications).

§ 7.07 TURNKEY CONSTRUCTION

Page 7-19, add to note 25:

A "turnkey" power plant is generally known in the construction industry as an arrangement whereby a contractor agrees to engineer, design, construct, commission, and start-up the facility. Input from the owner is limited to establishing price, performance specifications, site and local conditions, and completion date. In contrast, an "owner-satisfaction" project assumes regular input from the owner and potential modification of design specifications. Fluor Daniel Intercontinental, Inc. v. General Elec. Co., 1999 U.S. Dist. LEXIS 12983 (S.D.N.Y. Aug. 20, 1999).

Chapter 8
RECOGNIZING AND DEALING WITH DELAYS AND OTHER DISRUPTIONS

§ 8.06   NOTICE

Page 8-13, add to note 18:

In Clifford R. Gray Inc. v. City Sch. Dist., 277 A.D.2d 843, 716 N.Y.S.2d 795 (2000), the contractor was not entitled to damages incurred before August 1995, the month that the contractor forwarded correspondence specifically complaining of delays. The plaintiff was, however, awarded damages totaling $175,583 encompassing the period from September 1995 to July 1996, for extended site overhead, labor rate increases, loss of labor productivity, expenses for small tools, and consumables and lost profit. It was denied reimbursement for extended home office overhead and warehouse worker and truck expenses. The owner argued that the contractor's request for damages should have been rejected in its entirety because the August 1995 correspondence was not sufficiently particularized to comply with the notice requirement. The contract required only the submission of "a claim in writing" and provided that one claim would be sufficient in the event of a continuing delay. Having previously notified the owner of its intent to file a claim for pecuniary losses due to the project delays, the contractor detailed the continuing delays in an August 2, 1995, letter.

CHAPTER 9
PROCESSING CLAIMS

§ 9.02   SUBMISSION OF THE CLAIM

[A]   Subcontractor Claims

Page 9-7, add after note 30 in first full paragraph:

In submitting claims to general contractors, subcontractors should act in accordance with the claim procedures spelled out in the subcontract. For example, in *Ferguson Electric Co. v. Kendal at Ithaca, Inc.,* 274 A.D.2d 890, 711 N.Y.S.2d 246 (2000), Ferguson was awarded a subcontract for the mechanical work at a nursing home by the general contractor. The dispute resolution provision required any claim to be submitted to the general contractor's designated representative for decision. Although that decision would be conclusive, final, and binding, it could be reviewed in court to determine whether it was "arbitrary, capricious or grossly erroneous to evidence bad faith." When the subcontractor encountered a payment dispute with the general contractor, it submitted a written demand but not a request for a final decision. The general contractor refused to make payment, and the subcontractor sued. In considering the matter, the New York Supreme Court, Appellate Division, noted that under New York law the parties must comply with a clear and unequivocal alternative dispute resolution agreement before taking the matter to court. The court determined that the contract clause was more than just an optional step in processing claims; it was an enforceable alternative dispute resolution (ADR) provision. Although the general contractor never appointed a representative to render a decision on the dispute, it was not necessary to do so until the subcontractor submitted its claim in accordance with the ADR clause.

§ 9.05   RELEASES

Page 9-14, add after third full paragraph:

A contractor's release of its claims against the owner did not release the contractor's claims against the designer. For example, in *Crown Corr, Inc. v. Wil-Freds Construction, Inc.,* 2000 U.S. Dist. LEXIS 17961 (N.D. Ill. Dec. 11, 2000), Bertrand Goldberg Associates, Inc., was hired as the architect and construction coordinator of the Wright Junior College Project by the City of Chicago, acting through its Public Building Commission. Wil-Freds was hired to construct the floors of the five buildings. The project was delayed. Wil-Freds claimed loss of productivity, wage and benefit increases, and extended general conditions. Wil-Freds and the city compromised on Wil-Freds's claims. The settlement agreement included a table that allocated dollar amounts of the settlement into various categories. Goldberg claimed that the "release" provision of the Wil-Freds/City settlement agreement precluded Wil-Freds from recovering any damages from Goldberg.

The "release" provided that "the Commission agrees to pay to Wil-Freds the sum of $720,000 as full and complete settlement of all amounts claimed against the Commission." The settlement agreement also provided that "specifically excluded from the forgoing release and waiver are any claims, demands or actions that Wil-Freds has or may have against any other entity not a party to this Settlement Agreement." Thus, the release in the Wil-Freds/City settlement agreement not only stated that it was solely releasing the city, it also made clear that it did not affect claims against any other possible defendants.

However, the designer was entitled to offset the contractor's claims by the amounts allocated by the owner in its settlement with the contractor. Goldberg argued that the allocation was binding on Wil-Freds. Wil-Freds asserted that the court could not use the allocation table for purposes of assessing whether Wil-Freds had already recovered money for its current claims against Goldberg. Wil-Freds asserted that it had received $720,000 under the settlement agreement, to allocate any way it wanted. Wil-Freds's position conflicted with the parol evidence rule. The settlement agreement provided that "the Commission agrees to pay to Wil-Freds the sum of $720,000 . . . Exhibit 'B' provides an allocation of the settlement amount." By signing the writing, Wil-Freds unambiguously accepted the allocations set forth in Exhibit B of the settlement agreement. Therefore, Wil-Freds was precluded from admitting evidence outside the four corners of the settlement agreement to contradict or explain its terms, and Wil-Freds was bound by the terms outlined in the agreement. The allocation table of the settlement agreement provided that $69,707 of the $720,000 went to the wage and benefit increases claim and $188,500 of the $720,000 went to the extended general conditions claim. Any recovery Wil-Freds would receive from Goldberg for wage rate increases was offset by $69,707. Any recovery Wil-Freds would receive from Goldberg for extended general damages must be offset by $188,500.

Page 9-15, add after note 48 in first paragraph:

For example, in *Eagle Asphalt & Oil, Inc.*, IBCA No. 4173-1999, 01-1 B.C.A. (CCH) ¶ 31,234 (2000), the contractor submitted two claims for suspension of the work against the federal government but neither claim was properly certified nor did the submissions request a final decision as required by federal contracting claim procedures. The contracting officer indicated that the contractor should resubmit the claims in a proper manner, but the contractor failed to do so. When the contract work was completed, the contractor signed a general release, noting that it "reserved the right to submit a claim on the above-referenced contract" without providing any further specifics. The contractor later resubmitted its suspension of work claims and the matter came before the Board of Contract Appeals to determine whether the release precluded the contractor from proceeding on the claims. The Board found that the broad language in the release exception did not put the government on notice as to the specific nature and amount of the claims. The original submissions for suspension did not constitute "claims" under federal contract law, and the exception in the release was vague — a "naked intention to file an indeterminate future claim in an undetermined amount." The contractor was not allowed to proceed on the suspension of work claim.

Page 9-17, add to note 56:

Centex Bateson, VABCA Nos. 4613, 5162, 5165, 99-1 B.C.A. (CCH) ¶ 30,153 (1999) (to succeed on a cumulative impact claim the claimant to provide a reasonable explanation of how the number of changes or other incidents caused the cost overruns. To demonstrate causation, a claimant might be required to show that there are no other reasons for the loss of productivity or cost overrun. This may amount to a requirement that the claimant prove a negative — that there were no other causes of the cost overrun. Keating & Burke, *Cumulative Impact Claims: Can They Still Succeed?*, 30 Constr. Law. (Apr. 2000).

Page 9-18, add to note 57:

Uhle v. Tarlton Corp., 938 S.W.2d 594 (Mo. Ct. App. 1997).

Page 9-20, add after second full paragraph:

Release of lien in payment application does not bar a delay and acceleration claim. Consider *Battaglia Elec., Inc. v. Bancroft Construction Co.*, 2003 Del. Super. LEXIS 100 (2003). Bancroft Construction Co. subcontracted with Battaglia Electric, Inc. on a research center construction project. Both the contractor's steel and concrete subcontractors experienced delays in their performance, which the subcontractor averred significantly delayed the entire project schedule. Because of the impediments, the contractor then unilaterally decided to accelerate the project schedule. The subcontractor requested that it either be allowed some adjustment in its schedule or a provision be made to help it cover the costs of accelerating the schedule. The contractor responded that until the subcontractor demonstrated a meaningful effort to adhere to the construction schedule, no additional time or compensation would be given. The subcontractor executed two waiver and release forms. The first form, executed on April 26, 2000, was related to work the subcontractor performed before April 30, 2000. The second form, executed on May 24, 2000, was related to work the subcontractor performed before the date of execution of that release. Both forms were captioned "Waiver and Release of Lien Rights," and both contained language that upon receipt of payment as satisfaction in full for all labor, services, and materials furnished to the subcontractor, the document was effective to release pro tanto any mechanics' liens, stop notices, or bond rights the subcontractor had in connection with the project. The only apparent difference between the two forms was the typewritten assertion inserted by the subcontractor into the May 24, 2000 document that the release excluded all claims for delays, disruptions and inefficiency. The subcontractor then filed a complaint, alleging that it had incurred a significant increase in the cost to perform its work, and that it was entitled to damages. The contractor moved for summary judgment.

The contractor argued that the April 26, 2000 release covered all claims arising from work through April 30, 2000, and that the intent of the parties to include all claims was supported by the subcontractor's addition of language in the May 24, 2000 release. The contractor argued that the additional language would not have been necessary if the April 26, 2000 release did not include such claims for delays and disruptions. The subcontractor argued that the releases it executed applied only to claims for mechanics' liens. Each release executed by the subcontractor in the contractor's and the owner's favor was captioned "Waiver and Release of Lien Rights" and released any mechanics' liens, stop notices or bond rights the subcontractor may have had in connection with the project. Thus, the scope of the subcontractor's April 26, 2000 release related solely to claims to secure payment for debt-type actions. The subcontractor's complaint was for breach of contract and not for any claim to a mechanics' lien it may have asserted. The contractor's argument that insertion of the additional language into the May 24, 2000 release showed that the subcontractor intended the April 26, 2000 release to preclude delay claims was not determinative. Even before execution of the May 24 release, the subcontractor was in the process of preparing a claim for the already-existing delays. The contractor was not entitled to summary judgment.

§ 9.06   PROCESSING THE DISPUTED CLAIM

[A] Federal Contract Claims Procedures

Page 9-21, add after note 77 in first full paragraph:

The written submission must be a clear and unequivocal statement that gives the contracting officer adequate notice of the basis and amount of the claim. *Contract Cleaning and Maintenance v. United States*, 811 F.2d 586 (Fed. Cir. 1987). The written statement of the claim should be sufficient to inform the contracting officer of what is being claimed, providing enough information to allow a meaningful review. This may include factual allegations, the reasons that the claimant thinks the government is liable, supporting documentation, contract clauses, and references to specifications and drawings. Enough detail should be provided to allow the parties to begin negotiations. *Lee Ann Wyskiver*, PSBCA Nos. 3621, 94-3 B.C.A. (CCH) ¶ 27,118 (1994).

In some instances, the claim may not have to be submitted directly to the contracting officer, if the contractor gives the claim to its primary government contact, requesting a final decision with a reasonable expectation that the claim will be honored, and the claim is actually delivered to the contracting officer. *D.L. Braugher Co., Inc. v. West*, 127 F.3d 1467 (1997); or if the submission of the claim is reasonably calculated to ensure receipt by the contracting officer. *Roy McGinness & Co., Inc.*, ASBCA No. 40004, 91-1 B.C.A. (CCH) ¶ 23,395 (1991).

Page 9-21, add after note 79 in carryover paragraph:

In consideration of the $100,000 limit for the use of the accelerated appeals procedure, a contractor need not combine claims that are factually and legally distinct. For example, in *Linda Newman Constr. Co., Inc.*, VABCA Nos. 6307, 00-2 B.C.A. (CCH) ¶ 31,027 (2000), the claimant sought accelerated processing of its $42,533 claim for the impact of multiple change orders on unchanged work, and the normal processing of its $100,000 claim for late notice to proceed. The government unsuccessfully sought to remove both claims from the accelerated docket and consolidate the claims on the regular docket. The Board found the claims were factually and legally distinct, and further found that the contractor's actions were not an abuse of the accelerated appeals procedure. However, the Board partially consolidated the two cases for the purposes of conducting a hearing, but allowed them to proceed under the accelerated procedure.

Page 9-26, add after first sentence in first full paragraph:

The Contract Disputes Act itself does not give the definition of what is a claim; rather, *claim* is defined in the Federal Acquisition Regulations at § 33.201:

> Claim, as used in this subpart, means a written demand or written assertion . . . seeking as a matter of right, the payment of money in a sum certain, the adjustment or interpretation of contract terms. . . . [A] written demand or written assertion by the contractor seeking payment of money exceeding $100,000 is not a claim under the Contract Disputes Act of 1978 until certified by the Act and 33.207. A voucher, invoice, or other routine request for payment that is not in dispute when submitted is not a claim. The submission may be converted into a claim, by written notice to the contracting officer as provided in 33.206(a) if it is disputed either as to liability or amount or is not acted upon in a reasonable time.

There is a four-prong test to determine if a submission is truly a claim: (1) a written submission to the contracting officer claiming specific rights and requesting specific relief; (2) the amount requested is a sum certain; (3) a request is made to the contracting officer for a final decision; and (4) a claim over $100,000 must be certified. *Cubic Corp. v. United States*, 20 Cl. Ct. 610 (1990); *RSH Constructors, Inc. v. United States*, 14 Cl. Ct. 655 (1988).

Page 9-26, add after note 111 in first full paragraph:

An invoice certified in accordance with the requirements of the Contract Dispute Act and submitted after termination for default may be a claim, particularly when the government and the contractor dispute the percentage of completion. It may be an indication of the contractor's attempt to enforce its rights under the Contract Dispute Act. *American Service Supply, Inc.*, ASBCA No. 50606, 00-1 B.C.A. (CCH) ¶ 30,858 (2000).

Page 9-26, add after note 113 in first full paragraph:

The pricing of a claim based upon estimates may be adequate. *P.J. Dick Inc. v. General Serv. Admin.*, GSBCA Nos. 11783, 94-3 B.C.A. (CCH) ¶ 27,172 (1994); *Production Corp.*, DOTBCA Nos. 2424, 92-2 B.C.A. (CCH) ¶ 24,796 (1992); but a claim for an amount "in excess of" has been held to be inadequate. *Corbett Technology Co, Inc.*, ASBCA Nos. 47742, 95-1 B.C.A. (CCH) ¶ 27,587 (1995).

Page 9-27, add after first full paragraph:

The contracting officer's decision to delay making a final decision, which also delays the contractor's ability to appeal, is effective upon issuance of the decision to delay. Title 41 U.S.C. § 605(c)(2) provides that:

> A [contracting officer] shall, within sixty days of receipt of a submitted certified claim over $100,000—
> (A) issue a decision; or
> (B) notify the contractor of the time within which a decision will be issued;

Title 41 U.S.C. § 605(c)(5) provides that:

> Any failure by the [CO] to issue a decision on a contract claim within the period required will be deemed to be a decision by the [CO] denying the claim and will authorize the commencement of the appeal or suit on the claim as otherwise provided in this Act;

and 41 U.S.C. § 609(a) provides that:

> (1) . . . a contractor may bring an action directly on the claim in the United States Court of Federal Claims, notwithstanding any contract provision, regulation, or rule of law to the contrary; . . . .
> (3) Any action [on the claim] under paragraph (1) . . . shall be filed within twelve months from the date of the receipt by the contractor of the decision of the [contracting officer] concerning the claim, and shall proceed de novo in accordance with the rules of the appropriate court.

In *Logicvision, Inc. v. United States*, 54 Fed. Cl. 549 (Fed. Cl. 2002), Logicvision delivered to the United States Department of Commerce (DOC) a $259,177.82 claim for adjustment due to delay and disruption on October 12, 2001. The CO, by certified mail, sent plaintiff a letter, dated and issued on December 4, 2001, notifying plaintiff that a final decision would be issued by March 15, 2002. The CO's letter was not received by plaintiff until December 13, 2001. The 60-day deadline for issuance of a decision by the contracting officer under Section 5(c) of the Contract Disputes Act of 1978 expired two days earlier, on December 11, 2001. The complaint was filed on December 28, 2001. DOC argued that the court lacked subject matter jurisdiction to entertain plaintiff's complaint because it was filed before the CO issued a final decision and over two weeks after plaintiff received the CO's decision, issued within the 60-day period, that the final decision would be delayed.

Plaintiff contended that "notify" in 41 U.S.C. § 605(c)(2) meant actual receipt of a notice by the contractor. Reading the word "notify" to mean "the CO's making known or reporting" or even to turn on "issuance" rather than the contractor's receipt would not be unfair or adverse to a contractor, since it easily could call the contracting officer to inquire as to the status of its CDA claim prior to filing suit. Had plaintiff done so in this case, it would have learned, as it in fact did over two weeks before filing its complaint in this court, that the contracting officer had extended the 60-day period for issuing a final decision.

Dismissing the complaint on jurisdictional grounds also would not seriously prejudice plaintiff financially because interest under the CDA was paid "from the date the CO receives the claim . . . from the contractor until payment thereof." In addition, even if the claim was dismissed and subsequently denied by the contracting officer, plaintiff still would be able to file a complaint, and be entitled to otherwise payable interest from the date the contracting officer received the claim.

Plaintiff's suggested reading of the statute, on the other hand, seriously may prejudice defendant, and was inconsistent with the purposes of the CDA. The contracting officer in this case issued the notification seven days before the deadline for a final decision, which, generally, should provide a reasonable and adequate period for ensuring actual notice/receipt. Under plaintiff's reading, however, a notification letter mailed even several weeks before the 60-day deadline for a final decision could not be assured to arrive in time to extend the 60-day period. Requiring unduly early mailings to compensate for unknown mail delivery delays would force government agencies to decide large and complex monetary claims in significantly less time than the 60 days provided by statute, and thus, presumptively, in less time than intended by Congress.

Plaintiff's interpretation also would require the courts and Boards of Contract Appeals to act on claims that were not ripe and that might have been resolved more fairly, economically, and efficiently in the first instance, by those more familiar with the contract's administration, at the agency level. Moreover, if the date hinged on actual receipt, contractors would unilaterally determine the date and thus might have an incentive for manipulation. The contracting officer having issued a decision notifying plaintiff of an extension of the time for issuing a final decision on plaintiff's claim within the 60-day period provided by law, there was no "deemed denial" to trigger plaintiff's statutory right to immediately appeal its claim.

Page 9-30, add after note 138:

If the claimant desires to drop a specific claim, it must formally amend its complaint, and may not informally withdraw a claim and then attempt to pursue it later in another appeal after a decision has been made on the original claim. *Hitt Contracting, Inc.,* ASBCA No. 51594, 99-2 B.C.A. (CCH) ¶ 30,442 (1999).

[B] Other Contract Claims Procedures

Page 9-31, add after note 146 in first carryover paragraph:

Other dispute resolution clauses require that claims first be submitted to a designated representative of the other party for a written decision that is final and conclusive, subject only to judicial review to determine whether the decision was fraudulent, arbitrary, or so grossly erroneous as to evidence bad faith. Such clauses are often upheld by courts, and failure to submit the claim as required may result in the claimant being barred from pursuing the matter in court. *Metropolitan Dade County v. Recchi America, Inc.,* 734 So. 2d 1123 (Fla. Dist. Ct. App. 1999); *Ferguson Electric Co. v. Kendal at Ithaca, Inc.,* 277 A.D.2d 843, 711 N.Y.S.2d 246 (2000).

Nebraska Revised Statute § 16-726 requires, as a condition precedent to maintaining an action against a first class city, that "the claimant . . . file such claim within ninety days of the accrual of the claim in the office of the city clerk." Neb. Rev. Stat. § 16-726. Section 16-726 functions as a statute of limitations, resulting in the time bar of suits not filed within the requisite 90 days. *Centric Jones Co. v. City of Kearney, Nebraska,* 324 F.3d 646 (8th Cir. 2003), *citing Sinn v. City of Seward,* 3 Neb. App. 59, 523 N.W.2d 39, 51 (Neb. 1994).

In *Centric Jones Co. v. City of Kearney, Nebraska,* 324 F.3d 646 (8th Cir. 2003), Centric Jones Co. contracted with the City of Kearney, Nebraska for completion of the construction portion of the Kearney Wastewater Treatment Plant for $12,950,000. CH2M Hill, an engineering firm, served as the City's project engineer. The contract defined CH2M's duties: among other things, CH2M was to act as the City's representative during the construction period; receive payment applications from Centric and make recommendations to the city council regarding progress payments; and act as an impartial initial interpreter of the contract requirements and judge of the acceptability of the work, if and when disputes arose. If CH2M was unable to resolve an issue to the parties' satisfaction, either party could invoke the contract's dispute resolution procedures. If those dispute resolution procedures were unsuccessful, the contract provided that a party could institute suit in a court of competent jurisdiction. Centric submitted 30 payment applications to CH2M. CH2M reviewed the applications and forwarded them to the City's Utilities Director, along with either a certification that the application should be paid in full or a recommendation to pay a different amount. The applications were placed on the city council's agenda. The City adopted CH2M's certifications, resulting in full payment of 12 payment applications, refusal to pay in whole or in part 12 applications, and six instances of payment in excess of that actually requested on the application. As a result of the refusals to pay Centric the full amount requested, Centric requested that the parties mediate the dispute pursuant to the contract. The parties participated in an unsuccessful mediation. Centric sent a letter to the City's Utilities Director demanding payment of $1,266,486.53 within 30 days. The City rejected Centric's demand, proposing instead a final payment of $670,256.00. Centric filed suit against the City asserting causes of action for breach of contract and unjust enrichment. Centric sought damages in excess of $2,000,000. The district court granted the City's motion for summary judgment based on the affirmative defense that Centric had failed to comply with the claim statute governing claims against the City, Neb. Rev. Stat. § 16-726, and dismissed the whole case with prejudice.

On appeal, the Eighth Circuit held that substantial compliance was a limited concept under Nebraska law and inapplicable in this case. Moreover, under the existing case law, a clear requirement for substantial compliance was that the claim be filed with the statutorily mandated recipient, in this case the city clerk. Finally, there was no evidence that Centric ever filed a claim or payment application with anyone for the damages it sought in its complaint: namely, damages in excess of $2,000,000. Centric also argued that evidence of waiver of a contractual or statutory right by one party generally precluded summary judgment in favor of that party. The contract terms required compliance with the statutory notice-of-claim procedures, as well as all other applicable laws and regulations. There was not enough evidence of waiver to create a genuine issue of material fact. Thus, there were no genuine issues of material fact precluding summary judgment for the City.

Page 9-31, add after first full paragraph:

In *International Fidelity Insurance Co. v. County of Rockland,* 51 F. Supp. 2d 285 (S.D.N.Y. 1999), IFIC, the surety for NANCO (the original construction contractor), attempted to enjoin SWCF Architects Engineers Planners (SWCF) from adjudicating the parties' disputes over delay damages on two grounds: first, that the claims resolution clause requiring submission to the project architect did not include a dispute over post-completion delay damages; and second, that even if it did, the county's claim was not submitted to the architect for decision within 21 days after it arose, as required by the claims resolution clause.

The contract that NANCO signed contained a claims resolution clause which read:

> 4.4.2 Decision of Architect/Engineer. Claims, including those alleging an error or omission by the Architect/Engineer, shall be referred initially to the Architect/Engineer for action as provided in Paragraph 4.5.4, shall be required as a condition precedent to litigation of a Claim between the Contractor and Owner as to all such matters arising prior to the date final payment is due, regardless

of (1) whether such matters relate to execution and progress of the Work or (2) the extent to which the Work has been completed. The decision by the Architect/Engineer in response to a Claim shall not be a condition precedent to litigation in the event (1) the position of Architect/Engineer is vacant, (2) the Architect/Engineer has failed to render a decision within agreed time limits, (3) the Architect/ Engineer has failed to take action required under Subparagraph 4.5.4 within 60 days after the Claim is made, (4) 90 days have passed after the Claim has been referred to the Architect/Engineer or (5) the Claim relates to a mechanic's lien.

When it became clear that NANCO would be unable to complete the project in a timely manner, IFIC exercised its option to step into the contractor's shoes. Accordingly, it executed a Takeover Agreement, pursuant to which IFIC agreed to complete the contract in exchange for receipt of the payment of the remaining proceeds under the contract. The Takeover Agreement provided that all the terms of the underlying contract were incorporated by reference. It also provided that nothing in the Takeover Agreement affected any of IFIC's rights as surety under its payment and performance bonds.

IFIC engaged Harani Contracting Corporation to complete the project. Unfortunately, Harani proved unable to get the work done within the completion period. The county did not default IFIC and continued to pay under the contract through the Spring of 1995. Even after the county ceased payment in May 1995, IFIC and Harani continued work, and the project was accepted as substantially complete by SWCF, acting as the county's representative, on October 5, 1995. Harani thereafter ceased work on the project and filed for bankruptcy protection. The county defaulted IFIC on March 6, 1996, but ultimately permitted it to return and finally complete the project with another contractor.

Shortly before substantial completion, Rockland County served IFIC with a Notice of Claim for alleged delay damages totalling $4,554,735. The Notice of Claim stated that the county intended to submit the matter to SWCF, but the county did not submit the matter for decision to the architect at that time. By letter to counsel for the county, IFIC denied that delay damages were properly submissible to the architect, and further contended that the county had failed to submit the claim withing 21 days after it arose. Rockland County neither responded to these contentions nor sent the matter to SWCF until after final completion of the project, when it served IFIC with a more detailed analysis of claim and forwarded the matter to the architect for resolution.

IFIC then brought this proceeding, seeking compensatory damages against the county for money alleged to be due under the Takeover Agreement and a declaratory judgment that the claims resolution procedure was not applicable to it. IFIC also joined SWCF as a defendant and moved for a permanent injunction against resolution of the delay damages issue by the architect.

IFIC first asserted that the question of delay damages could not be submitted to the architect because it was not bound in any manner, shape or form by the claims resolution clause contained in § 4.4.2. The court stated that when it signed the Takeover Agreement, which incorporated all the terms of the underlying construction contract by reference, IFIC bound itself to send all disputes falling under §§ 4.4.1 and 4.4.2 of that contract to the architect for its review.

IFIC also argued that delay damages could not be decided by the architect, even if it fell within the clause, because Rockland County did not submit the dispute to SWCF within 21 days of the time when the dispute arose or when it first became aware of the matter giving rise to the dispute (whichever was later), as required by § 4.4.3. IFIC further contended that, even if the issue was timely submitted, the failure of the architect to take action on the matter within 60 days after the claim was first made removed an obligation on IFIC's part to wait on a decision by SWCF as a condition precedent to litigation.

Rockland County took the position that it made the claim when it served IFIC (but not the architect) with a notice of claim for over $4 million in delay damages. The contract stated that pursuant to § 4.4.2 of the contract, the decision by the architect in response to a claim was not a condition precedent to litigation in the event that the architect failed to take action required under Subparagraph 4.5.4 within 60 days after the claim was made. There could be no dispute that the architect had not taken action on the claim within 60 days. Therefore, by the express terms of the contract, IFIC was freed from any restriction that may have limited its right to have a court determine whether the county is owed delay damages.

If, on the other hand, the claim was not actually made until the dispute over delay damages was submitted to SWCF for resolution, then the conclusion that it was made too late was inescapable. The county asserted in a brief to the court that it first became aware that it had a claim for delay damages on September 12, 1995. Section 4.4.3 of the contract gave it 21 days from that date to submit the claim to the architect for resolution under the alternative dispute resolution clause. There was no dispute that the information needed to resolve the dispute was not sent to SWCF until the Spring of 1997, well beyond the brief limitations period agreed to by the original parties to the contract.

According to the court, New York courts examining such clauses have rejected the notion that architects are empowered to resolve delay damages disputes. Citing *Liebhafsky v. Comstruct Assocs., Inc.,* 62 N.Y.2d 439, 440, 466 N.E.2d 844, 844, 478 N.Y.S.2d 252, 252 (1984) (authority of architect under resolution clause was centered on the operational phases of construction and a claim for delay damages, asserted two years after substantial completion need not be submitted to the architect); *County of Rockland v. Primiano Construction Co.,* 51 N.Y.2d 1, 11, 409 N.E.2d 951, 956, 431 N.Y.S.2d 478, 484 (1980) (claims, disputes and other matters in question between the contractor and the owner that must first be referred to the architect are those relating to the execution or progress of the work, but claims asserted after substantial completion of the work do not fall within the scope of the duties of the architect); *Tsombikos v. Grager,* 147 Misc. 2d 995, 999, 559 N.Y.S.2d 460, 462 (Sup. Ct. 1990) (where claims were made subsequent to the termination of contractor's role as a contractor, architect's responsibility to supervise the contractor's performance and, by extension, initially mediate the dispute was at an end). Delay damages by their nature arise after the construction project is complete—a time when the architect has ceased to be responsible for supervising the contractor's performance. IFIC's claim for a declaratory judgment was granted, and SWCF was enjoined from entertaining the county's claim.

In *County Commissioners of Caroline County v. J. Roland Dashiell & Sons, Inc.*, 747 A.D.2d 600 (Md. 2000), the contractor's suit for unjust enrichment was dismissed because the contractor failed to submit its claim in a timely manner as required by the contract. The County awarded a contract to Dashiell for the renovation and expansion of a correctional facility. The contract included the American Institute of Architect's General Conditions (Doc. A201-1987) that required the submission of a claim to the other party within 21 days of the event giving rise to the claim or 21 days after the claimant recognizes the conditions giving rise to the claim. Dashiell allegedly experienced an increase in its performance costs due to design errors and differing site conditions that were claimed to be the responsibility of the County, but Dashiell did not submit a claim until after substantial completion of the contract. The County denied the claim for various reasons, and Dashiell brought suit under two theories — breach of contract and unjust enrichment. The trial court dismissed the suit under both theories, and an appeal reached the Court of Appeals of Maryland. The court of appeals ruled against the contractor on both theories. The court reasoned that the contractor failed to pursue its contractual claim in a timely manner. Further when a claim was covered by the express terms of the contract, a party may not recover under a quasi-contractual theory of unjust enrichment.

CHAPTER 11
USING THE SCHEDULE TO PROVE DELAY AND DISRUPTIONS

§ 11.01   WHY USE A SCHEDULE?

Page 11-3, add after note 2 in first full paragraph:

In order to be awarded delay damages, one multiple prime contractor must demonstrate that the delays by another multi prime contractor specifically affected its work performance. In *Biemann & Rowell Co. v. Donohoe Cos., Inc.,* 147 N.C. App. 239, 556 S.E. 2d 1 (2001), Biemann & Rowell Co. and Donohoe Cos., entered into separate contracts on June 1, 2002, with the State of North Carolina to build a multi-million dollar neuropsychiatric hospital. Delays occurred throughout the project and the contractors were frequently forced to complete work out of the anticipated sequence. To accelerate completion of the project, it was the understanding of the contractors, architect, and schedule coordinator that Donohoe would "dry-in" the building by installing a moisture seal. Donohoe never installed the building seal. The architect indicated that Donohoe failed to complete work according to the project schedule and to fulfill its duties as project expediter. Meeting minutes and observation reports indicated that Donohoe also contributed to overall project delay. Biemann and Rowell maintained that the contractor's failure to install the building seal, and its failure to supervise and properly schedule its subcontractors, caused delays to Biemann and Rowell's work. The installation of the temporary seal first appeared as an activity on the critical path long after the project began experiencing delays. Biemann and Rowell merely presented a chart of instances of delay allegedly attributable to Donohoe and relied on anecdotal testimony about the delays. The trial court rendered judgment in favor of Donohoe. Biemann and Rowell argued on appeal that it was not necessary to prove that Donohoe proximately caused injury to it because an injured contractor may recover delay damages by merely demonstrating that such damages were within the contemplation of the parties at the time the contract was entered. Donohoe had a duty to the other prime contractors for the full performance of all duties and obligations due under the terms of the separate contracts and in accordance with the plans and specifications. To recover damages, Biemann and Rowell had to show that Donohoe breached the contract and that the breach caused Biemann and Rowell's damages. Although there was evidence that

Donohoe may have contributed to overall project delay, Biemann and Rowell failed to show how delays specifically caused by Donohoe affected its work performance. Biemann and Rowell also failed to take into account delays attributable to other causes.

§ 11.05   DEMONSTRATING SCHEDULE RELIABILITY

[B]   Reliable Schedule Is Updated

Page 11-29, add to note 40:

Blinderman Constr. Co. v. United States, 39 Fed. Cl. 529 (1997), *aff'd mem.*, 178 F.3d 1307 (Fed. Cir. 1998).

§ 11.06   MANIPULATION OF THE SCHEDULE

Page 11-38, add after carryover paragraph:

One common problem is the failure to submit a schedule at the beginning of construction. The failure to submit the schedule prior to the start of construction provides a claimant with the opportunity to develop an "after-the-fact as-planned" schedule that may depict its intended sequence of construction in ways that would reflect delays and problems of others. For example, an after-the-fact schedule could be developed with the critical path running through the activities later discovered to be affected by the delays of the owner. To prevent the development of after-the-fact schedules, many owners have developed detailed scheduling specifications requiring the submittal and acceptance of the project schedule as a prerequisite to receiving payment for mobilization or for the entire first progress payment. Some owners require the contractor to submit a preliminary schedule prior to receiving notice to proceed.

Schedule manipulation may also occur in updates. Despite the initial accuracy of the schedule logic, some activities may actually begin prior to the completion of activities that are depicted as "precedessor" activities—follow-on activities start out of sequence. Some scheduling software allows the scheduler to employ two different approaches to automatically deal with this common situation. One technique is known as "retained logic" where if an activity starts out of sequence but is not completed in the update period, the remaining duration of the activity is shown starting after the predecessor activities are completed. Another technique is "progress override" that allows the scheduler in essence to ignore the activity relationships and depict the activity start without being tied into the previously established logic. Rather than allow the software to use either "retained logic" or "progress override" as the "default" technique in updating schedules, a better approach may be to require the scheduler to redefine the logic relationships between activities to reflect the current plan for completing the activities.

Software may also automatically assign start and completion dates for activities, rather than reflect its actual start and finish dates. This is often referred to as "percent complete updating." For example, when a schedule is updated on the first day of every month, if an activity started on May 25 and was worked on for five days, the June update would indicate that the activity started on June 1 and was 50 percent complete with five days remaining duration. In reality, the activity began on May 25 and may require more than five days to complete. This schedule updating technique may also distort the project schedule. Therefore, many owners require the scheduler to use actual dates in reporting on updates.

Page 11-45, add at end of section:

Features and functions available on software programs have facilitated the manipulation of schedules. Some commentators have opined that the problems are so widespread that it is "an industry crisis" that has its origin in the failure of scheduling software to require the users to employ discipline and realism in planning and scheduling. Wickwire & Ockman, *Use of Critical Path Method on Contract Claims—2000,* 19 Const. Law. 12 (Oct. 1999).

Several scheduling software features or techniques that may distort schedules include:

- Scheduling reports and updates that do not list predecessor and successor relationships, listing only activities that the scheduler deems to be on the critical path;

- Program options that allow the scheduler to hide flawed logic, such as restraints that interrupt the calculation of the critical path;

- Software manuals that instruct schedulers on how to fix certain dates as driving the schedule rather than the logic and duration of activities;

- Software manuals that encourage schedulers to misrepresent the status of the project and distort the impact of events and problems on the project schedule;

- Software tools that allow the scheduler to mask or delete key information from scheduling reports;

- Linking cost-loaded schedules developed for project billing purposes with schedule activities in such a way as to distort updates;

- Extensive use of leads and lags in such a way that the critical path is no longer sequential;

- Scheduling reports that do not identify which part of a critical "overlapping" activity is truly critical and which part has float;

- Scheduling reports that do not identify how much of any given activity must be in place before its immediate successor can start;

- Use of multiple calendars that allow the scheduler to apply different calendars for various parts of the schedule;

- Reporting activity status by its percentage of completion rather than recording actual start and completion dates—for example, automatically assigning an activity's start date as the schedule status date when the activity progress was first reported as more than 0 percent, rather than its actual start date;

- Misusing the "retained logic" function in updating schedules. If a follow-on activity has started before its predecessor activities are complete, the remaining duration is shown as starting only after all of the predecessor activities are complete. This may have the affect of distorting the relationships between the activities;

- Misusing the "progress override" function in updating schedules. If a follow-on activity has started before its predecessor activities are complete, the relationships are ignored or "overridden" to allow activities to start out of sequence. *Id.* at 17–19.

The authors suggest several procedural and software changes that will help resolve some of these problems: audit trails programs that identify changes in the schedules; monthly reports for predecessor-successor relationships; program requirements for the reporting of actual start and completion dates of activities; restricted use of arbitrarily assigned milestones or other constraints; reports that highlight schedule changes made in each update or revision; restrictions on the automatic use of "progress override" or "retained logic" features in schedule updating; and restrictions on the use of inappropriately calculated start and completion dates for activities. *Id.* at 20.

§ 11.07   METHODS OF SCHEDULE ANALYSIS

[A]   As-Built Schedules

Page 11-47, add after carryover paragraph:

Courts may also find the as-built schedule methodology to be unreliable if only a single activity or portion of the schedule is analyzed without consideration of the progress on other portions of the schedule. In *Galaxy Builders,* ASBCA No. 50018, 00-1 B.C.A. (CCH) ¶ 31,040 (2000), the contractor was required to develop a critical path method schedule for its work in building an Air Force support facility. Once it was approved by the government, the schedule was to be updated monthly, and be the basis for determining time extensions and delays. The contractor submitted shop drawings for the roofing system, and the government took longer than the 60-day period for response. The contractor submitted a delay claim for the late approval, using an as-built schedule that isolated the roofing activities only. This was "proof" that the submittal response problem delayed the other activities and overall project completion date. The contractor's analysis did not track the progress of other activities. The government submitted an alternative analysis indicating that there were concurrent contractor delays in the HVAC and masonry activities, such that the late roofing submittal and the roofing activities were never on the critical path. The board found that the government had rebutted the contractor's as-built schedule analysis. The contractor's focus on a single line of activities, excluding the actual progress information of all other activities, was a distortion of the schedule and not a proper delay analysis.

In *Morganti National, Inc. v. United States,* 49 Fed. Cl. 110 (2001), an as-built delay analysis was rejected and a time impact analysis substituted. Morganti was required to prepare a schedule, using critical path method scheduling, for the Federal Bureau of Prisons. The contractor's progress was to be tracked in monthly schedule updates. The contract also required that Morganti submit a time impact analysis (TIA) in support of any time extension requests. The contract did not allow the contractor to add time to the contract schedule until the time was approved by a bilateral modification. The contractor brought in a scheduling expert to produce a project schedule. The schedule expert prepared a schedule that eventually became known as "Schedule B." The parties agreed that the activity durations and schedule logic in one Schedule B update (WC04) would serve as the baseline schedule for measuring any impacts to the schedule.

The contractor was required to redesign 387 cell panels of the 5,800 cell panels required for the project. Because of the impact these changes had on cell-panel production, installation of cell panels and follow-on work had to be resequenced. The WC04 update took into account the additional delay caused by the disruption to the sequencing of cell-panel installation activities. Contemporaneous with the first panels arriving on site, the contractor submitted a TIA prepared by the scheduling expert that indicated a time extension of 213 work days.

The contractor abandoned the TIA analysis at trial. Another expert provided a different scheduling analysis on behalf of the contractor at trial, based on an as-built analysis. The other expert testified that the as-built critical path of the project ran through cell-panel installation and explained that the "total time" until project completion represented the duration of the government-caused delay, which entitled the contractor to a time extension of 511 calendar days.

The court found that the cell-panel change caused some delay to the critical path, and thus caused delay to the project as a whole. The contractor's trial expert's as-built delay analysis never referenced the durations or logic in the contractor's schedule updates. Rather, the other expert determined the number of days of excusable delay by comparing the as-built schedule with the initial schedule. According to the court, the contractor's trial expert's as-built analysis was a "total time" approach, which was of virtually no value. The court stated that the "total time" theory of proving delay was insufficient to prove that government-caused delay actually delayed overall completion of the project. The court used the TIA prepared by the contractor's first expert to measure the delay. According to the court, the contractor's trial expert's "total time" analysis was "wholly lacking" in the face of contemporaneous schedule updates showing other causes for the contractor's remaining delay.

[C] As-Planned Method

Page 11-61, add after note 110 in first full paragraph:

For example, it may be a distortion of the schedule merely to insert additional activity days to reflect change-order work without considering the impact of other delays or the actual effect of the change orders on the progress of the work. Additional activity days for change orders inserted into a schedule do not necessarily equate to day-for-day delays to overall project completion. *J.T. Jones Construction Co.,* ASBCA No. 48303, 98-2 B.C.A. (CCH) ¶ 29,892 (1997).

[E] Other Delay Analysis Methods

Page 11-66, add to note 123:

See C&D Lumber, Inc., VABCA No. 2877, 91-1 B.C.A. (CCH) ¶ 23,544 (1991); Norair Eng'g Corp., ENG BCA No. 3804, 90-1 B.C.A. (CCH) ¶ 22,327 (1990); Blackhawk Heating & Plumbing Co., GSBCA No. 2432, 75-1 B.C.A. (CCH) ¶ 11,261 (1975).

Page 11-72, add after note 130 in third full paragraph:

In *Kinetic Builders, Inc. v. Secretary of Air Force,* 226 F.3d 1307 (Fed. Cir. 2000), the Air Force awarded Kinetic the contract for alteration of a building. The government took beneficial occupancy of the building 37 days after the scheduled completion date and withheld liquidated damages. The contractor submitted multiple claims to the contracting officer (CO) for government-caused delays. The CO determined that the contractor was permitted 30 days of delay. The contractor appealed to the Board. The contractor contended that progress in completing the contract had been delayed because of the Air Force's delay in providing a solution to a defective restroom design. The contractor contended that the progress schedule indicated that the defective design and the Air Force's slow response caused it to go from 4.2 percent ahead of schedule to 5.8 percent behind schedule, clearly indicating that its progress had been negatively affected by the defective design. Moreover, the contractor contended that the progress reports for drywall work indicated that it went from 60 percent completion of the work, at the time the Air Force was notified of the defect, to 14 percent behind schedule when the Air Force solved that defect, also evidencing that the defect caused delay. The contractor further contended that the evidence of progress on the drywall work at least entitled it to a contract extension to restart and complete the drywall work. The Board noted that the mere fact that the progress rate declined, between the time the contractor notified the Air Force about the design defect to the time the Air Force corrected that defect, did not establish a causal connection between the defect and the slowing of the progress. The Board noted indications in the record that other drywall installation and other work could have been completed, but was not, during the time the defective design was being resolved. Moreover, the Board noted that 0.7 percent of the drywall work was not completed until after resolution of the design defect. The Board also found that the contractor failed to show that the design defect itself delayed or prevented any drywall work. The Board determined that the contractor was entitled to 17 days of excusable delay because of the Air Force's delay, and referred the quantum to the parties. The contractor appealed the Board's decision to the Federal Circuit court. The Federal Circuit court concluded that the contractor's method of delay analysis did not establish that the Air Force's delay in correcting the defective design had caused the contractor's overall slowing of progress or slowing of the progress on drywall installation.

§ 11.08   CHOOSING A SCHEDULE ANALYSIS METHOD

Page 11-77, add after first full paragraph:

Of course, when the contract specifies a particular method, there is no choice: the contract method must be used. Consider *P.J. Dick, Inc. v. Principi*, 324 F.3d 1364 (Fed. Cir. 2003). The Department of Veterans Affairs (VA) selected P.J. Dick, Inc. (PJD) to construct the Clinical Addition to a VA Medical Center. Under the contract, PJD was due to complete the work by January 12, 1998. The specifications required:

> The Contracting Officer's determination as to the total number of days of contract extension will be based upon the current computer-produced calendar-dated schedule for the time period in question and all other relevant information.

During the contract, the government issued over 400 orders changing the contract and causing various delays to different aspects of the project. These modifications increased the contract price by over 5 percent and caused the VA to grant 107 days of additional contract performance time. PJD completed the contract 260 days after the original contract completion date and 153 days after the revised date. PJD presented to the government contracting officer claims for additional relief as a result of the delays to the contract. All of the claims were denied by the contracting officer (CO). PJD timely appealed the CO's denials to the Board. PJD claimed it was entitled to a time extension for all 260 days of delayed performance and sought field and home office overhead damages for most of these delays. A large portion of the extension (201 days) granted by the Board resulted from PJD's claim for delays due to the "combined directives." The "combined directives" were six separate contract change orders issued by the DVA over a ten-month period, all relating to installation of certain equipment in the Clinical Addition. The Board analyzed the effect of each of the changes as of the date of the earliest change, which gave PJD a larger delay than it would have received were the effects of the change orders analyzed separately on the dates the DVA issued them. The Secretary and PJD each appealed different aspects of the Board's decision. The Secretary argued that the Board erred in its determination that the "time period in question" for all six of the changes included in the "combined directives" was November 1995—the date the DVA issued the first of those change orders.

The language of the contract required the Board to analyze the changes of the "combined directives" separately utilizing the most recent monthly update of the "computer-produced calendar-dated schedule." The express language of the contract established that the "current" schedule "will be" the basis for determining the extent of the delay. By using "will" the contract indicated that this was the sole method of calculating the delay. The Board circumvented this language by crediting litigation arguments that the six unrelated changes issued over ten months had a unitary effect, making the "time period in question" the date the DVA issued the first change order. This was error because the language of the contract required the use of the "current" computer schedule as the basis for making such a determination. In other words, regardless of what the testimony showed, under the contract, the only way of determining the effect of the changes was to analyze each of them using the current computer schedule. Thus, if the changes did have a unitary effect, it had to be demonstrated by the computer model, not the testimony PJD presented. The Board's determination was reversed that the "combined directives" should all be analyzed utilizing the October 1995 schedule update—the update most current as of November 1995—and remanded for a damages analysis in accordance with the contract. On remand the Board should determine whether PJD's delay claims that it found were not controlling because of the "combined directive" delay (the underground conduit and the radiology and cardiology claims) become controlling as a result of any reduction in the "combined directive" delay and analyze them accordingly.

Page 11-77, add after fifth full paragraph:

The study in the *Journal of Construction Engineering and Management* indicated that different delay analyses methods provide different results with the same facts. Three accepted methods were considered. The As-Planned Method; the As-Built Method; and the Modified As-Built Method. Two analyses were performed using the As-Planned Method. First, after representing the delay as activities, the delays were input one at a time and the schedule was calculated after each input. The resulting project completion date and total float available were recorded. Second, the six delays were input to the As-Planned Schedule, then the schedule was calculated. The results were the same for both variations. A. Bubshait & M. Cunningham, *Comparison of Delay Analysis Methodologies,* 124 J. Constr. Eng'g & Mgmt. 315, 322 (No. 4, July/Aug. 1998).

The As-Planned Method considered all delays at once, therefore, the completion date was adjusted to the largest delay on the most critical path. Of the six delays, the results showed that the project completion date had been delayed by 56 days caused by delay No. 2-B, which was the late delivery of electrical duct heaters. After the delay, the total float was reduced to 56 days, delaying project completion by 56 days to 8/18/93. Delay No. 6-A caused two days delay to two activities, however these two days were included into the larger delay caused by delay No. 2-B. Bubshait & Cunningham, at 319–320.

The As-Built procedure compared original float to float available after the delay. Delay No. 2 delayed two activities on the work plan by a total of 127 days. The first activity initially had 169 days positive float, and the second had 71 days positive float. After the delay, activity was reduced to 256 days total float, thus delaying project completion by that amount. The result was 22 days to the project completion date. The As-Built Method calculation showed that the project completion date had been delayed by 58 days. Bubshait & Cunningham, at 320.

Using the Modified As-Built Method, impacts were incorporated as they occurred, the network recalculated, and the results immediately evaluated. After delay No. 2, there was no positive float available. Negative float was 70 days and the revised completion date was 9/1/93. Delay 5 had an impact on the completion date by increasing negative float from 217 to 268 days and resulted in a revised completion date of 8/31/93. The Modified As-Built Method resulted in delays of 70, 51, and 87 days, for delay Nos. 2, 5, and 6 respectively. Bubshait & Cunningham, at 320–321.

The As-Planned Method accessed a penalty duration of 56 days. The As-Built Method penalized the project by 58 days. Under the Modified As-Built Method, the project completion date was delayed by 87 days. Bubshait & Cunningham, at 321.

Page 11-78, add after first full paragraph:

The importance of the skill of the scheduler and the methodology used is underscored by the case of *Cogefar-Impresit U.S.A., Inc.,* DOTCAB No. 2721, 97-2 B.C.A. (CCH) ¶ 29,188 (1997). In the *Cogefar* case, both the government and the contractor retained scheduling experts to perform analyses of the delays and to provide expert witness testimony at the board hearings. The parties' experts employed different methods of schedule analysis. The contractor's expert measured delays by comparing the as-planned schedule against the as-built schedule. The contractor's expert took great pains to document the as-built schedule, reviewing daily reports, monthly progress reports, field reports, cost reports, payroll records, submittal log, and depositions. The contractor's experts also viewed videos and interviewed 20 contractor employees. The government's expert used a "contemporaneous time frame analysis," using information available at the time of the delay and evaluating the delay in a "window" of time using two successive schedule updates contemporaneous with the timeframe in which the delay occurred. The court noted that the conclusions of the experts were "heavily slanted" towards the position of the party that retained them, but found the contractor's expert to be more reliable because of its "thorough" review and attempt to determine the "as-built critical path." The government's expert relied on the contractor's updates without changing the update logic to reflect the "actual logic on the job." The board determined that the approach used by the government's expert did not use a current CPM schedule, and yielded a less precise result.

Page 11-78, add at end of section:

In selecting a scheduling method to analyze the impact of project delays, one commentator developed guidelines to ensure proper schedule analysis based on recent case law. The guidelines were stated as the "Ten Commandments" of schedule analysis:

1. Do not rely upon a schedule that was not followed during the project.
2. Consider actual performance.
3. Avoid "as-planned plus impact" analyses.
4. Establish a correlation between the plan, changes, actual performance, and contemporaneous records.
5. Consider your own delays in a delay analysis.
6. Keep schedules concurrent and reflect delays as they occur.
7. Involve the right people in the delay analysis.
8. Be objective and avoid adversarial interests that damage credibility.
9. Recognize the right to finish early.
10. Recognize reasonable resource leveling.

Wickwire, *The Scheduling Expert's Commandments,* The Millenium Construction Superconference (Dec. 9, 1999).

§ 11.09   APPORTIONING CONCURRENT DELAYS

Page 11-81, add after carryover paragraph:

In *Clark Construction Group, Inc.,* No. VABCA-5674, 00-1 B.C.A. (CCH) ¶ 30,870 (2000), Clark originally planned to construct a VA hospital using a "horizontal" construction sequence. Clark intended to complete the structure of each floor of all three wings before constructing the next floor. Clark developed an "interim" schedule that reflected scheduling logic using a horizontal construction sequence. As a consequence of a stop order, Clark re-sequenced the job from the planned horizontal to vertical construction. Consequently, Clark commenced vertical construction of the West Tower where the foundation was complete while concurrently, on a limited basis, continuing East and Center Wing foundation work. The interim CPM schedule required by the contract, still under development at the time the first stop work order was issued, was abandoned.

However, the change to vertical construction took place well before the major part of the subcontractors' work began. Apparently, the subcontractors took no actions to adjust their material delivery or packaging schedules to mitigate the disruption. The fact that Clark did not seek nor did the subcontractors attempt any input or apparent influence on the development of the vertical construction CPM schedule provided some explanation for the subcontractors' failure to adjust their material deliveries. Also providing some reason for the subcontractors' material handling difficulties, the record showed that Clark did not progress the job according to the schedule and the subcontractors were reduced to looking out the window to see where Clark was working in order to assign its forces. The subcontractors' claims did not consider all the other delays identified in the record, but blamed all the delay on the government. The board concluded that the subcontractors failed to adequately prove that the change in working conditions resulting from the sequence change was the sole cause of its material handling inefficiencies.

Similarly, in *Par Painting, Inc. v. Greenhorne & O'Mara Inc.*, 61 Conn. App. 317, 763 A.2d 1078 (2001), the Connecticut appellate court refused to permit a subcontractor to collect its delay damages when the delays were concurrent with the subcontractor's own delays. A subcontractor that sandblasted and repainted steel structures brought an action against a bridge inspector on the repainting projects, alleging that it had inspected the subcontractor's work too slowly and in bad faith, resulting in the subcontractor's inability to perform under the contract to repaint a bridge. The subcontractor claimed tortious interference with business relationships. A jury found in favor of the subcontractor. However, the trial court granted the inspector's motion to set aside the verdict.

According to the appellate court, the jury could not properly have concluded that the inspector's action was the cause of the subcontractor's delayed completion. Despite evidence of the subcontractor's very late start and other difficulties performing its work, employees' high blood lead levels that prevented work, and lapse of the subcontractor's certification, the jury found that the conduct of the inspector was the factor that kept the subcontractor from finishing its work on time. Even when viewing the evidence most favorably to the subcontractor and assuming that duplicate two-hour inspections in fact occurred, the jury could not with reasonable certainty have concluded that such inspections were the reason the subcontractor had completed only 33 percent of the work well after the contract period had expired. The reviewing court agreed with the trial court's determination that it was impossible for the jury to find (without speculating) that the inspector's tortious conduct, as opposed to its legitimate inspections or the subcontractor's own delays, caused the subcontractor's losses, considering the many nonactionable delays that occurred on the project. The court held that there was no showing of a causal connection between the inspector's conduct and the subcontractor's delays. The inspector presented ample evidence that the subcontractor's work was inadequate and that the inspectors were merely doing what they were hired to do. The trial court judgment was affirmed.

In *Net Construction, Inc. v. C & C Rehab and Construction, Inc.*, 2003 U.S. Dist. LEXIS 6141 (E.D. Pa. 2003), C & C Rehab and Construction, Inc. served as the general contractor for the Chester Housing Authority. From February 3, 1997 through March 25, 1999, when C & C was removed from the project by a federally appointed receiver, Net Construction, Inc. performed installation of concrete site work services. Net's work was delayed and its performance costs increased. Net filed suit, claiming $383,366.29 in consequential damages as a result of C & C's breach of its contract with Net.

A default judgment hearing determined the amount of damages suffered by Net. Net's only witness was its president who testified that the project proceeded in two "phases" each of which involved work on ten to twelve homes that were basically identical. As the concrete site work contractor, Net performed work directly related to the construction of the buildings, and involved pouring concrete "footers" and "base slabs." Net also performed miscellaneous site-work, including the construction of curbs and sidewalks. Work on Phase I was supposed to be completed in July 1997, but it did not end until April of 1998. Net lost $103,188 on Phase I of the project. The whole project, including the completion of Phase II, was supposed to end in April 1998, but the project was not complete until April 1999. Net lost $139,000 on Phase II. The delay in finishing the project was due primarily to C & C's poor management, especially during of Phase I of the project. However, there were other problems with the construction site that led to delay, including the existence of asbestos at the site, unsuitable soils, and weather related issues. Furthermore, Net itself contributed to the delay of the project's completion because Net experienced problems with its concrete supplier and with pouring a floor.

The court found that Net failed to establish a reasonable allocation of its extra costs as a result of particular delays caused by C & C. While Net established that there were delays in completing the construction project, it failed to demonstrate that its damages for lost productivity were the result of delays for which C & C was responsible. "No basis appears for even an educated guess" as to the increased costs suffered by Net as a result of delays for which C & C was responsible. Net failed to distinguish losses suffered as a result of delays by C & C from losses that it might have suffered because of Net's own performance problems, weather, unsuitable soils, or the existence of asbestos at the site. Net was not entitled to recover damages on its claim of lost productivity and extended home office overhead.

Page 11-80, add after note 144 in second full paragraph:

In the United Kingdom there are competing approaches that are being considered to define and apportion concurrent delays. One approach is to attempt to differentiate the various causes of delay in terms of their "causative potency." One delay may not have the same potential impact as the other, only being a minor cause, in which case, it is treated as if it did not cause the delay at all. Only the "effective cause" of delay would be considered in the delay analysis. The responsibility to make decisions under the "dominant cause approach" could be given to the architect to determine which delay was "dominant." The architect may already have the contractual authority, as it has the responsibility under many standard form agreements to decide claims and time extensions. This approach may help sort out concurrent delays in some situations, but there are instances where more than one event is of "approximate equal causative potency." This is in essence a winner-take-all approach that actually treats the delays as not being truly concurrent in equal value. Martin, *Concurrent Delay*, 18 Constr. L.J. 6, 436-48, at 437, 445-46 (2002).

Another approach is to apply a "but-for" test. For example, in the event of two concurrent delays, one caused by extra work ordered by the architect and one caused by the contractor is delaying the performance of the extra work, the contractor may argue that the delay would not have occurred at all but for the extra work. The but-for approach may assist in sorting out such delays; however, the but-for test does not seem to have a basis in English case law for determining contract claims. *Id.* at 443.

Another approach is known as the "Malmaison approach," based upon the rationale of the case, *Henry Boot Construction (U.K.) Limited v. Malmaison Hotel (Manchester) Limited*, 70 Con. L.R. 32, QBD (TCC) (1999). In *Malmaison*, the court distinguished between "relevant events" and events that were not relevant, both of which were concurrent delays. Relevancy of an event is determined through consideration of the contractual allocation of risk between the parties. For example, do the terms of the contract specifically allocate the risk of certain delays, such as "exceptionally inclement weather" but remain silent concerning delays due to labor shortage? The contract would be examined to determine if one of the concurrent delays were specifically stated to be grounds for relief under the contract. If so, such a delay would be deemed to be relevant under the terms of the contract, and be more important to the parties. *Id.* at 447-48.

Canadian law also permits the apportionment of concurrent delay. Rather than simply permit a "winner-take-all" approach, a contractor proceeding on a breach of contract theory for delay may be able to sort out its own delays and yet still recover for the delay of the employer (owner). Martin, *Concurrent Delay*, 18 Const. L.J. No. 6 at 439 (2002), *citing Tompkins Hardware Limited v. North Western Flying Services Limited*, 139 D.L.R.3d 329 (1982); *Ribic v. Weinstein*, 140 D.L.R. (3d) 258 (1982); and *Doiron v. Caisse Populaire D'Inkereman Ltee*, 17 D.L.R. 4th 660 (1985), and *citing Convert-A-Wall Limited v. Brampton Hydro-Electric Commission*, 65 Or. 2d 385, 441 (1988).

[A] Apportioning Consecutive Concurrent Delay

Page 11-82, add to Abrahamson cite at note 154:

at 139 (4th ed. 1979).

Page 11-83, add after fourth full paragraph:

In *Essex Electro Engineers, Inc. v. Danzig*, 224 F.3d 1283 (Fed. Cir. 2000), the federal court found that shop drawing submittal and approval are inherently apportionable, but may distort the overall measurement of delay. In *Essex,* the Marine Corps Research, Development and Acquisition Command awarded Essex a contract to manufacture, test, and deliver a number of skid-mounted floodlights. The contract required Essex to produce and test two prototypes. Essex notified the government that the drawings contained errors and omissions that had to be corrected before Essex could assemble the prototypes. Essex stopped work because of the errors. The government's technical project officer contacted Essex by telephone on May 10 and provided additional details and revised dimensions that addressed some of Essex's concerns. Then, on May 21, the contracting officer sent Essex a letter advising that changes to the drawings appeared to be indicated and directing that the proposed changes to the drawings be submitted as engineering change proposals (ECPs) pursuant to the contract. On November 26, Essex submitted the ECPs on the correct form, providing the total proposed cost for each ECP, but no cost details. The government, on February 11, 1992, notified Essex that it had approved some of the ECPs but had rejected others. Two of the disapproved ECPs concerned the dimensional errors and detail omissions that were the subjects of the government's May 10, 1991, telephone call to Essex. The government informed Essex that Essex needed to submit additional cost details and a revised delivery schedule to complete the approved ECPs. Essex submitted the required cost details on May 5, 1992.

The Board found that the government had provided Essex with defective drawings and was liable for the resulting harm. The Board awarded Essex recovery of the engineering and production costs to incorporate the disapproved ECPs into the design. In addition, the Board found the government liable for Essex's costs associated with the 25-day delay between Essex's notice to the government of the drawing defects and the government's May 10 telephone call providing additional detail and revised dimensional information, because that delay affected the production of the prototypes. For the period after May 10, however, the Board concluded that Essex had acted unreasonably in stopping work pending the government's acceptance of the ECPs. Any government-caused delays after that date were concurrent with Essex-caused delays and precluded Essex from further recovery based on delays associated with the erroneous drawings.

On appeal to the Federal Circuit court, Essex argued that the government's liability for the defective drawings did not end with the May 10 telephone call in which the government allegedly provided Essex with correct dimensions and details. The telephone call from the government required Essex to choose whether to produce sets that did not conform to the official drawings, and thus could be rejected by the government; or to defer further prototype development pending formal ECP approval by the contracting officer. Neither the contract nor case law required Essex to proceed at its peril following the government's telephone call. The Federal Circuit court did not, however, accept Essex's contention that the government's liability extended to all the delays associated with approval of the ECPs. Essex caused delay in approval of the ECPs by failing to follow the applicable standards prescribed by the contract to provide cost information. Both Essex and the government may have delayed the approval of the ECPs in other ways as well. The government requested ECPs for the defective drawings on May 21, 1991, and Essex submitted them on July 30. The government was liable for whatever period of time Essex reasonably needed to respond to the government's written request for the ECPs, but not for any longer. The Board on remand had to determine whether Essex acted reasonably in taking 70 days to submit the original ECPs, and if not, what constituted a reasonable period for preparing the ECPs. Even though Essex submitted the ECPs on the wrong form and may have taken an unreasonable amount of time to submit the original ECPs, Essex's conduct in turn did not relieve the government of its obligation to proceed reasonably thereafter. After Essex's initial ECP submission on July 30, 1991, the government took 48 days to respond simply that Essex had not followed the applicable standard. Within 15 days of the government's response, Essex requested a meeting with government officials concerning the ECPs. Thirty-nine more days elapsed before the government met with Essex on November 8 and stated that the ECPs required cost data. Essex then submitted ECPs with estimates of total costs. The record suggested that the government did not respond again for another 77 days, when it notified Essex that some of the ECPs had been approved, subject to the submission of cost details. On remand, the Board had to determine whether the government acted reasonably in the substance and pace of its responses to Essex's various submissions, keeping in mind that the need for the ECPs arose from the government's defective specifications in the first place. A finding that the government did not act reasonably in responding to Essex's ECP submissions may affect the Board's conclusion that most government-caused delays were concurrent with Essex-caused delays. The sequential nature of Essex's submissions and the government's responses rendered each party's delays inherently apportionable, at least in the case of ECP-related delays.

The amount of any overall delay chargeable to the government should be equal to the period between the time the submissions would have been approved absent culpable delay by the government and the time Essex actually began testing. This inquiry required the Board to focus on the overall effect that government-caused delay had on the beginning of prototype testing, and not to focus on each discrete period of delay and then automatically treat as concurrent delay any period of government-caused delay during which Essex was also causing unrelated delay. That type of instance-by-instance analysis of the delays could result in distortion of the proper measure of overall delay. In the absence of any government-caused delay, Essex's unrelated delays might have been concurrent with each other (rather than concurrent with government-caused delays), so that the overall delay in contract completion would not have been as great.

Page 11-84, add after first paragraph:

In *Alcan Electrical & Engineering Co. v. Samaritan Hospital*, 2002 Wash. App. LEXIS 33 (2002), the court concluded that subcontractors that each contribute to project delay were not jointly and severally liable for the entire project delay if their delays can be apportioned. Gilbert H. Moen Company was the general contractor for the renovation and expansion of Samaritan Hospital. Alcan Electrical & Engineering Co. was a subcontractor on the project. Alcan sued Moen for payment. Moen filed a counterclaim against Alcan, arguing that any payment was subject to an offset for liquidated damages resulting from Alcan's delay of the project. The trial court found a 201-day delay was the result of another subcontractor's unauthorized installation of nonconforming pipe, as well as Alcan's failure to submit fire alarm shop drawings to the Fire Marshall in a timely manner. The court determined that the other subcontractor's installation of the wrong pipe delayed the project 170 days. The court found Alcan's untimely submission of fire

117

alarm shop drawings caused a 31-day delay. Alcan's award was reduced for its 31-day delay. Claiming Alcan was responsible for more than 31 days of the delay, Moen appealed.

Moen asserted that the two subcontractors caused a concurrent delay and were therefore both liable for liquidated damages for the same period of time. Moen claimed that both Alcan and the other subcontractor should have been held to be jointly and severally liable for the entire delay. However, the appellate court decline to so hold. Moen also took issue with the court's apportionment of the delay between the two subcontractors. It argued that Alcan was responsible for more than 31 days of the delay. During November and December 1991, Alcan was working with the Fire Marshall to prepare satisfactory drawings. In December 1991, Alcan wrote to Moen, asking when it would get a response from the architect regarding the fire alarm system and when it would be able to complete its work. During this time, tests of the other subcontractor's nonconforming pipe were being done. These tests required the removal of walls and ceilings. The pipe testing process went almost into January 1992. It could be inferred that, until the pipe testing was complete, Alcan could not have installed the fire alarm system. Therefore, it was reasonable for the court to find that Alcan was only responsible for the 31-day delay from January 4 to February 4, 1992.

§ 11.10   USING THE SCHEDULE TO PROVE OUT-OF-SEQUENCE WORK AND OTHER DISRUPTIONS

Page 11-97, add at end of section:

Contractors' efforts to protect their productivity rates also are hampered by the prevailing view that total float is "owned by the project" and is freely available on a first-come-first-serve basis to both owners and contractors. When attempting to analyze the disruptive impacts of delays, however, there are two arguments in favor of using free float rather than total float. First, while total float determines delays to overall project completion, free float is a more relevant schedule characteristic when looking for delays to activities and increases in activity overlaps. Since disruption is largely caused by activity overlaps, it may be reasonable to analyze disruptive results using free float and leave total float to delay analyses. Second, total float indicates the amount of float available to a chain or path of activities. Total float is shared by all activities along a given chain, and does not necessarily represent the float available to a specific activity. M. Finke, *Schedule Density as a Tool for Pricing Compensable Float Consumption,* 42 Cost Eng'g 34, at 35 (No. 6, June 2000).

Changes in schedule density are practical indicators of the disruptive effects of free float consumption. Schedule density adds the total of all activities' free float to determine the proportion of activity durations to free float. Reducing the free float of activities that have high labor costs should be more disruptive than if the activities had relatively low labor costs. Disruption may be measured by adding labor costs to the density determination and then measuring the effect of any reduction of free float. If such information were provided for activities in the schedule, weighted schedule densities could be calculated for specific locations, trades, and/or supervisors to more narrowly focus on specific causal mechanisms. Finke, at 35.

Increases in schedule density should never reduce a contractor's costs, instead, they should tend to increase activity-specific costs for the remainder of the work. Changes in (remaining) weighted schedule density should be considered in light of the schedule's total remaining labor costs. A given change in weighted schedule density may have a greater effect if the schedule's remaining labor costs total $500,000 rather than if they total only $100,000. Conversely, a given schedule change also will tend to cause smaller changes in weighted schedule density if it occurs earlier in a schedule. Without any revisions to logic or activity descriptions, a noncritical delay should always cause a potentially disruptive increase in weighted schedule density because the sum of activity durations will stay the same while the sum of activity free floats will decrease. On the other hand, a critical delay will decrease a schedule's weighted density because the sum of activity durations will stay the same while the sum of activity free floats will stay the same or increase. As a result, a critical delay could very well be less disruptive than a noncritical delay. Finke, at 36–37.

CHAPTER 12
DELAY DAMAGES

§ 12.01   THE IMPORTANCE OF PROVING DAMAGES

Page 12-3, add after first paragraph:

In *Clark Construction Group, Inc.,* No. VABCA-5674, 2000 VA B.C.A. LEXIS 4 (Apr. 5, 2000), the VA did not contest that it took extended periods to respond to some RFIs, primarily because of the failure of its A/E to act promptly. The average response time to RFIs relating to the ten systems or areas impacting Clark's subcontractors ranged from 38–235 days which appeared, according to the board, to raise questions. However, the reasonableness of RFI response time, in terms of disruption of installation labor, must be gauged from the context of when the RFI was submitted and when the work was to be performed. Most of the RFIs at issue were submitted beginning in the last quarter of 1991 through 1992. The VA's failure to respond until mid-1992 to an RFI submitted in December 1991 relating to an installation scheduled for December 1992 was not necessarily unreasonable and, by itself, did not result in VA's liability for a labor disruption experienced in that installation.

In addition, proof that the late RFI response caused the disruption of its labor required corroboration by reference to contemporaneous documentation. Disruption should leave a trail through the project documentation, including daily logs, CPM fragments, correspondence, and other contemporaneous contract documentation to support that the late RFI responses changed the expected working conditions and that the change to working conditions disrupted labor and the extent of the disruption. The board inferred, in light of the subcontractor's failure to cite any of the extensive contemporaneous documentation in the record to support late RFI response caused disruption, that the documentation in the record did not support the disruption. The board concluded that the subcontractors failed to prove by a preponderance of the evidence that the VA's response to any particular RFI was unreasonably late or that a late RFI response by the VA caused a loss of labor productivity.

§ 12.04   DAMAGE CALCULATION THEORIES

[B]   Total Cost Method

Page 12-13, add after second sentence in first paragraph:

Federal courts hearing contract disputes also take a conservative approach to the use of the total cost method of calculating damages. The U.S. Court of Federal

Claims stated, "Trial courts are advised to use this method with caution because bidding inaccuracies can create an unrealistically low estimate of the contractor's costs, and performance inefficiencies can increase the costs incurred." *Baldi Brothers Constructors v. United States*, 50 Fed. Cl. 74, 79-80 (2001).

[1]   Permissible Uses of the Total Cost Method

Page 12-20, add at end of subsection:

In *McKie v. Huntley*, 620 N.W.2d 599 (S.D. 2000) the concrete contractor priced its claims for delay and extra costs upon the actual labor and material costs for amount of concrete placed, and then subtracted the amount of the payments it received. The trial court granted summary judgment to the defendant because the damages as calculated by the claimant were vague and speculative. On appeal, the South Dakota Supreme Court reversed the summary judgment because the lower court failed to recognize that the total cost method has legitimacy under certain circumstances. If the claimant was able to prove the prerequisite elements or modify the total cost calculation for its own problems, the court might entertain use of the total cost method. However, to reject the total cost methodology as a matter of law was inappropriate.

In *Baldi Brothers Constructors v. United States,* 50 Fed. Cl. 74, 79-80 (2001), the contractor was awarded a contract by the government to construct a tank training range where extensive earthwork was required. However, the project was located on federally protected wetlands, a fact that was not indicated in the contract documents. After award, the government provided the contractor with a wetlands designation map indicating that 80 percent of the site was affected. The government admitted that its failure to disclose the wetlands was a Type II differing site condition but rejected the contractor's pricing of the claim on a total cost basis. The court found the modified total cost method of calculation to be acceptable because nearly all of the work was impacted — this was not a situation where only discrete work activities were subject to increased performance costs. The court did modify the total costs claimed by the contractor based upon what it found to be overly optimistic equipment production rates.

§ 12.05   EXTENDED GENERAL CONDITIONS

Page 12-23, add after note 79 in first paragraph:

Courts have allowed extended general conditions to be paid on a daily rate basis. For example, in *Techdyne Systems Corp. v. Whittaker Corp.*, 427 S.E.2d 334 (Va. 1993), a prime contractor calculated its extended general conditions as a daily rate of $2,068 and was able to recover these costs against a subcontractor that delayed the critical work activities.

Page 12-24, add at end of third full paragraph:

Extended general conditions may also include additional subsistence costs for onsite supervisory personnel, transportation expenses and sanitary facilities. Such costs should be demonstrated to be time-related. For example, the time-related rental costs for a dumpster may be properly recovered, but the roll-off charge disallowed as it would have been incurred whether or not the project time was extended. *Adventure Group, Inc.*, ASBCA No. 50188, 97-2 B.C.A. (CCH) ¶ 29,081 (1997)

Page 12-26, add after note 86 in carryover paragraph:

In seeking to recover its general conditions cost on change orders, contractors often use the percentage markup on the change order cost. If the change order involves a time-extension, a contractor may also seek to recover a per diem for the extended general conditions. Using both methods on a given contract may be problematic. Two key cases on this issue are *M.A. Mortenson Co.*, ASBCA No. 40750, 97-1 B.C.A. (CCH) ¶ 28,623 (1997), *aff'd on recons.* 98-1 B.C.A. (CCH) ¶ 29,658 (1998) and *Caddell Construction Co., Inc.*, ASBCA No. 49333, 00-1 B.C.A. (CCH), ¶ 30,702, *aff'd on recons.*, 00-1 B.C.A. (CCH) ¶ 30,859 (2000). In *Mortenson*, the contractor added a percentage markup for general conditions for change order work that did not extend the performance time and used a daily rate for extended general conditions costs when the change order involved a time extension. The government allowed a three and one-half percent markup for home office overhead but did not allow a markup for field overhead costs without an extension in the performance time. For example, if the project already required a full-time supervisor in the field, the performance of change order work would not increase its supervision costs, unless the change order involved a time extension requiring the supervisor to be on-site for a longer duration. The Board found in favor of the government in the original appeal and upon reconsideration. Switching between a per diem rate and a percentage markup on the same contract would allow the contractor to include the field general conditions costs in two different overhead pools. According to the Board's reading of Federal Acquisition Regulation (FAR) 31.203 (b) this is not allowed. The *Mortenson* rule was confirmed in *Caddell Construction*. The contractor building a wastewater treatment plant for the Corps of Engineers used a percentage mark-up for general conditions costs on change order proposals that did not involve time extensions and a per diem rate for general conditions on change order proposals involving a request for compensable extension of time. After an audit by the Defense Contract Audit Agency, the Corps gave the contractor the option of choosing either, but not both methods. In considering the matter on appeal, the Board ruled that the contractor must use one method in order to comply with the requirement of FAR 31.203 (b) for a single distribution base for allocating an overhead pool. The "single cost pool" requirement was the basis for the decision.

However, in *The Sherman R. Smoot Corp*, ASBCA No. 52261, 01-1 B.C.A. (CCH) ¶ 31,267 (2001), the Board did not preclude the practice of using both a percentage markup and a per diem to compensate the contractor for general conditions costs in limited situations. The fixed-price contract for renovation of buildings stipulated overhead and profit percentage markups for change orders up to ten percent of the original contract value, and that field overhead was not to be a direct cost to change orders. The contractor received unilateral modifications granting time extensions providing for extended field overhead on a per diem basis, in addition to the amount of overhead paid on previous change orders. The contractor submitted a claim for extended field overhead calculated on a per diem basis, arguing that the percentage markup limitation did not apply to delays *not* associated with change orders. The board denied the government's motion for summary judgment because a fact issue existed as to whether the government waived the percentage limitation by issuing the unilateral modifications authorizing a daily rate for extended field general conditions.

The issue of paying general conditions as a daily rate or a percentage of the cost of change orders was also raised in *W.M. Schlosser, Inc. v. United States*, 50 Fed. Cl. 147 (2001), where the contractor argued that the government's approval of the pricing of extended field overhead on a per diem basis for three change orders established an implied agreement for future change orders to alter the contract provisions that extended field overhead was to be priced as a percentage of the cost of a change order. The contractor claimed that the extended field overhead also should be priced as a daily rate for other changes. Only three of the 95 change orders issued by the government priced extended field overhead on a per diem basis, and the government argued that this was a mistake. The court determined that an implied agreement to alter the terms of the contract requires proof of mutual intent and found the three change orders pricing field overhead on a daily rate were inadvertent. Further an explicit provision like the percentage markup pricing method cannot be changed by an implied agreement.

§ 12.06   HOME OFFICE OVERHEAD

Page 12-29, add after second full paragraph:

Broward County v. Russell, Inc., 589 So. 2d 983 (Fla. App. 1991); *Department on Transportation v. Herbert R. Imbt, Inc.*, 630 A.2d 550 (Pa. Cmmw. Ct. 1993); *Chilton Ins. Co. v. Pate & Pate Enterprises, Inc.*, 930 S.W.2d 877 (Tex. Ct. App. 1996); *Fairfax County Redevelopment and Hous. Auth. v. Worcester Brothers Co., Inc.*, 257 Va. 382, 514 S.E.2d 147 (1999).

[A]   *Eichleay* Formula

Page 12-32, add after second sentence in first paragraph:

For instance, the *Eichleay* formula has been approved by Florida's Fourth Judicial Court of Appeals. *See Triple R Paving, Inc. v. Broward County*, 774 So. 2d 50 (Fla.

Dist. Ct. App. 2000), *citing Broward County v. Russell, Inc.,* 589 So. 2d 983 (Fla. Dist. Ct. App. 1991).

[B] Establishing That Home Office Overhead Expenses Were Affected

Page 12-36, add to last sentence of first paragraph:

, and (4) the contractor's performance is extended by change order work. Courts reason that the contractor's home office overhead has been absorbed by the value of the change order overhead mark-up. (See **§ 12.06[E]**.)

Page 12-39, add after note 149 in first full paragraph:

In *Interstate General Government Contractors v. West,* 12 F.3d 1053 (Fed. Cir. 1993), the Federal Circuit stated that a contractor proving that it is on "standby" does not need to prove that it has workers or equipment idly standing around waiting for productive work tests. The standby requirement can be met by the contractor demonstrating that the delay or suspended performance is for an uncertain duration during which period the contractor remains ready to perform. However, if the contractor continues to progress the work in any substantial manner, there has been no standby sufficient to support home office overhead claims.

The Federal Circuit in *P.J. Dick, Inc. v. Principi,* 324 F.3d 1364 (Fed. Cir. 2003), explained in much greater detail how a public owner should make a standby analysis. In making the standby inquiry, the court should first determine whether the contracting officer (CO) has issued a written order that suspended all the work on the contract for an uncertain duration and required the contractor to remain ready to resume work immediately or on short notice. *P.J. Dick, Inc. v. Principi, citing Interstate,* 12 F.3d at 1055, 1057 n.4. In such a case, the contractor need not offer further proof of standby. In the cases where the CO does not issue such a written order, the contractor must then prove standby by indirect evidence. To do so, the contractor must show three things.

First, the contractor must show that the government-caused delay was not only substantial but was of an indefinite duration. *P.J. Dick, Inc. v. Principi, citing id.* at 1058. For example, where the government suspends all work on the contract, but tells the contractor work will begin again on a date certain, the contractor could not be on standby. *P.J. Dick, Inc. v. Principi, citing Melka,* 187 F.3d at 1376.

Second, the contractor must show that during that delay it was required to be ready to resume work on the contract, at full speed as well as immediately. Once the suspension period is over, the contractor must be required to be ready to "resume full work immediately." *P.J. Dick, Inc. v. Principi, citing id.* at 1375; *All State Boiler,* 146 F.3d at 1373. Thus, where the government gives the contractor a reasonable amount of time to remobilize its work force once the suspension is lifted, the contractor cannot be on standby. *P.J. Dick, Inc. v. Principi, citing Mech-Con Corp. v. West,* 61 F.3d 883, 887 (Fed. Cir. 1995) (holding the contractor could not be on standby where the government gave the contractor three months to remobilize its work force on site). Presumably, the same result would follow if the government required immediate resumption of the work, but only with a reduced work force and allowed the contractor to gradually increase its work force over some reasonable amount of time. *P.J. Dick, Inc. v. Principi, citing Melka,* 187 F.3d at 1375. In addition, satisfaction of this element of standby clearly requires something more than an uncertain delay. The implication is that the contractor must be required to keep at least some of its workers and necessary equipment at the site, even if idle, ready to resume work on the contract (i.e., doing nothing or working on something elsewhere that allows them to get back to the contract site on short notice). *P.J. Dick, Inc. v. Principi, citing Sergent Mech. Sys. v. United States,* 54 Fed. Cl. 47, 49-50, 54 Fed. Cl. 636 (2002).

Third, the contractor must show effective suspension of much, if not all, of the work on the contract. *P.J. Dick, Inc. v. Principi, citing Melka,* 187 F.3d at 1375. Early decisions contained some statements that supported the notion that suspension of the work and idleness are not prerequisites to a determination that the contractor is on standby. *P.J. Dick, Inc. v. Principi, citing Altmayer v. Johnson,* 79 F.3d 1129, 1134 (Fed. Cir. 1996) ("There is no requirement that a contract be suspended before a contractor is entitled to recover under *Eichleay.*"); *Interstate,* 12 F.3d at 1057 n.4 ("Although idleness of workers is evidence that a contractor is on standby, i.e., performance has been suspended, it is neither conclusive nor required."). At no time, however, has the Federal Circuit court held that a contractor has been placed on standby merely because a government-caused delay of uncertain duration occurred, at the end of which the contractor must be ready to resume work. According to the Federal Circuit, *Altmayer,* oft cited for that proposition, held no such thing. *Altmayer* merely held that a contractor's performance of "minor tasks" during a suspension does not prevent it from recovering *Eichleay* damages. *P.J. Dick, Inc. v. Principi, citing Altmayer,* 79 F.3d at 1134. Nor does *Interstate*'s statement that idleness is not a prerequisite to standby support the idea that a contractor can be deemed on standby where there is no delay or suspension of the work. *P.J. Dick, Inc. v. Principi, citing Interstate,* 12 F.3d at 1057 n.4. *Interstate* indicates that its reference to "idleness" simply means the workers need not be "physically standing by idly." *P.J. Dick, Inc. v. Principi, citing id.* at 1057 n.5 (referencing a quote in a previous opinion and stating "these two phrases ["stand by idly and suspend its work"] clearly refer to standing by in the sense that no work is being performed on the contract, not that there must be workers physically standing by idly"); *see also id.* at 1057 n.4 ("If the test were whether the contractor's work force assigned to the contract in issue was standing by, the contractor would be penalized for, and thus deterred from, mitigating its damages for direct costs by reassigning its employees to other jobs or laying them off during the period of delay."). Every case where the Federal Circuit has held a contractor to be placed on standby has involved a complete suspension or delay of all the work or at most continued performance of only insubstantial work on the contract. *P.J. Dick, Inc. v. Principi, citing E.R. Mitchell Constr. Co. v. Danzig,* 175 F.3d 1369, 1372, 1374 (Fed. Cir. 1999) (holding subcontractor was entitled to *Eichleay* damages where it performed "some work" on the contract, but where most "work could not proceed until the faults [causing the suspension] were cured"); *All State Boiler, Inc.*, 146 F.3d at 1370, 1373 (holding contractor was entitled to *Eichleay* damages where the government suspended all work on the contract); *Satellite Elec. Co. v. Dalton*, 105 F.3d 1418, 1421 (Fed. Cir. 1997) (holding contractor was on standby where all the work on the contract was stopped, but denying recovery of *Eichleay* damages for other reasons); *Altmayer*, 79 F.3d at 1134; *Mech-Con*, 61 F.3d at 887 (holding contractor was entitled to *Eichleay* damages where work on the contract was completely suspended); *see also Interstate*, 12 F.3d at 1058 (noting that the record "could support" a conclusion that a contractor was on standby where all work on the contract was suspended).

Later decisions by the Federal Circuit explicitly state that such a suspension or delay of the work on the contract is a prerequisite to a finding that the government placed the contractor on standby. *P.J. Dick, Inc. v. Principi, citing Melka*, 187 F.3d at 1375-76; *see also Interstate*, 12 F.3d at 1057 (discussing standby as requiring "suspension of work on the contract"). In *Melka*, the Circuit Court held that a contractor was not on standby where it "was working on the contract and the government had not suspended all contract work." *P.J. Dick, Inc. v. Principi, citing Melka*, 187 F.3d at 1375. There, the government stopped work on one type of work, but, by resequencing the work under the contract, the contractor was able to perform substantial work on another type of work with comparable direct cost billings. *P.J. Dick, Inc. v. Principi, citing id.* at 1375-76. Subsequent decisions by the Court of Federal Claims and the Contract Boards also followed this view of the law. *P.J. Dick, Inc. v. Principi, citing Pete Vicari, Gen. Contractor, Inc. v. United States*, 53 Fed. Cl. 357, 368-70 (2002); *Carousel Dev., Inc.*, ASBCA No. 50719, 2001-1 B.C.A. (CCH) ¶ 31,262 (Jan. 23, 2001) (concluding contractor was not on standby where it continued to perform substantial amounts of work on the contract — here "approximately one quarter of the entire scope of the contract work"). So too does a major treatise on government contracts. *P.J. Dick, Inc. v. Principi, citing* John Cibinic, Jr. & Ralph C. Nash, Jr., Administration of Government Contracts 737 (3d ed. 1995) ("The standby test precludes a contractor from receiving extended or unabsorbed overhead unless there has been some period when the work was significantly slowed or stopped."). Thus, even though it is the typical scenario, formal suspension is not an absolute prerequisite. Contract performance also could be stopped or significantly slowed by government inaction, such as failure to vacate spaces in which the contract was to be performed.

In short, a court evaluating a contractor's claim for *Eichleay* damages should ask the following questions: (1) was there a government-caused delay that was not concurrent with another delay caused by some other source; (2) did the contractor demonstrate that it incurred additional overhead (was the original time frame for completion extended or did the contractor satisfy the *Interstate* three-part test); (3) did the government CO issue a suspension or other order expressly putting the contractor on standby; (4) if not, can the contractor prove there was a delay of indefinite duration during which it could not bill substantial amounts of work on the contract and at the end of which it was required to be able to return to work on the contract at full speed and immediately; (5) can the government satisfy its burden of production showing that it was not impractical for the contractor to take on replacement work (i.e., a new contract) and thereby mitigate its damages; and (6) if the government meets its burden of production, can the contractor satisfy its burden of persuasion that it was impractical for it to obtain sufficient replacement work. Only where the above exacting requirements can be satisfied will a contractor be entitled to *Eichleay* damages.

In *P.J. Dick, Inc. v. Principi*, 324 F.3d 1364 (Fed. Cir. 2003), the Department of Veterans Affairs (DVA) selected P.J. Dick, Inc. (PJD) to construct the Clinical Addition to the DVA Medical Center in Ann Arbor, Michigan. Under the contract, PJD was due to complete the work by January 12, 1998. During the contract the government issued over 400 orders changing the contract and causing various delays to different aspects of the project. These modifications increased the contract price by over 5 percent and caused the DVA to grant 107 days of additional contract performance time. In accepting the additional days to complete the contract, PJD reserved its right to seek additional impact and suspension costs. PJD completed the contract on September 29, 1998, 260 days after the original contract completion date and 153 days after the revised date. PJD presented to the government contracting officer claims for a time extension for all 260 days of delayed performance and sought field and home office overhead damages for most of these delays.

After the CO denied the claims, the Board concluded that PJD was not entitled to *Eichleay* damages because it failed to prove that it was placed on standby. The Board found that PJD was not placed on standby because "PJD was able to progress other parts of the work during the time periods it alleges it was suspended." The Board determined that PJD's direct billings remained substantial during the several suspension periods and that it accelerated the work on the contract was irrelevant. The Secretary and PJD each appealed different aspects of the Board's decision.

First, PJD argued the Board committed legal error because a contractor was automatically on standby any time there was a government-caused delay of an uncertain duration extending the performance of the contract, at the end of which the contractor can be required to immediately resume work. Second, PJD argued that substantial evidence did not support the Board's findings that its direct billings "showed no appreciable diminution during the alleged suspension periods" and that it accelerated performance of the contract.

The Board applied the correct legal standard for standby. The contractor must show a suspension, whether formal or functional, of all or most of the work on the contract. Consequently, PJD's legal argument failed. The evidence, at worst, showed that in one of these delay periods PJD billed 53 percent less than it had the month before. There was, however, no evidence that PJD's direct billings were less than they would have been absent the suspensions—that was the controlling test. A comparison of pre- and intra-delay billings or intra- and post-delay billings was not the test. Regardless, PJD's direct billings during the delay periods could hardly be characterized as "minor." At worst, PJD's direct billings during one of the periods of suspension were 47 percent of what they were in prior months; thus, PJD continued to perform substantial amounts of work on the contract during the suspension periods. The Board's conclusion that PJD was not on standby was affirmed.

Page 12-39, add after note 152 in second full paragraph:

Another board of contract appeals supplemented the proof requirements for recovery of *Eichleay* damages with "disruption in stream of income" standard and also held that *Eichleay* damages cannot be recovered after substantial completion. In *Young Enterprises of Georgia, Inc. v. General Services Administration*, GSBCA No. 14437, 00-2 B.C.A. (CCH) ¶ 31,148 (2000), the contractor was awarded a contract for the renovation of a historic courthouse. During the course of construction, the contractor alleged its performance was delayed by the need to remediate unanticipated asbestos, various change orders and constructive suspension at the end of the project. The contractor received time extensions and additional compensation for the asbestos delays and change orders, but the government denied the constructive suspension claim. The government's defenses to the constructive suspension claim were that there were concurrent subcontractor delays, and that some of the delays occurred after substantial completion. Before the board of contract appeals, the government also argued that the contractor should not be able to recover *Eichleay* damages where there was no disruption of cash flow from the contract.

The Board agreed with the government in these two points. It ruled that the recovery of unabsorbed home office overhead is not appropriate for delays after substantial completion because the contractor did not demonstrate that it was unable to increase its bonding capacity or obtain additional work. Thus, the board recognized that substantial completion is a milestone event, precluding the contractor from recovering *Eichleay* damages as well as precluding the owner from assessing liquidated damages.

"The stream of income" standard was applied to preclude recovery of home office overhead damages. The board found that because the contractor received continuous progress payments, and performed change order work during the alleged delay period, there was no basis to find that the contractor's home office overhead was unabsorbed or that there was disruption in the stream of income emanating from the contract.

Page 12-41, add after second full paragraph:

In *Melka Marine, Inc. v. United States*, 187 F.3d 1370 (Fed. Cir. 1999), the Federal Circuit court determined that a contractor's ability to bid or perform other work during suspension or delay did not by itself indicate replacement for delayed or suspended project. The Navy awarded Melka a contract for dredging work, construction of a breakwater, repairs to an existing boat ramp, quay wall, finger pier, and various other repair work. The contract required the government to obtain a dredging permit prior to the commencement of the dredging and breakwater work, but not for the repair work. The government notified Melka that the permit had not yet been obtained, but was expected at any time. The government noted that construction repairs were not dependent on the permit. Melka mobilized all of its equipment to the job site by November 15, 1994. On November 16, 1994, Melka sent a letter to the government stating that Melka's proposed schedule for completing the work would be negatively impacted by the government's failure to timely obtain a permit and that it would re-sequence the work to avoid inactivity. On November 21, Melka began the re-sequenced work by starting work on the boat ramp. Work was suspended the next day, however, due to the discovery of a six-inch pipe in the ramp and the discovery of a prior boat ramp beneath the existing ramp, which required a revised ramp design. Modification P00003 was a unilateral modification compensating Melka for overhead and field costs associated with performing the work out of sequence and for its dredging and breakwater equipment for 12 days.

As a result of these delays and the delay in obtaining a permit, on November 29 the government issued a formal "Suspension of Work" order. The order suspended the commencement of dredging and breakwater work for an indefinite period. Two days later the government revised its Suspension of Work order to permit work on the repairs to the quaywall and the finger pier, and also suggested that equipment on site that would not be utilized on the repairs to the boat ramp, quaywall, or finger pier could be demobilized. The government requested that Melka take any other steps necessary to minimize costs due to the suspension of permit related work. By December 27, 1994, Melka had demobilized its dredging and breakwater equipment while it continued the re-sequenced repair work, which was substantially completed by January 4, 1995. Melka later mobilized its dredging and breakwater equipment for use on another project from January 4–18, 1995, and a second project from January 20, 1995 through March 31, 1995. Melka originally scheduled these jobs to be performed after the government project, but the government-imposed delay allowed Melka to perform these jobs earlier. Melka also bid on other projects during this period which it did not receive, but that it would have been able to perform had they been awarded them.

On February 2, 1995, the government informed Melka that work on the dredging and breakwater, rather than commencing in February 1995, could not begin until October 15, 1995, and requested that it agree to perform this work under the original contract price. Melka agreed and proposed a completion date of February 29, 1996. All work was completed by February 1996.

Melka asserted that it was entitled to recovery of its unabsorbed overhead from November 16, 1994 through March 30, 1995 as calculated by the *Eichleay* formula. The Court of Federal Claims denied Melka's claims and dismissed Melka's complaint. Melka appealed. From November 16 (the beginning of Melka's alleged damages period) to November 29, 1994 (the date the government issued the formal Suspension of Work order), the Court of Federal Claims found that no government-imposed delay in fact occurred and Melka could not have been on "standby." Although the government had failed to obtain a permit for the dredging and breakwater work, the parties had agreed that Melka would re-sequence its work so that work not related to the permit could be done. From November 29, 1994 to January 4, 1995 (the approximate end of Melka's performance of all those contract tasks not dependent upon issuance of the permit), the Court of Federal Claims found that although the government issued a suspension of work order at the beginning of this period, that order directed Melka to perform non permit-related work and indicated that the dredging permit would not be obtained until 1995. After the Suspension of Work order, Melka continued to work on the contract (with re-sequenced work) and did so on a virtually uninterrupted basis through January 3, 1995. Melka argued that because the dredging and breakwater work accounted for a significant amount of the work in the government contract, once such work was suspended indefinitely, Melka was on standby.

The Federal Circuit Court found that Melka could not establish that it was on standby by dividing the contract into one portion that was able to be performed (the repairs) and another that was on standby (the dredging and breakwater work), because the contract required that both types of work be performed. If work on the contract continued uninterrupted, albeit in a different order than originally planned, the contractor was not on standby. Given these facts, the Court of Federal Claims did not clearly err in finding that Melka was not on standby and not entitled to *Eichleay* damages during this period. From February 2, 1995 (when the government informed Melka that permit-related work could not begin until October 15, 1995) to March 30, 1995 (the last date for which Melka sought recovery), the Court of Federal Claims found that Melka could not have been on standby because it knew then with certainty that it could not be called on to perform the work before October 15. The Federal Circuit found this was not clearly erroneous because "standby" requires an uncertain delay period when the government can require the contractor to resume full-scale work at any time. Melka knew that it would not be called on to work on the contract until October 15 and the government did not require Melka to keep its dredging and breakwater equipment at the site. Thus, *Eichleay* damages could not be awarded for this time period either. The Federal Circuit affirmed those portions of the Court of Federal Claims decision.

January 4, 1995 (when Melka completed those contract tasks not dependent upon receipt of the permit) to February 2, 1995 (the date when the government and Melka agreed that the permit-related work would not commence until October 15, 1995), presented a different issue because the government conceded that Melka was on standby of indefinite duration. The issue became whether the government satisfied its burden of showing that it was not impractical for Melka to obtain replacement work, or that Melka's inability to obtain replacement work was due to circumstances not related to the government-caused delay. In an effort to satisfy its burden, the government argued that the work Melka was able to perform on the two projects constituted replacement work. Those projects, according to the government, could not have been performed if Melka had been performing the dredging and breakwater parts of the government contract because it could only take on one large dredging project at a time. The government also argued that Melka would have taken on more work had its bids been successful and the economy been stronger, both reasons unrelated to the government's delay and suspension of work. Melka argued that the projects it took on were not replacement work because they were relatively small in comparison to the work on the government contract and were merely moved up in its schedule in order to mitigate its losses as a matter of good faith.

The Court of Federal Claims noted that Melka performed several other projects while on standby and bid unsuccessfully on several others, and it held that Melka was not entitled to any *Eichleay* damages for this time period. The Federal Circuit held that the Court of Federal Claims applied the wrong legal test when it focused on Melka's ability to take on any other work during the delay period as a basis to deny any *Eichleay* damages. The appropriate inquiry was whether Melka was able to take on replacement work, not just any additional work. Because the Federal Circuit was unable to discern from the record whether the work performed or bid on by Melka during this time frame was replacement work, producing sufficient support to absorb all the overhead costs that the government contract would have if work had not been suspended, the case was remanded to the Court of Federal Claims for a determination of that issue.

The court stated that a heavy burden falls on the government once a contractor has established its prima facie case of entitlement to *Eichleay* damages because in very few cases will the government be able to demonstrate that it was not impractical for the contractor to take on replacement work. Nevertheless, the government may be able to show that Melka was not injured by the delay. For example, the government argued that part of Melka's inability to obtain work was due to cold winter weather, rather than the government-caused delay and requirement to stand by. Such evidence related directly to the issue of what caused Melka's inability to obtain adequate replacement work; if in fact it was unable to obtain such work, or if bad weather prevented performance of work that was obtained. Bidding on other projects can also support, rather than undercut, a contractor's argument that it was impractical for it to obtain replacement work, particularly if the projects that were bid on could not be commenced and/or completed within the government-caused delay.

Melka argued that it could not obtain replacement work by bidding on other projects because such work involved substantial lead times that would render it impossible to begin the project in a reasonable period of time, much less before the suspension is lifted. For example, three and a half months elapsed from the time the project was advertised until Melka actually commenced work on the delayed contract. Such commercial realities in the market may be highly material when determining whether it was impractical to obtain any replacement work or sufficient replacement work. Finally, the relative sizes of the projects at issue in terms of dollar amount, timing, and duration are relevant when determining whether a particular project was in fact replacement work, as opposed to merely additional work in the ordinary course of business for a contractor that routinely performs multiple contracts. The key was the potential for the new work to contribute a comparable amount to the contractor's overhead, as the government contract would have absent the suspension, assuming that the time durations are also comparable. However, replacement work need not be identical in size, duration, or type as compared to the delayed work. If the same amount of money was not contributed to the overhead costs in the same period by the replacement work, then the contractor should be able to obtain at least some *Eichleay* damages. Partial replacement entitles the contractor to reduce its *Eichleay* claim, not substitute for it.

Another board of contract appeals case indicates that change order work that is subcontracted out may not constitute "replacement work" for the prime contractor for purposes of determining the recovery of *Eichleay* damages. In *Able Products Co. v. Department of the Treasury*, GSBCA No. 15167-TD, 01-2 B.C.A. (CCH) ¶ 31,554 (2001), the contractor, Able, was awarded a contract to renovate the HVAC system, and during the course of performance discovered the presence of asbestos that had to be abated. The asbestos abatement work was performed by a subcontractor under a change order to Able because Able's personnel were not properly qualified to do the task. Able filed a delay claim alleging that its own HVAC renovation work was on standby while the subcontractor performed the asbestos abatement. The delay costs included unabsorbed home office overhead calculated according to the *Eichleay* formula.

The government moved for summary judgment as to the *Eichleay* damages, arguing that the change order work for the abatement was replacement work for the delayed HVAC work. The Board denied summary judgment, reasoning that there was a factual question as to whether the change order for asbestos abatement by the subcontractor was truly replacement work.

Page 12-42, add after first paragraph:

The second prerequisite to use of the *Eichleay* formula requires that the contractor be unable to take on additional work. In *Safeco Credit v. United States,* 44 Fed. Cl. 406 (Ct. Cl. 1999), the Court of Claims found that the contractor failed to prove it was not able to take on additional work. Safeco cited a statement made by its president in response to a government interrogatory that the suspensions prevented it from undertaking any other work because its resources (employees, equipment, and finances) were committed to the completion of this project. The government stated that the fact that Safeco was able to do the change order work demonstrated that the contractor was not prevented from doing additional work as would be required to use the *Eichleay* formula. The court determined that Safeco's proof was not sufficient to show that they could not have taken on any other jobs during the contract period.

The court found the modifications to the contract required Safeco to perform change order work for which it was compensated; the revised completion dates were clearly set forth in the modifications. Furthermore, aside from the unsubstantiated conclusory allegation of Safeco's president, Safeco failed to show an inability to take on other work. Unlike other cases, the Federal Circuit had decided that the element of uncertainty was absent in *Safeco*. Accordingly, the Navy was determined not to be liable for *Eichleay* damages.

Page 12-42, add after note 161 in second full paragraph:

For example, in *Idela Construction Co.*, ASBCA No. 45070, 01-2 B.C.A. (CCH) ¶ 31,437 (2001), the contractor demonstrated that it repeatedly encountered uncharted and unanticipated water lines, and was required to stop work on the installation of a sewer line until the government determined whether the water lines were active. This required the contractor to suspend work for an uncertain duration, and extended the completion of its work beyond the contractually required completion date.

However, if the contractor is able to perform some of the contract work, more than "minor" work items, it may not be in a true standby mode. For example, in *Carousel Development, Inc.*, ASBCA No. 50719, 01-1 B.C.A. (CCH) ¶ 31,262 (2001), the contractor was awarded a contract to renovate 24 military family housing units, to be released to the contractor in groups of four units every 21 days, and each group to be completed by the contractor within 75 days of release. The government became dissatisfied with the contractor's work, and did not release additional units to the contractor until it completed work on 12 units that were only about 50 percent done. The contractor filed a claim alleging suspension and requesting *Eichleay* damages. Although the Board found that the government suspended work on the 12 remaining units by refusing to release them, the contractor was performing contract work on first 12 units and never came to a standstill. Thus, the contractor was not entitled to recover *Eichleay* damages.

Page 12-42, add after second paragraph:

An owner may avoid paying the contractor's unabsorbed home office overhead by permitting a remobilization period after the suspension ends. For example, in *Complete General Construction Co. v. Ohio Department of Transportation*, 94 Ohio St. 3d 54, 760 N.E.2d 364 (2002), Complete General Construction filed a complaint to recover the unabsorbed home office overhead costs it incurred for the Ohio Department of Transportation's two extensions of contract. The court of claims awarded the contractor $184,947 on its claim for unabsorbed home office overhead. The owner appealed.

According to the owner, the court of claims erred because the contractor failed to establish that it was on standby during the suspension period. The owner conceded that the length of the suspension period was uncertain and that the contractor could have been called back to work at any time during the suspension period. However, the owner contended that the contractor was not on standby when work on one part of the project was suspended but the contractor continued to work on other parts of the project.

The appellate court stated that whether the contractor was able to perform other work on the contract during the suspension period was not relevant to whether the company incurred unabsorbed overhead during the extension period. The uncontroverted evidence showed that the suspension period was of uncertain duration, that the contractor was subject to being called back to work at any time during the suspension period, and that the contractor was required to work on the contract beyond the original completion date due to the suspension. This was sufficient to establish a prima facie case that the contractor incurred unabsorbed overhead as a result.

The owner further contended that the court of claims erred in utilizing *Eichleay* because the evidence showed that the contractor was able to reallocate whatever unabsorbed overhead it incurred as a result of the delay to replacement work. The contractor had successfully bid on $78 million worth of work during the contract, and the annual value of the contractor's work, as well as the company's bonding capacity, increased by $10 million. The appellate court stated that the evidence did not establish that the contractor had "replaced" the work lost during the delay, thereby offsetting unabsorbed overhead. The rule that work obtained as part of a contractor's normal, ongoing bidding process does not constitute replacement work permits few instances in which the owner can successfully rebut a prima facie showing of entitlement to *Eichleay* damages, because the responsibility for a contractor being on standby rests with the owner. By fixing, at the outset of the suspension period, a future date on which the contractor may return to work, or by allowing the contractor a remobilization period at the end of the suspension period, the owner may avoid keeping the contractor on standby during the suspension and thus avoid liability for unabsorbed overhead expenses in the future. Judgment affirmed in part and reversed in part, and case remanded.

Page 12-43, add after first paragraph:

In *Safeco Credit v. United States,* 44 Fed. Cl. 406 (Ct. Cl. 1999), the Claims Court repeated that change orders that extended the performance period did not suspend the work as required to collect unabsorbed home office overhead damages under the *Eichleay* formula. The dispute arose from a 1985 contract for berthing improvements to a naval dock. Safeco Credit was the surety to Fraley Associates, Inc., and the contractor and succeeder to its responsibilities and interests. The contract was divided into seven construction phases identified as 1A, 1B, 2A, 2B, 3A, 3B, and 3C, and a mobilization phase. The Navy added or changed work on the project by 53 modifications to the contract. Many of the modifications extended the time period for completion of phases 1A, 1B, 2A, and 2B—those phases of the project which (with the exception of phase 1B, which was to begin before the completion of phase 1A) were to run consecutively. The parties disagreed about the effect of these modifications on the contract completion dates and, in turn, on Safeco's possible liability for failure to complete the project on time.

Safeco contended that it was entitled to reimbursement for home office overhead as a result of extensions to the project for $663,707.47. The government asserted that Safeco failed to apply the *Eichleay* formula correctly. The court stated that the first prerequisite to use of the *Eichleay* formula was the occurrence of a government-imposed delay which placed the contractor on standby. Safeco asserted that *Eichleay* applied to contract extensions which cause uncertainty as to future performance on a project, as well as suspensions. Safeco also alleged that the government's conduct, evidenced by the number of modifications to the contract, created uncertainty in the length of performance of the contract. The government contended that Safeco performed additional work throughout the extension period and therefore was not on "standby." The court found that Safeco misinterpreted Federal Circuit precedent by asserting as a general rule that "*Eichleay* applies to contract extensions in addition to suspensions."

The contract was extended as a result of modifications issued by the government. These modifications did not suspend work, but rather required Safeco to perform additional and change order work for which it was given additional compensation. The Federal Circuit had determined that *Eichleay* was not applicable to a situation involving additional work due to contract modification as opposed to a suspension without evidence that the contract changes resulted in a delay which required the contractor to stand by idly and suspend its work. The work performed by Safeco during the period of suspension was significant. Furthermore, the modifications added by the government did not make the length of performance uncertain. Rather, the modifications expressly set forth dates by which the contract was lengthened.

Page 12-44, add after eighth sentence in carryover paragraph:

It is unreasonable to expect a contractor who has been delayed to factually prove that, except for a delay on one contract, he was not able to bid for another contract and as a consequence thereof was unable to generate sufficient income to fund his overheads. In reality, except where a contractor carries out only one contract at a time or where the delayed contract is a high proportion of the company turnover, it is almost impossible to obtain the necessary definitive, contemporaneous evidence to prove that a contractor could have obtained profitable work elsewhere which he was unable to do, but for the claimed delay. Such evidence that can be obtained is usually inconclusive. Notwithstanding these problems, it is clear that if a contractor has entered into a contract which generates turnover and contribution to overheads and is prevented from earning these amounts, overheads will be underfunded and he will incur a loss. J. Pettet, *Claims for Head Office Overheads—Alternatives to Formulae,* 65 Arbitration 130, at 139 (No. 2, May 1999).

[C]   Adjusting the Formula Calculations

Page 12-46, add after first paragraph:

The period for calculating extra home office support expenses is not limited to the contract duration plus any allowable extensions when the notice to proceed is delayed by the designer's error. For example, in *Crown Corr, Inc. v. Wil-Freds Construction, Inc.,* 2000 U.S. Dist. LEXIS 17961 (N.D. Ill. Dec. 11, 2000), Bertrand Goldberg Associates, Inc., was hired as the architect and construction coordinator of the Wright Junior College Project by the City of Chicago, acting through its Public Building Commission. Wil-Freds was hired to construct the floors of five buildings. The contractor was delayed and submitted a claim. Wil-Freds's claims included loss of productivity, wage and benefit increases, and extended general conditions. Wil-Freds and the city compromised on Wil-Freds's claims. The settlement agreement included a table that allocated dollar amounts of the settlement into various categories. Wil-Freds sought $701,798 from Goldberg for extra home office support. Goldberg argued that Wil-Freds had used the wrong starting date in calculating its damages, utilizing the contract award date as opposed to the date of notice to proceed. Goldberg also argued that the appropriate time period to be used was the contract period plus any extensions allowed. Part of Wil-Freds's claim against Goldberg for extra home office support was premised on the allegation that certain notices to proceed were unreasonably delayed because of Goldberg's failure to coordinate the Wright Project properly. Based on this allegation, it would be unreasonable to require Wil-Freds to compute damages beginning with its receipt of the notice to proceed. The reviewing court found the starting date used by Wil-Freds to be reasonable. This was not a breach of contract case whereby a contractor was suing an owner for delay damages. This case involved a contractor suing a construction coordinator (designer) for delay damages. The appropriate time period to be utilized to determine extra home office support damages was the equitable period already applied by Wil-Freds.

[D] *Hudson* Formula in English Law Cases

Page 12-50, add to note 196:

Manshul Constr. Corp. v. Dormitory Auth., 436 N.Y.S.2d 724, 79 A.D.2d 383 (1981) (court used formula similar to the *Hudson* formula to calculate home office overhead after project completion).

[E] *Eichleay* and Change Order Overhead

Page 12-51, add after first paragraph:

The award of unabsorbed home office overhead according to the *Eichleay* formula must credit the portion of change order markup attributed to home office overhead. In *Complete General Construction Co. v. Ohio Department of Transportation,* 94 Ohio St. 3d 54, 760 N.E.2d 364 (2002), the contractor recovered its unabsorbed home office overhead costs, incurred for two time extensions, in the Ohio Court of Claims. The public owner appealed, arguing that the court of claims should have deducted a portion of the more than $2 million worth of change order work performed on the contract from the contractor's unabsorbed overhead award. Given the court of claims finding that change orders for additional work included a 5 percent markup for overhead, the court was required to deduct 5 percent of the change order work from the award. The appellate court agreed. The appellate court stated that the trial court's exclusion of a 60-day extension period from the general contractor's compensable period showed that the court of claims should have deducted a portion of the change order overhead on the contract from the contractor's unabsorbed overhead damage award. Given the trial court's finding that home office overhead was built into change order payments for additional work, to the extent that the change orders also granted the contractor compensation for additional work, the change orders granted compensation for additional overhead. The court of claims' failure to deduct 5 percent of the value of any of the change orders from the amount of the contractor's unabsorbed overhead damage award resulted in excessive compensation for unabsorbed overhead. Nonetheless, deducting the entire 5 percent would result in an excessive reduction of the damage award, as the total value of all contract change orders included payments to subcontractors. On remand, the court of claims had to determine the amount by which change orders compensated the contractor for extra work, and deduct 5 percent of that amount from the *Eichleay* damage award. Judgment affirmed in part and reversed in part, and case remanded.

[F] Alternative Calculation Methods

Page 12-52, add after note 208 in third full paragraph:

A different measure of damages for home office overhead may be applied for delays that occur after the scheduled completion date. In *Manshul Construction Corp. v. Dormitory Authority,* 436 N.Y.S.2d 724, 79 A.D.2d 383 (1981), the court compensated the contractor for the home office overhead incurred during delays subsequent to the project completion by applying a formula involving a four step process similar to the *Hudson* formula. (See **§ 12.06[D]**). In the first step, the court estimated the direct cost of the work performed after the scheduled completion date. This assumed that the contractor used a 15 percent overhead and profit factor. So 100/115 or 87 percent of the billings during the post-completion period were used as the basis for calculating the direct cost of the work. In the second step, the court applied an overhead factor. Assuming that the contractor's 15 percent factor was for both overhead and profit, the court determined that overhead was 7.25 percent and profit was 7.25 percent. In the third step, the court multiplied the direct cost of the work times the 7.25 percent overhead factor to calculate the additional overhead that the contractor incurred for post-completion delays. In the fourth step, the court determined that the contractor was responsible for 5 percent of the delays, so it multiplied the post-completion overhead by 95 percent to calculate the additional overhead that the contractor was entitled to recover for the delays caused by the owner that forced the contractor to continue work after the scheduled completion date. This complex calculation was used because of concerns with the application of the *Eichleay* formula based upon the New York Court of Appeals case in *Berley Industries, Inc. v. City of New York,* 45 N.Y.2d 688, 385 N.E.2d 281, 412 N.Y.S.2d 589 (1978).

Page 12-53, add after first full paragraph:

In *Complete General Construction Co. v. Ohio Department of Transportation*, 94 Ohio St. 3d 54, 760 N.E.2d 364 (2002), the Ohio Supreme Court accepted the *Eichleay* formula to calculate unabsorbed home office overhead damages in public construction delay cases. The Ohio DOT argued that the *Eichleay* formula allowed contractors to recover for breach of contract without establishing causation. To the contrary, before the formula could be applied, a contractor must prove an extraordinary set of circumstances that demonstrated causation and damages. A contractor may recover only if there is an owner-caused construction delay. Moreover, the "standby" character of the delay must also be caused by the owner, and must prevent the contractor from finding replacement projects to cover the overhead. Thus, *Eichleay* did no violence to contract law. A court in Ohio could also utilize the direct cost formula. The direct cost method compared the direct costs actually attributed to a project as a portion of all of the direct costs incurred by the business over a particular period. The result was a ratio by which the percentage of indirect costs could be calculated, including home office overhead applicable to a particular project.

[G] Unallowable Overhead Costs by Contract

Page 12-55, add after second paragraph:

A contractor will inevitably incur overhead costs which have no relevance to the particular contract on which the claim is being made. Such items will therefore have to be excluded from the aggregate balance of overheads. Such non-applicable exclusions may be:

- Administration of non-contracting activities such as manufacturing, maintenance work, repair services, domestic work, property development, management services, housing developments, and other similar activities;

- Management resources dealing with previous claims, delays and abnormal problems on earlier and concurrent contracts;

- Allowance for grants;

- Redundancy payments;

- Interest and finance charges;

- Losses on other contracts;

- Goodwill costs.

J. Pettet, at 139.

[1]   By Regulation

Page 12-56, add after second full paragraph:

In *Complete General Construction Co. v. Ohio Department of Transportation*, 94 Ohio St. 3d 54, 760 N.E.2d 364 (2002), the Ohio Supreme Court concluded that the costs prohibited by Federal Acquisition Regulations (FAR) should not be recovered in claims that involve Ohio public contracts. Complete General Construction Company constructed part of I-670 for the Ohio Department of Transportation (ODOT). Early in the project, design errors attributable to ODOT caused a fourteen-month delay. Complete General sued ODOT to recover unabsorbed home office overhead, among other costs. The Court of Claims awarded Complete General $184,947 for unabsorbed home office overhead. ODOT appealed the part of Complete General's award based upon the *Eichleay* formula. According to the Ohio Supreme Court, differences between federal and Ohio public contracting law allowed contractors to recover inappropriate costs when the *Eichleay* formula was applied in Ohio. The federal government adopted the FAR to determine which costs were allowable and which were not. FAR prohibitions included interest on borrowings, entertainment expenses, contributions and/or donations, bid and proposal costs, and bad debts. The idea that the government should fund a contractor's parties, sports tickets, political contributions, or other expenses that brought nothing tangible to the government's project was unreasonable. Such costs should not be recoverable in an Ohio case applying the *Eichleay* formula. The trial court erred in applying the *Eichleay* formula without allowing ODOT to dispute items of overhead.

§ 12.07   IDLE EQUIPMENT COSTS

Page 12-59, add after fourth full paragraph:

The contractor must connect the cause of idled equipment during winter shutdown with the acts of the owner. In *Complete General Construction Co. v. Ohio Department of Transportation,* 94 Ohio St. 3d 54, 760 N.E.2d 364 (2000), Complete General Construction filed a complaint to recover its idle and extended equipment costs incurred during the Ohio Department of Transportation's two extensions of contract. The court of claims awarded the contractor $62,622.50 on its claim for idle equipment costs. However, the court of claims found against the contractor on its claim for extended equipment costs. The owner appealed.

At trial, the contractor claimed three types of equipment costs as a result of the delay: (1) the costs incurred as a result of having equipment idle on the job site during the suspension period; (2) the costs incurred as a result of having equipment idle on the job site during the extension period; and (3) the costs of owning equipment used during the extension period. The owner challenged the court of claims' damage award for idle equipment costs incurred during the suspension period. The contractor had presented no evidence to establish a causal link between the delay and the equipment that was idled during the suspension period. The appellate court stated that the actual delay had been fully resolved by the end of December 1991. The fact that the owner did not require the contractor to resume work on the project until after April 29, 1992, or that the owner granted the contractor a 12-month extension for what was actually a 7-month suspension, was not sufficient to make the owner responsible as a matter of law for equipment being idle during the period after the actual delay ended. Although it is possible that the equipment was idle until April 29, 1992, as a result of some lingering problem related to the delay, the record was devoid of any evidence establishing such a causal connection. No evidence was presented to show that the equipment was on the job site due to the delay, as opposed to some other cause such as a scheduling choice by the contractor. Judgment affirmed in part and reversed in part, and case remanded.

[C]   Challenging Equipment Rates

Page 12-64, add after carryover paragraph:

Under a cost reimbursement contract, a contractor is entitled to recover rental costs paid for equipment it rents. When a contractor uses its own fully depreciated property, the rental value of that property ordinarily is not an allowable cost. However, the government may agree to pay the contractor a reasonable amount for the use of the contractor's fully depreciated property. In *Union Boiler Works, Inc. v. Caldera,* 156 F.3d 1374 (Fed. Cir. 1998), the Court of Appeals for the Federal Circuit affirmed the Court of Federal Claim's denial of a contractor's claim for the rental costs of fully depreciated property when the contractor had not entered into an agreement with the government regarding payment of those costs.

In 1989 the Army contracted with Union Boiler Works, Inc. to repair three boilers at Aberdeen Proving Ground, Maryland. After work began, the contracting officer directed Union Boiler to replace insulation on two of the three boilers. As part of the contract modification, the government granted Union Boiler a 90-day extension to accommodate the changed work.

Because it was running behind schedule, in October 1989, Union Boiler installed a temporary boiler in the affected building. Union Boiler owned the temporary boiler, which was fully depreciated on Union Boiler's books. Union Boiler completed the repairs on the boilers affected by the contract change 70 days after the 90-day extension period had passed.

The ASBCA sustained its earlier decision that the government's direction to replace the boiler insulation caused Union Boiler to install a temporary boiler 90 days earlier than the contract required. The decision left a quantum of compensation up to the parties to resolve. In July 1995, the contracting officer denied Union Boiler's claim for cost to hook up and start up the temporary boiler, as well as the rental value of the temporary boiler. The government argued that because Union Boiler did not complete the added work within the allocated 90-day period, it would have incurred hook-up and start-up costs even without the change. The board agreed and granted the government's motion for summary judgment.

With respect to rental costs, Union Boiler contended that it was entitled to recover the rental value of its boiler, $4,500 a month, as lost opportunity costs for rents it could have collected had the equipment not been needed by the government. To assess the allowability of the rental costs, the board first looked to the recovery of costs for construction equipment under FAR 31.105(d)(2). This section of the FAR permitted the government to specify a schedule of predetermined rates to be used when actual cost data was not available. The board found that Union Boiler had no evidence of actual costs, and the contract did not prescribe a predetermined rate schedule. Accordingly, the board concluded that the allowability of the costs claimed would be determined under FAR Subpart 31.2.

§ 12.08   LOST PRODUCTIVITY

[B]   Measured Productivity Method

Page 12-77, add at end of section:

A measured mile analysis compares work performed in one period, not impacted by events causing a loss of productivity with the same or comparable work performed in another period, that was impacted by productivity affecting events. *Clark Construction Group, Inc.,* No. VABCA-5674, 2000 VA B.C.A. LEXIS 4 (Apr. 5, 2000). The measured productivity method has also been called the "measured mile analysis." Although there are different ways to calculate the measured productivity, the goal of the measured productivity method is to compare productivity during undisrupted periods (or locations) with productivity during disrupted periods (or locations). Ideally, the comparison will be made on the same project, but some practitioners will make a comparison between what they consider to be similar projects. Measured productivity obviates the need for the claimant to prove the reasonableness of its estimated productivity, because estimated productivity is not used as the basis for comparison.

Courts have accepted the measured productivity method as a way to establish disruption and to quantify the productivity loss. For example, the court decisions in *General Insurance Co. v. Hercules Construction, Natkin & Co. v. George A. Fuller Co.,* and *Groves-Black* (all discussed in the main text) all accepted lost productivity calculated by the measured productivity method. In addition, in *U.S. Industries, Inc. v. Blake Construction, Inc.,* 671 F.2d 539 (D.C. Cir. 1982), the plaintiff, U.S. Industries, sued its joint venture partner, Blake Construction, alleging disruption, among other things, from the failure to schedule and coordinate the work. U.S. Industries submitted financial and statistical evidence along the lines of a measured mile to prove that its labor costs increased dramatically when it was disrupted by the defendant.

Experts are often engaged to perform and present measured productivity analyses. In *Danac, Inc.,* ASBCA No. 33,394, 97-2 B.C.A. (CCH) ¶ 29,184

(1997), *aff'd*, 98-1 B.C.A. (CCH) ¶ 29,454 (1998), the claimant's expert prepared an analysis purportedly using the measured mile approach. The expert's analysis calculated the ratio of the number of labor hours expended to the number of units completed in various time periods. According to this analysis, the claimant experienced a 55 percent productivity loss in one period and a 25 percent productivity loss in another period when compared to one of the more efficient time periods that was used as the baseline for measuring productivity.

The use of the measured productivity approach has its limitations, according to some courts. For example, the comparison to work in different time periods or locations should be similar in terms of complexity or difficulty of the work activities, skill level of the workers and supervisors, and work environment. If the work tasks are not comparable, courts may reject or adjust the measured mile analysis. In *United States ex rel. Shields v. Citizens & Southern National Bank,* 367 F.2d 473 (4th Cir. 1966), it was determined that the work in the "disrupted" areas was by nature more time-consuming than the work in the measured mile areas, and the analysis was neither a reasonable comparison nor a reasonable basis for quantifying disruption damages. Industry commentators have also identified other limitations, adjustments, or problems with the use of the measured productivity:

- The lack of an unimpacted time period or location to develop a measured mile baseline, because disruption occurs throughout the project.

- "Learning curve" or worker orientation and familiarization should be taken into account.

- Time and price requirements, such as accelerated work, change order work, and time and material compensation, may require special consideration.

- Environmental factors, such as temperature, wind, and other weather conditions, may affect the comparison.

- The measured mile period or location may not represent a reasonably sustainable level of productivity.

Thomas & Sanvido, *Quantification of Losses Caused by Labor Inefficiencies: Where Is the Elusive Measured Mile?,* 1 Constr. L. & Bus. 3 (Summer 2000); Patton & Gatlin, *Claims for Lost Labor Productivity,* Constr. Law. 21 (Apr. 2000); Loulakis & Santiago, *Getting the Most Out of Your Measured Mile Approach,* Civil Eng'g 69 (Nov. 1999); Ginsburg & Dickson, *Loss of Efficiency/Edition II,* Constr. Briefings No. 99-11 (Oct. 1999).

Some of these factors might be adjusted by using a baseline approach rather than a strict measured productivity analysis, according to the studies and recommendations of Penn State University professors Thomas and Sanvido. Thomas & Sanvido, *Quantification of Losses Caused by Labor Inefficiencies: Where Is the Elusive Measured Mile?,* 1 Constr. L. & Bus. 3 (Summer 2000). The baseline approach uses a comparable period of work time when the contractor achieves good productivity even though it may be hampered by its own inefficiencies. Nor does the baseline period have to be free of impacts caused by the other party, as is required when using a measured mile analysis. Further, the baseline time frame need not be comprised of consecutive work periods—the baseline may include sporadic workdays, weeks, or months. To ensure that the baseline is a realistic representation of the contractor's potential productivity, the professors recommend that it comprise at least 10 percent of the time when the measured work activities were being performed.

The baseline approach described by Thomas and Sanvido may raise concerns because it is an analysis based upon the contractor's "best productivity." This may exclude conditions reasonably encountered on a project, such as learning curves, normal corrective work, and reasonably anticipated mobilization requirements. Therefore, a baseline productivity analysis may be bolstered by a demonstration that it represents a reasonably attainable and sustainable level of productivity, taking into consideration the field conditions anticipated by the contract documents and other conditions inherent in the work.

§ 12.10   INTEREST

[C] Prejudgment Interest for Denied Use of Funds

Page 12-87, add after second paragraph:

A flow-through agreement in a subcontract does not include an interest clause in the general contract when the subcontract work is limited to the work provisions of the general contract. For example, in *Thor Electric, Inc. v. Oberle & Assocs.,* 741 N.E.2d 373 (Ind. Ct. App. 2000), the Richmond Hotel Limited retained Oberle as the general contractor on a renovation project. Oberle retained Thor as a subcontractor to perform specified work on the project, including plumbing, heating, ventilation, and air conditioning. Under the contract, Oberle would pay Thor 95 percent of the invoiced amounts five days after Oberle was paid by the owner. Thor would receive the 5 percent retainage upon satisfactory completion of the work. Should Oberle fail to pay Thor, the subcontract provided that Thor could stop work until payment of the amount owed, and the contract price would be adjusted for the additional costs of shutdown, delay, and startup. In its cross-claim, Thor sought payment of its retainage from Oberle. Thor was entitled to $82,633.30 in retainage under the subcontract. Additionally, Thor sought prejudgment interest on the retainage. The trial court rendered its judgment, awarding Thor attorneys' fees, prejudgment interest, and damages against Oberle.

Thor argued that its subcontract with Oberle contained a flow-through provision that incorporated the provisions of the contract between Oberle and the owner. Based on the flow-through provision, Thor contended that the proper interest rate was the local prime rate plus two percent. The language of the flow-through provision clearly provided, however, that incorporation was limited to the work provisions of the general contract as applicable to Thor. The work provisions were limited to the specific performance of the work—materials used, labor, and timing—and as such did not include the payment provisions of the Oberle/owner contract. Consequently, the flow-through provision did not incorporate the interest-rate provision of the Oberle/owner contract into the subcontract. Furthermore, whereas the general contract provided for interest in the event of late payment, the subcontract provided for stoppage of work in the event of late payment and was silent on the issue of interest. In addition, the court recognized a public policy interest in allowing subcontractors to negotiate a price without being constrained by the contractor and owner's negotiated price and method of payment. A subcontractor would look to the agreement between the owner and contractor for the project specifications and materials requirements in submitting a bid to the contractor. However, the subcontractor is free to negotiate its own financial arrangements. This subcontract did not provide the interest rate to be applied in calculating prejudgment interest.

[F]   Computing Prejudgment Interest

Page 12-95, add after third sentence in second full paragraph:

For example, in *Thor Electric, Inc. v. Oberle & Assocs.,* 741 N.E.2d 373 (Ind. Ct. App. 2000), the court held that retainage due on substantial completion is readily ascertainable for calculation of prejudgment interest. Richmond Hotel Limited retained Oberle as the general contractor on a renovation project. Oberle retained Thor as a subcontractor to perform plumbing, heating, ventilation, and air conditioning. Under the contract, Thor was required to submit monthly invoices to Oberle. Oberle would then pay Thor 95 percent of the invoiced amounts five days after Oberle was paid by the Owner. Thor would receive the five percent retainage upon satisfactory completion of the work. Should Oberle fail to pay Thor, the contract provided that Thor could stop work until payment of the amount owed, and the contract price would be adjusted for the additional costs of shutdown, delay, and startup. The contract did not expressly provide for the recovery of attorneys' fees or other damages. Thor sought payment of its retainage from Oberle. Thor was entitled to $82,633.30 in retainage under the Oberle/Thor contract. The trial court awarded Thor prejudgment interest. Oberle appealed.

Oberle argued that the award of prejudgment interest was improper because the damages and the due date were not readily ascertainable. Oberle contended that the damages were not readily ascertainable because Thor had not completed approximately $10,000 of the work. Further, Oberle argued that the due date was not ascertainable because it was uncertain when Thor satisfactorily completed the work. Here, the damages were readily ascertainable. Oberle retained five percent of the contract amount until Thor satisfactorily completed the work. Thus, the amount of damages could be easily determined by a simple mathematical computation. The due date was also readily ascertainable: Thor was entitled to payment upon completion of the work. A project manager for Oberle created a punch list of things to be completed, which Thor fulfilled. Thor notified Oberle of the completion, and Oberle acknowledged receipt of operation manuals and drawings. Another building inspector testified that Thor had not completed approximately $10,000 of the work. However,

$10,000 represented approximately one-sixth of 1 percent of the contract price, and therefore, Thor had substantially completed the work. Consequently, Thor was entitled to its retainage on March 26, 1987. As the damages were readily ascertainable, there was no error in the trial court's conclusion that Thor was entitled to prejudgment interest.

§ 12.14 RECOVERY OF ATTORNEYS' FEES IN STATE COURT ACTIONS

Page 12-108, add to note 434:

Thor Elec., Inc. v. Oberle & Assocs., 741 N.E.2d 373 (Ind. Ct. App. 2000) (subcontractor may recover attorneys' fees for contractor's failure to pay retainage only if permitted by agreement, statute, or rule; because there was no contract provision or applicable statute authorizing an award of attorney fees, trial court erred in awarding attorneys' fees to subcontractor).

§ 12.19 OWNER'S DAMAGES

Page 12-122, add after second full paragraph:

If a contractor's defective work causes the performance of the contract to be more expensive or burdensome, the owner is entitled to damages including compensation for stopping business while corrected or delayed work is completed. For example, consider *Pelshaw Co. v. City Motors*, 2003 Iowa App. LEXIS 266 (2003). R.L. Pelshaw Co. agreed to build a new 175-foot metal building addition for City Motors. Pelshaw proposed to receive $30,000 for construction of the addition, plus $39,000 for installation of the concrete foundation and flooring, including a floor drainage system. The floor drainage system failed to work and the parties disputed the best method to correct the system. City Motors concluded the building was not completed in a workmanlike manner and declined to pay Pelshaw. Pelshaw filed a claim for $35,280 based on breach of contract. City Motors filed a counterclaim for damages resulting from Pelshaw's poor workmanship and delays caused by the installation of a new drainage system. The district court awarded Pelshaw $34,280, but also awarded City Motors $24,000 as replacement costs for the floor and $15,000 as reasonable compensation for closing the business while the floor was repaired. Pelshaw has appealed, and City Motors has cross-appealed.

Pelshaw contended the district court erred in awarding City Motors $15,000 as compensation for down time resulting from any business closure due to efforts to correct the faulty drainage system. Pelshaw contended that while there was no dispute the floor's installation was defective, City Motors was not entitled to extra compensation for "down time" since it was denied the opportunity to correct its mistakes. City Motors initially determined such a shut down would cost it over $129,527 over a 15-day period. The district court concluded that $24,000 would put City Motors in a position the same as if the floor been correctly installed and that $15,000 was reasonable compensation for a five-day shut down. Pelshaw's poor workmanship caused considerable delays in the building's construction, and the failure to properly install the drainage system caused City Motors to incur additional expenses in correcting it. Affirmed.

Page 12-123, add after second full paragraph:

On the other hand, the simplicity of owner damages does not excuse an obligation to calculate and prove them. For example, in *Cut Bank School District No. 15 v. Rummel*, 2002 Montana 248 (S. Ct. 2002), Cut Bank School District No. 15 solicited bids from area contractors to repair and patch the steps and sidewalk in front of the Cut Bank High School, resurface the steps and sidewalk with a concrete texture finish and apply an epoxy sealant on all the surfaces. Rummel's bid proposing to complete the work at a cost of $7,950 was accepted. The District desired that the work be completed on or before August 29, 1999, because students and staff would be returning to the school on the following day. There was no written documentation that this timeliness element was a requirement of the contract between the parties, but the District contended that Rummel guaranteed the work would be finished by August 29, 1999. In contrast, Rummel contended he made no guarantee, but told the District he would make his best effort to complete the project by that date. On August 15, 1999, the District accepted another bid from Rummel for $1,500 to repair and patch a second sidewalk on the north side of the high school. Again, the District contended Rummel guaranteed completion of the project by August 29, 1999. On August 30, 1999, the District terminated the contracts with Rummel because the work had not been completed. The District subsequently filed a complaint asserting that Rummel's failure to complete the projects by August 29, 1999, was a breach of the contracts and requesting monetary damages. The district court entered an order granting judgment in favor of Rummel based in its determination that, even assuming Rummel's failure to complete the projects was a breach of the contracts, the District failed to present evidence establishing that damages resulted. The District appealed.

The District argued that it proved damages resulting from the breach of the first contract via Rummel's testimony. On cross-examination, Rummel was asked to give a rough estimate of what it would cost in materials and labor to complete the first contract project from the point at which he left it on August 29, 1999. In response, Rummel testified "I don't know off the top of my head . . . between three and 4,000, total, maybe." The District presented no evidence of the actual cost to complete the project originally contemplated in the first contract because the District contracted in the summer of 2000 with another construction company to repair the front steps and sidewalk using an entirely different method and materials. Thus, the only evidence relating to the District's damages for breach of the first contract was Rummel's purely speculative statement. Such speculation was insufficient to prove damages to a reasonable degree of certainty and, consequently, the District Court's finding of fact in that regard was not clearly erroneous.

[B]   Limitations to Owner's Delay Damages

Page 12-128, add after note 534 in carryover paragraph:

General damages are those that are so usual an accompaniment of the kind of breach or wrongdoing that the mere allegation of the wrong gives sufficient notice. 2 McDonald, Texas Civil Practice 124, § 6.17.1 (1970). If an item of damage is not peculiar to only a particular plaintiff, the damage is not consequential, but direct. Consequential damages may be recovered only if proved to be "the natural, probable, and foreseeable consequence" of the defendant's breach. *CMC Steel Fabricators, Inc. v. Harrop Constr. Co.*, 131 F. Supp. 2d 882, *citing Mead v. Johnson Group Inc.*, 615 S.W.2d at 687. For example, in *Roanoke Hospital Assoc. v. Doyle and Russell, Inc.*, 215 Va. 796, 214 S.E.2d 155 (1975), the owner claimed three types of interest costs: (1) added interest costs (including expenditures on borrowed funds and interest revenue lost on invested funds) during the construction period arising from the longer term of borrowing necessitated by the contractor's unexcused delay (extended financing costs); (2) added interest costs during the construction period attributable to higher interest rates during the extended term (incremental construction interest costs); and (3) added interest costs for the permanent loan attributable to higher interest rates (incremental permanent interest costs). The court concluded the extended financing costs were direct damages because customarily construction contracts, particularly large contracts, required third-party financing and a delay in completion ordinarily required an extension of the term of construction financing. The interest costs incurred and the interest revenue lost during such an extended term were predictable results of the delay and were, therefore, compensable direct damages. Only the incremental construction interest costs were consequential damages. *See also Hemenway Co. v. Bartex, Inc.*, 373 So. 2d 1356 (La. Ct. App.), *cert. denied*, 376 So. 2d 1272 (La. 1979). Similarly, in *Chandler v. Madsen*, 197 Mont. 234, 642 P.2d 1028 (1982), the supreme court explained that the necessity of moving from a residence undergoing massive repairs and of renting a temporary residence was likely to result from design errors that caused major damage to a structure. The court found that costs for moving, storage, and temporary rental were improperly deleted from the damage award. In *Miracle Mile Shopping Center v. National Union Indemnity Co.*, 299 F.2d 780 (7th Cir. Ind. 1962), the district court allowed $8,500 for the increased cost of mechanical work that resulted from the contractor's abandonment of the project. The appellate court distinguished the additional cost of completion from special or consequential damages. Miracle Mile Shopping Center, *citing Johnson-Johnson Inc. v. Farah*, 123 Ind. App. 87, 108 N.E.2d. 638 (1952). *See also Walker Builders, Inc. v. Lykens*, 628 So. 2d 923 (Ala. Ct. App. 1993) (homeowner's mental anguish damages were actual, not special damages); *Grossman v. Sea Air Towers, Ltd.*, 513 So. 2d 686 (Fla. Dist. Ct. App. 3d Dist. 1987) (architect was held liable for lost rents when tenants vacated owner's building due to noise and dust of construction resulting from collapse of an improperly designed parking garage without mentioning consequential damages); *Apfel v. D.A. Bennett, Inc.*, 109 A.D.2d 1039, 487

N.Y.S.2d 159 (1985) (costs awarded for the owner's excess heating fuel consumption due to the contractor's defective insulation installation without mentioning consequential damages); *Lenz Constr. Co. v. Cameron,* 207 Mont. 506, 674 P.2d 1101 (1984) (temporary rental costs for comparable equipment awarded as compensatory damages in negligence action, where the owner's equipment was damaged by the contractor).

"The potential for delay damages should always be within the contemplation of parties entering into a construction contract." *Construction Law* § 6.10[5] (S. Stein, ed. 2001). Many industry commentators agree and include those damages that should be expected from acts that delay a construction program or project. A treatise on Texas construction law suggested those damages may be:

> If there is no liquidated damage clause in the contract, the owner is entitled to recover actual damages suffered because of the delays. The measure of damages is normally the value of loss of use of the building for the duration of the delay, *or expenses caused by the delay.* J. Canterbury, Texas Construction Law Manual § 10.20 (2d ed. 1992) (emphasis added) citing *Ryan v. Thurmond,* 481 S.W.2d 199, 1972 Tex. App. LEXIS 2458 (1972) (A contractor who has not performed the contract in due time is generally liable in damages for the delay. The measure of damages for failure to complete the work within the time fixed by the contract is generally the value of the use of the building).

Professor Justin Sweet in his work, *Legal Aspects of Architecture, Engineering and the Construction Process,* stated that:

> Direct losses can occur in any construction contract. They are usually measured by conventional objective formulas, such as lost use for unexcused contractor completion delay, cost of correction or diminished value for other contractor defaults, interest for owner-delayed payment, the balance of the purchase price for nonpayment, and the additional costs caused by owner disruption or delay.
>
> Sometimes a claimant claims consequential damages, those that go beyond *direct* losses. Consequential damages are abnormal, related to the particular transaction, and more subjective. . . .

Sweet, Legal Aspects of Architecture, Engineering and the Construction Process 608 (5th ed. 1994).

The American Institute of Architect's (AIA) Standard Form of General Conditions of the Contract for Construction, AIA Document A201 (1997 ed.), includes at Paragraph 4.3.10 a mutual waiver of consequential damages that defined consequential damages to include, " . . . damages incurred by the Owner for rental expenses, for losses of use, income, profit, financing, business and reputation, and for loss of management or employee productivity or of the services of such persons." Similarly, the Associated General Contractor's of America's (AGC) Standard Form of Agreement and General Conditions Between Owner and Contractor, AGC

Document No. 200 (2000 ed.), contract also contains a mutual waiver of consequential damages at Paragraph 10.2. The AGC defines consequential damages,

> ... including but not limited to the Owner's loss of use of the Project, any rental expenses incurred, loss of income, profit or financing related to the Project, as well as the loss of business, loss of financing, principal office overhead and expenses, loss of profits not related to this Project, or loss of reputation.

Assuming these definitions are a good bright line for the industry generally, the AIA and AGC standard excludes most traditional delay damages in their definition of consequential damages: cost overruns occasioned by the delay; payments to contractor's for delay claims; escalated costs, and all the others.

In *H. Shurter v. M. Butler*, 43 Tex. Civ. App. 353, 94 S.W. 1084 (1906), the appellate court stated that delay damages that included a payment to a third party, additional labor caused by the delay, and security costs were *not* too remote to be "direct" damages. H. Shurter contracted with the city of Houston to build sewers in 120 days, or in default to pay $10 per day liquidated damages. M. Butler subcontracted to furnish the brick and knew the terms of the contract. By the terms of the subcontract, the bricks were to be furnished at such time and in such quantities as they were called for. Instead of completing the work in 120 days it was not done for nearly a year, the delay caused by the failure to furnish brick as required for the work. The contractor claimed delay damages, including the $10 per day paid to the city for the delay in completing the sewer; the expense of a watchman required to watch the excavation made for the sewer, for the time the work was delayed; a large sum expended for extra labor rendered necessary by the delay; and the amount expended for re-excavation occasioned thereby; as well as the difference between the amount paid for brick, which the contractor was compelled to buy elsewhere. The trial court refused proof as too remote of any of the delay damages claimed. According to the reviewing court, the delay damages were not too remote to be recovered as matter of law. The subcontractor knew that the work had to be completed in 120 days and that the completion of the work depended upon furnishing the brick promptly as needed in the prosecution of the work. The subcontractor was liable for such damages as were the proximate result of the breach, "that is, for all such damages as resulted directly from such breach and which might be reasonably supposed to have been in contemplation of the parties, at the time of making the contract, as likely to result therefrom." *Id.* at 1085. Reversed and remanded.

In *U.S. for the Use and Benefit of CMC Steel Fabricators, Inc. v. Harrop Constr. Co.*, 131 F. Supp. 2d 882, 891 (S.D. Tex. 2000), the Federal District Court stated that "the direct damages that are available . . . are virtually the same under any theory of liability and causation" and stated a wide variety of incidental damages were also recoverable. *Id. citing Kish v. Van Note*, 692 S.W.2d 463, 466-67 (Tex. 1985). The court identified as direct damages "offsets" in the form of direct damages it took to correct subcontractor's errors.

In *Hess Die Mold, Inc. v. American Plasti-Plate Corp.*, 653 S.W.2d 927 (1983), the court allowed an owner the cost to replace a plastic mold that the contractor failed to supply. American Plastic was in the business of injection molding of plastics. Hess manufactures die molds. One of American's molds no longer performed satisfactorily, and it solicited bids for a new one. Hess submitted a quote to American to design and build a suitable mold at a price of $23,445.00. Hess never completed a mold that would perform or operate properly in American's business. As a result, American was forced to contract with another manufacturer for the production of a suitable mold at a contract price of $47,500. The cost to American for this mold, over and above its contract price with Hess, was $24,065. American sued Hess. The court rendered judgment for $24,065 and Hess appealed. Appellant's points of error all attacked the award of $24,065.00 on the ground that such losses were "special damages," as opposed to "general damages." The trial court stated the damages represented the benefit of the bargain for American. The Texas 12th District Court of Appeals found the damage award of $24,065.00 was properly characterized as an item of general damages. Hess contracted to replace an existing mold, which American was actively using in its manufacturing process. It should have been clearly foreseeable to Hess that if it failed to supply a suitable new mold to American within the time specified, American would be forced to obtain a mold from another manufacturer in order to meet its commitments to its customers. Since the cost was an item of general damages, it followed that allegations and/or findings of contemplation of said loss were not necessary to support the judgment. Appellant's points one through three were overruled.

Costs for re-performance are recoverable even with a limitation of liability clause that limits a party's liability to re-performance. In *CBI NA-CON, Inc. v. UOP Inc.*, 961 S.W.2d 336 (1997), Fina contracted with UOP for the designs for a fluidized catalytic cracking unit (FCCU) at Fina's Port Arthur refinery. UOP's liability to Fina was limited to re-performing at UOP's expense. UOP's contract with Fina also waived any special, consequential or indirect damages, including loss of use, loss of profits, plant or unit downtime, or suits by third parties. Fina also contracted with CBI to construct a catalyst cooler, which was part of the FCCU. UOP did not have a contract with CBI. Fina also entered into contracts with other parties, to modify the design, inspect, install, fabricate and manufacture certain components of the catalyst-cooling unit. The catalyst-cracking unit stopped operating properly, because the catalyst cooler failed. After the unit failed, Fina filed suit against CBI and the other companies, but not UOP, to recover damages in replacing the catalyst cooler and for $17,450,000 in consequential damages until replacement of the catalyst cooler. Fina made claims against CBI for negligence, breach of contract, breach of warranty, and strict products liability. Fina alleged CBI negligently breached warranties in connection with the construction of the catalyst-cooling unit. CBI filed a third-party claim against UOP for contribution. UOP moved for summary judgment. The trial court granted UOP's motion for summary judgment. CBI appealed.

The Fina/UOP contract expressly limited UOP's liability to Fina for any breach, loss or damage to re-performance. The only direct damages recoverable by

Fina against UOP for negligence was re-performance *or the cost of re-performance*. If Fina had pursued UOP for negligence in designing the catalytic cooler, UOP would be obligated to re-perform at UOP's expense. If UOP had not re-performed the work, then Fina would have been limited to a breach of contract claim for UOP's refusal to re-perform the work. CBI's claim was also so limited. Even if CBI could bring a tort claim, based on the derivative nature of CBI's claim, CBI's recovery was limited to that of Fina. Affirmed.

In *Anderson Development Corporation v. Coastal States Crude Gathering Co.*, 543 S.W.2d 402 (1976), Anderson Development agreed to construct two steel pipelines for Coastal States Crude Gathering Company. Anderson sued to recover damages for breach of contract, payment of retainage withheld by Coastal, and payment on an invoice for work performed. Anderson alleged Coastal's failure to supply proper right-of-way as required by the contract caused work to be done in the inclement fall months instead of the more desirable summer months; forced Anderson to construct in a piecemeal fashion; prevented completion of the job until 76 days after the date required in the contract; and caused Anderson $267,525.33 in excess of the amount Coastal was obligated to pay under the contract. Anderson's petition alleged that Anderson spent $267,525.33 over the $544,799.47 Coastal owed Anderson under the contract's Unit Price Schedule, that these sums represented the reasonable value of work done for Coastal, and that Coastal was obligated to pay the excess because its failure to supply proper right-of-way caused the expenditures. Trial to the court for recovery of the retainage and for the amount of the invoice resulted in a $69,943.59 judgment for Anderson, plus interest and costs. Anderson appealed.

Coastal asserted that Anderson claimed special damages, which were not specifically stated. According to the Texas Court of Appeals, because Coastal contracted to furnish proper right-of-way, which was a prerequisite to Anderson's doing any work, it was foreseeable that its failure to supply right-of-way would keep Anderson from progressing with construction and would cause Anderson additional expense in completing work. These were general damages. Anderson's points of error were sustained.

The date of the contract (and if amended, the date of the last modification) may also be important to distinguish direct from consequential damages. When the breach includes an unexcused delay in completion, if the completion date has been altered by consensual amendment, the contemplation of the parties is to be determined as of the date of amendment. *Roanoke Hospital Assoc. v. Doyle and Russell, Inc.*, 215 Va. 796, 214 S.E.2d 155 (1975). Knowledge that is not available at the time of contracting cannot be used later to prove that a contractor could foresee the damages. *Wills Elec. Co., Inc. v. Mirsaidi*, 2001 Tenn. App. LEXIS 915 (2001) (contractor held back $19,013 because the subcontractor had not fully paid all its suppliers or obtained lien releases. The subcontractor borrowed $25,000. The trial court ruled that the contractor was liable for consequential damages for the amount of interest associated with the subcontractor's loan. The appellate court found no evidence that at the time of contracting the contractor knew or suspected that failure to make complete payment would force the subcontractor to borrow money. After contracting, the contractor became aware that the subcontractor faced some financial difficulties).

All courts recognize that the difference in value of the building caused by the contractor or designer's breach is a direct damage. Whenever an item of owner damage strays from that formula the owner risks a court concluding the damage is consequential. For example, in *Wright Schuchart, Inc. v. Cooper Industries, Inc.*, (not published) 1994 U.S. App. LEXIS 31520 (9th Cir. 1994), an unpublished decision that also involved a waiver of consequential damages, the Ninth Circuit Court of Appeals rejected the contractor's claims for "direct damages" against an owner as calculated by its claims consultant as consequential despite the contractor's argument that otherwise it could not be made whole (because consequential damages are necessary to make any plaintiff whole); the direct damages were foreseeable (because foreseeability was immaterial); and if it could not collect its direct damages the contractor's exclusive remedy failed (because the contractor's lack of a remedy was the consequence of excluding consequential damages in the contract). The contractor sought:

> project supervisory personnel kept on payroll an extra 15 months; labor necessary to service and maintain equipment supporting the overall project; additional employee benefit costs (i.e. insurance, travel, rest breaks); provision of room and board to island personnel (46 man months); escalation in room and board costs that would not have occurred if project had been complete according to SWS schedule; additional electricity, telephone use, facsimile charges; opportunity losses from equipment tied up on the overall project; decline in value of assets due to harsh weather conditions on the island; costs incurred in demobilizing and mobilizing the island while Cooper [owner] redesigned the exciter control panels; loss of labor productivity and efficiency during delays and disruptions; loss of learning on the part of Wright employees due to disruption; additional site cleanup costs; additional subcontractor costs incurred due to change of schedule from the disruption; costs of preparing the claim against Cooper; and home office general and administrative costs.

According to the court, these damages were undeniably typical examples of consequential damages as that term was commonly understood. The court agreed with the contractor, however, that any costs it incurred by directly contributing to the repair of defective owner-furnished equipment were recoverable as direct damages. *Wright, citing Canal Elec. Co. v. Westinghouse Elec. Corp.*, 756 F. Supp. 620, 624, 627 (D. Mass. 1990). The contractor alleged direct repair damages under the label "back charges." The court did not agree that the contractor could recover amounts it expended facilitating the repair. The contractor could not also recover costs such as those associated with the demobilization and mobilization, for example.

However, restoration and replacement costs as means of determining damages may be allowed if diminution in the fair market value measure was unreasonable. In *Massachusetts Port Authority v. Sciaba Constr. Corp.*, 437 Mass. 1104, 766 N.E.2d 118 (2002), Massachusetts Port Authority was legislatively mandated to build a public park. The plan was to use an existing pier upon which to construct recreational improvements. The authority hired Sciaba Construction to perform the platform renovations. While the contractor was working with torches on the platform during a heavy windstorm, hot metal fell onto the creosote-treated wood members comprising the platform and its underlying pilings and supports, igniting them and causing severe damage. The authority filed suit, claiming that the contractor was negligent in performing "hot work" on a windy day without proper permission and without adequate safety precautions. The authority contended that roughly 61 percent of the platform, other than the pilings, needed to be replaced. The authority identified three options for completing the project. The first option was to completely remove the existing damaged structure and replace it with a new, entirely concrete, structure. The second option was to remove only the timber structure and replace it with concrete, but to leave the wooden pilings. The final option was to replace the timber members of the structure with new timber, while also leaving the existing pilings in place. A consultant arrived at net cost estimates for each option after deducting the amounts that would be saved by not proceeding under the pre-fire schedule of work. The contractor objected to evidence of the cost of repairs or replacement because the only relevant evidence on the question of damages was the difference in fair market value caused by the fire. The judge instructed the jury that ordinarily the measure of damages was the diminution of market value resulting from a wrongful act, but explained that an alternative method could be used. The jury awarded $1,049,130, which was identical to the net cost of replacing the pier as estimated under option 1. The contractor moved for a judgment notwithstanding the verdict and for a new trial. The judge denied the motions. The contractor appealed.

According to the appellate court, diminution in fair market value would not have been a fair and reasonable measure of damages. Even assuming that comparable sales of similar piers were available, or that expert testimony could have established the property's approximate fair market value before and after the fire, the judge had discretion to determine that the resulting figure would not compensate the authority for the special value the property held as a place to build a park, and would not have fairly represented the actual injury suffered by the authority. Replacing or restoring the pier was necessary because the fire had caused substantial damage. The authority was not in a position to sell the property and to find a new location on which to construct a park. Not only was the property part of a larger plan taking into account the surrounding area, but the authority was acting under legislative direction to build a park on the specific location. Prior to the fire, the pier was reasonably well adapted to the special purposes for which it was intended. The pier possessed a value to its owner that could not be properly weighed by using the ordinary methods of damage calculations. It was reasonable to allow the jury to hear evidence of restoration and replacement costs and to instruct them on the availability of those methods. Affirmed.

By presenting an owner's increased costs as part of the benefit of the bargain formula, a court fit owner delay costs into an accepted theory and avoid the risk of the court finding an owner's damages are consequential. The increased costs may be added to the square foot costs the building would cost, claiming the difference between the increased square foot costs to complete the building and the square foot costs estimated to complete the buildings. The added expenses also represent the *decreased* appreciation of the value of the space. Just because the space is worth more than now should not deprive the owner of the reduced appreciation costs. The court in *Noble v. Tweedy*, 90 Cal. App. 2d 738, 203 P.2d 778 (1949) (landlord refused to complete bowling alley for tenant. The court recognized the difference in value between the property as built and the value that it would have had if it had been built in accordance with contract plans and specifications as the exclusive measure of damage), allowed something similar when it affirmed an owner award for the difference in value of a bowling alley that included the additional costs to complete the project. Although no substantive difference from presenting its completion costs as "direct" costs as in *Wright*, the translation into a square foot costs permitted the appellate court to endorse the classic formula for calculating owner damages and eliminated the need for legal support for failure of remedy and other similar arguments.

Page 12-130, add at end of section:

Despite contractor delay, owner is not entitled to installation of more expensive fixtures that are installed quicker. For example, in *Harley Paws, Inc., d/b/a Three Dog Bakery v. Mohns, Inc.*, 249 Wis. 2d 488, 639 N.W.2d 203 (Wis. Ct. App. 2001), Mohns, Inc. and Harley Paws, Inc., contracted for the remodeling of a retail store. Mohns told Harley Paws that the construction should be completed in approximately five weeks, and estimated the cost to be $52,000. Based on that information, Harley Paws scheduled its grand opening for September 26, 1998. Construction commenced in early August 1998 and continued until September 11, when disputes developed primarily involving: (1) the modification, possible delay, and additional costs involving the construction of the store's cabinetry; and (2) the rescheduling of the faux finisher, who was scheduled to do the finishing painting on September 12, but could not because Mohns had failed to complete the preliminary painting. When Harley Paws discovered defects in the drywall and learned from Mohns' president, that the store would not be completed by the grand opening date, Harley Paws fired Mohns and arranged for other contractors to complete the remodeling. Harley Paws claimed that it cost $42,175.68 to complete Mohns' contract and sought damages of $28,958.82, including more expensive countertops necessary to complete the project on time. The replacement cabinetmaker could only guarantee the timely installation of Surrell countertops, as opposed to the less expensive Laminate countertops, for which Harley Paws had contracted with Mohns. Harley Paws subsequently sued Mohns for breach of contract. The court concluded "that the termination on the 11th of the contract and the hiring of replacement contractors was reasonable."

The trial court found that the subsequent cabinetmaker's use of the more expensive countertops required a $2,000-reduction in Harley Paws damages. The trial court's careful considerations were not erroneous, arbitrary, or excessive.

An owner's damages for cost to complete a project for a contractor may also have to be reasonable. The actual cost to complete may not be sufficient proof. Consider *Driver Pipeline Co. v. Mustang Pipeline Co.*, 2001 Tex. App. LEXIS 8403 (Dec. 20, 2001) (opinion withdrawn). Mustang wanted to build a 200-mile gas pipeline. Mustang hired Driver to dig the trenches and lay the pipe for the north 100 miles of pipeline. Because Mustang wanted to finish the pipeline by a specific deadline, it prepared a contract stating that the prices were based on 11 hours per day and seven days a week to meet a 14-week schedule (98 construction days), and specifying that the final completion of the pipeline within that time was of "great importance to the Company." And then the rains came. At the end of 58 days, Driver had finished only 15 miles of the pipeline and had laid off some of its crews and suspended operations. Driver proposed that Mustang give it additional time and money to finish the project. Driver took the position that rain delayed its work and that all parties understood that his bid was based on no weather delays. The owner of Driver testified that his bid took into account a 15-percent contingency for rain days. At trial, however, Driver testified that this was a "best-time" contract with no rain days included and that he relied on a clause allowing (but not requiring) Mustang to give them extra time in the event of weather delays. There was evidence that the builder of the south portion of the line sought and received a 30-day extension on its construction.

Mustang sued Driver for breach of contract, seeking costs to complete the project. Driver countersued for wrongful termination, seeking damages for termination, lost profits, and attorney's fees. Mustang sought damages of $4,065,286 because it cost that much more than the original contract price with Driver to complete the pipeline. At the conclusion of an eight-day trial, the jury found: Driver failed to comply with the contract; Mustang was not justified in terminating its contract with Driver; $2,104,601 would compensate Mustang for damages caused by Driver's failure to comply with the contract; and $2,515,958 would compensate Driver for damages caused by Mustang's unjustified failure to comply with the contract. The trial court found that the verdict was for Driver and that there was no evidence of probative force to sustain the jury's finding with respect to the damages question for Mustang. The court then rendered judgment in favor of Driver and Seaboard Surety against Mustang. The court awarded Driver actual damages of $3,146,728.33.

Mustang contended that the trial court erred by disregarding the jury's answer to its damage issue. There was substantial evidence of the amount that it cost Mustang to complete the pipeline. The jury charge contained language limiting any recovery to "the reasonable and necessary costs incurred to complete the pipeline less the amount agreed to between Mustang and Driver to construct the pipeline. The position taken by Driver and accepted by the trial court was that this evidence was legally insufficient because there was no evidence before the jury to show that the amount that was admittedly paid was "reasonable and necessary" to complete the work. Although there was substantial evidence about the extent of damages, there was no evidence from any source to suggest that the actual expenditures were reasonable or necessary—merely that those were the amounts expended in completing the pipeline. Mustang argued correctly that it was not necessary for the witnesses to repeat the magic words "reasonable and necessary" in order to provide evidence that expenses are in fact "reasonable and necessary." As long as the evidence sufficiently showed that the expenses were reasonable and necessary, it was not required that particular "magic words" be used by the witnesses. However, a plaintiff cannot recover damages just by proving how much it spent. It must also provide evidence that the amount spent was reasonable and necessary. Mustang presented no testimony that showed that the amount paid was reasonable or necessary. Evidence of the failure to complete the contract and the completion by another contractor did not suffice to show that the cost of the work was reasonable. The trial court correctly granted a j.n.o.v.

CHAPTER 13
ESTABLISHING THE BASIS OF LIABILITY

§ 13.02   BREACH OF EXPRESS PROMISES IN CONTRACT

[D]   Prime Contractor as Third-Party Beneficiary

Page 13-12, add after first carryover paragraph:

However, an electrical prime contractor was not a third-party beneficiary to the general prime contractor's contract with the owner as a result of clauses that made prime contractors liable to other primes for delay in *Kinback Corp. v. Quaker Constr. Man., Inc.*, 2001 U.S. Dist. LEXIS 16845 (M.D. Pa. 2001). Quaker was awarded the general trades contract and Kinback the electrical contract. The contract's general and supplementary conditions indicated that, "Costs caused by delays or by improperly timed activities or defective construction shall be borne by the party responsible therefor." The electrical contractor could perform its electrical work only after other trades had completed certain portions of their work. The construction project experienced delays as a result of the contractor being unable to meet any of its construction deadlines. The project began to operate out of sequence. Electrical work could not be installed in a productive manner until the building structure was reasonably complete. Because of the delays caused by the contractor, the electrical contractor had to accelerate staffing levels and work overtime. As a result, the electrical contractor incurred substantial additional costs by not being able to complete the project by its final completion date. The electrical contractor instituted an action against the contractor. The complaint alleged that the contractor breached its contract with the owner by not meeting its construction deadlines. As a result of the breach, the electrical contractor, an alleged third-party beneficiary to the deadlines in the contractor-owner contract, suffered injury.

The contractor filed a motion to dismiss because there was no privity between the electrical contractor and the contractor and the electrical contractor was not a third-party beneficiary of the contractor's contract with the owner. The electrical contractor contended that it was an intended third-party beneficiary to the time limits set forth in the contract between the contractor and the owner. The language did not explicitly confer third-party beneficiary status upon the electrical contractor. The benefit for the construction to be completed in a timely manner ran to the owner, not to the electrical contractor. There was no privity of contract between the electrical contractor and the contractor and the complaint's contract claim was dismissed.

[E] Other Third Parties as Beneficiaries

Page 13-14, add after carryover paragraph:

In *Jenne v. Church & Tower, Inc.*, 814 So. 2d 522 (Fla. Dist. Ct. App. 4th Dist. 2002), the court concluded that a course of dealing could not create third-party beneficiary status by. Church & Tower, Inc. contracted with Broward County to design and construct a detention center. The contract provided that the project was to be substantially completed within 548 days of the "project initiation" date. The anticipated completion date was October 4, 1997. Although the county began to occupy the facility in February 1998, a final Certificate of Occupancy was not issued until October 28, 1998. Sheriff Ken Jenne sued the contractor for breach of contract, alleging that the delay in completing the facility caused him to incur labor costs and expenses associated with transporting inmates to other counties, resulting in over $13 million in damages. The sheriff contended that he was the intended third-party beneficiary of the contract between the county and the contractor. The contractor moved to dismiss the complaint, arguing that the sheriff was not an intended third-party beneficiary and that damages were barred by the liquidated damages clause of the contract. The trial court dismissed the complaint with prejudice. The sheriff appealed.

The sheriff alleged that the parties intended that he primarily and directly benefitted from the contract. There was a federal court decree that ordered the sheriff to develop reorganization and jail population management plans for the jail system. The county requested construction proposals, which stated, "It is the intent of the County and the Broward Sheriff's Office that the program and schematic plans comply with the foregoing applicable laws." There was a proposal submitted by the contractor that the sheriff claimed "acknowledges that the contractor needed the sheriff's approval for performance under the contract and acknowledged that it would be working together with the sheriff throughout the project." The sheriff alleged that he purchased furniture for the jail, appointed his office personnel to the selection committee, and made decisions on site location and management. The factors did not confer third-party beneficiary status on the sheriff. Negotiations and dealings between the parties cannot modify a written contract to create the parties' "intent," when the lack of such intent was evident from the contract. The parties to the contract were the county and the contractor, and the contract involved the construction of a public facility funded by the county. The contract was intended to directly and primarily benefit the citizens of the county, not the sheriff. The sheriff received only incidental or consequential benefit from the contract's enforcement, so he was precluded from suing for a breach of it. An article concerning "Defective Work," gave the county, not the sheriff, the right to notify the contractor to make corrections. The liquidated damages clause allowing the county to recover delay damages indicated that the parties to the contract did not intend that the sheriff enforce a separate remedy for the same delay. Affirmed.

A subcontractor that is protected by owner's insurance coverage is not a third party beneficiary of the contractor's contract with the owner. In *Donald B. Murphy Contractors, Inc. v. King County,* 112 Wash. App. 192, 49 P.3d 912 (2002), Frank Coluccio Construction Company contracted with King County to construct a waterway project. The contractor subcontracted with Donald B. Murphy Contractors for the construction of a concrete access shaft. The contract assigned the contractor the responsibility of presenting subcontractor claims to the county for coverage. Any insurance proceeds were to be paid to the contractor, who would then have the obligation of paying to each subcontractor "a just share." The subcontractor encountered difficulties on the site, and completing the shaft cost more than anticipated. The subcontractor notified the contractor of the extra expenditures. The subcontractor submitted a claim to the county, through the contractor, for coverage under the county's Builders Risk Insurance policy. The county notified the contractor that it rejected the subcontractor's claim, stating that no coverage was available because the information supplied by the subcontractor did not describe any direct physical loss or damage to covered property. The subcontractor filed an action directly against the county. The basis of the action was a contractual provision between the county and the contractor, in which the county promised to procure and maintain "All Risk" builder's risk insurance on the project, including the interests of subcontractors. The county moved for summary judgment based on another contractual provision that expressly disclaimed any intent that subcontractors would be third-party beneficiaries to the contract. The trial court granted the county's motion for summary judgment. The subcontractor appealed.

On appeal, the subcontractor contended that the county's agreement to procure and maintain builder's risk insurance, including the interests of subcontractors, created an enforceable contract interest in favor of it under third-party beneficiary principles. The Washington appellate court explained that the plain language of the contract disclaimed any intent to have subcontractors be third-party beneficiaries. The contract provided instead for all claims by subcontractors to be handled through the general contractor. The procedure envisioned by the contract was clear, and the subcontractor initially followed it. The subcontractor corresponded with the contractor about its claim for a number of months before filing suit directly against the county. The provision for insurance including the interests of subcontractors showed the county's desire to benefit the subcontractor, but a desire to benefit a third party was not the same as an intent to assume a direct obligation to that third party. Because the contracting parties did not intend it, the subcontractor was not a third-party beneficiary to the contract. The subcontractor alternatively contended that the county breached an implied covenant of good faith and fair dealing. Because the county did not owe a contractual duty to the subcontractor, the claim was properly dismissed.

[F] Good Shepherds

Page 13-15, add after first full paragraph:

In breach of contract actions against the federal government, prime contractors have long been permitted to present subcontractors' claims on a pass-through basis against the government, even though the no-privity rule has barred subcontractors from recovering directly against the government. *Interstate Contracting Corp. v. City of Dallas, Texas*, 2003 U.S. App. LEXIS 2083 (5th Cir. 2003), *citing* Henry R. Kates, *Facilitating Subcontractors' Claims Against the Government Through the Prime Contractor as the Real Party in Interest*, 52 Geo. Wash. L. Rev. 146, 150 (1983); *see also Severin v. United States*, 99 Ct. Cl. 435 (1943), *cert. denied*, 322 U.S. 733, 88 L. Ed. 1567, 64 S. Ct. 1045 (1944) (in a breach of contract claim against the federal government, a prime contractor may recover damages on behalf of its subcontractor only if the prime contractor suffered actual damages); *J.L. Simmons Co. v. United States*, 158 Ct. Cl. 393, 304 F.2d 886, 888 (Ct. Cl. 1962) (a prime contractor suffers actual damages if the prime contractor (1) has reimbursed its subcontractor for the subcontractor's damages; or (2) if the prime contractor remains liable for such reimbursement in the future); *Folk Constr. Co. v. United States*, 2 Cl. Ct. 681, 685 (1983) (limiting the application of the *Severin* doctrine and holding that "a prime contractor is precluded from maintaining a suit on behalf of its subcontractor only when a contract clause or release completely exonerates the prime contractor from liability to its subcontractor").

Similarly, a number of states have permitted pass-through claims in cases involving state government entities. *Interstate Contracting Corp. v. City of Dallas, Texas*, 2003 U.S. App. LEXIS 2083 (5th Cir. 2003), *citing Clark-Fitzpatrick, Inc./Franki Found. Co. v. Gill*, 652 A.2d 440, 449 (R.I. 1994); *Frank Coluccio Constr. Co. v. City of Springfield*, 779 S.W.2d 550, 551-52 (Mo. 1989) (en banc); *St. Paul Dredging Co. v. State*, 259 Minn. 398, 107 N.W.2d 717, 724 (Minn. 1961); *Roof-Techs Int'l, Inc. v. Kansas*, 57 P.3d 538, 550-53 (Kan. Ct. App. 2002); *Metric Constructors, Inc. v. Hawker Siddeley Power Eng'g, Inc.*, 121 N.C. App. 530, 468 S.E.2d 435, 438-39 (N.C. Ct. App. 1996); *Schiavone Constr. Co., Inc. v. Triborough Bridge & Tunnel Auth.*, 209 A.D.2d 598, 619 N.Y.S.2d 117, 118 (1994); *Board of County Comm'rs v. Cam Constr. Co., Inc.*, 300 Md. 643, 480 A.2d 795, 795 (1984); *Kensington Corp. v. Michigan*, 74 Mich. App. 417, 253 N.W.2d 781, 783 (1977); *Buckley & Co., Inc. v. New Jersey*, 140 N.J. Super. 289, 356 A.2d 56, 73-74 (N.J. Super. Ct. Law Div. 1975); *D.A. Parrish & Sons v. County Sanitation Dist. No. 4*, 174 Cal. App. 2d 406, 344 P.2d 883, 888 (1959).

At least five states have not allowed a pass-through claim. *Interstate Contracting Corp. v. City of Dallas, Texas*, 2003 U.S. App. LEXIS 2083 (5th Cir. 2003), *citing Board of Governors for Higher Educ. v. Infinity Constr. Servs., Inc.*, 795 A.2d 1127, 1129 (R.I. 2002); *Farrell Constr. Co. v. Jefferson Parish*, 693 F. Supp. 490, 498 (E.D. La. 1988); *Dep't of Transp. v. Claussen Paving Co.*, 246 Ga. 807, 273 S.E.2d 161, 164 (Ga. 1980); *Barry, Bette & Led Duke, Inc. v. New York*, 240 A.D.2d 54, 669 N.Y.S.2d 741, 743 (1998); *APAC-Carolina, Inc. v. Greens-*

boro-High Point Airport Auth., 110 N.C. App. 664, 431 S.E.2d 508, 511-12 (1993).

Page 13-17, add after note 79 in carryover paragraph:

If the general contractor has entered into a liquidating agreement with the subcontractor, but fails to submit the subcontractor's claim, it may be liable to the subcontractor for the amount of the claim. *Shomar Construction Services, Inc. v. Lawman*, 693 N.Y.S.2d 784, 262 A.D.2d 956 (1999).

Some states permit pass-through claims only when there is a liquidating agreement in place that meets certain requirements, *Interstate Contracting Corp. v. City of Dallas, Texas*, 2003 U.S. App. LEXIS 2083 (5th Cir. 2003), *citing Bovis Lend Lease LMB Inc. v. GCT Venture, Inc.*, 285 A.D.2d 68, 728 N.Y.S.2d 25, 27 (2001) (a liquidation agreement has three basic elements: (1) the imposition of liability upon the general contractor for the subcontractor's increased costs, thereby providing the general contractor with a basis for legal action against the owner; (2) a liquidation of liability in the amount of the general contractor's recovery against the owner; and (3) a provision that provides for the "pass-through" of that recovery to the subcontractor); *Barry, Bette & Led Duke, Inc.*, 669 N.Y.S.2d at 743 (holding that a showing of actual contractual liability on the part of the contractor is necessary in order for a pass-through claim to be permissible), while other states permit pass-through claims when the prime contractor pleads the suit on behalf of the subcontractor and has an obligation to render the recovery to the subcontractor. *Interstate Contracting Corp. v. City of Dallas, Texas*, 2003 U.S. App. LEXIS 2083 (5th Cir. 2003), *citing Frank Coluccio Constr. Co.*, 779 S.W.2d at 551-52.

Page 13-17, add at end of first full paragraph:

A no damage for delay clause does not preclude a contractor from entering into a liquidation agreement with a subcontractor for the subcontractor's delay claim. In *Bovis Lend Lease LMB Inc. v. GCT Venture, Inc.*, 285 A.D.2d 68, 728 N.Y.S.2d 25 (1st Dep't 2001), GCT Venture, a developer retained Bovis Lend Lease LMB for the restoration and renovation of New York's Grand Central Terminal. The contractor was responsible to the developer for the performance of its subcontractors, although no contractual relationship was created between the developer and the subcontractors. The contractor had to submit a list of subcontractors for pre-approval to the developer for retail work. The subcontractors' contracts provided that the subcontractors' only recourse with respect to delays was to seek an extension of time for performance. The contractor alleged that the developer materially breached the general contract, which delayed and impeded the subcontractors' work, causing them to incur additional costs. The contractor alleged that it had entered into a Liquidation Agreement in which it had acknowledged its liability to the subcontractors for such claims, liquidated the amount of liability, and obligated itself to recover such amounts on their behalf. In its motion to dismiss, the developer asserted that the contractor had no contractual liability to its subcontractors due to the no damage for delay clauses in the subcontracts. The court granted the developer's motion. The contractor appealed.

The clause that the contractor would not be liable for any additional costs incurred as a result of delays caused by the developer was consistent with the general rule that, absent a contractual commitment to the contrary, a prime contractor was not responsible for delays that its subcontractors incurred unless the delays were caused by some agency or circumstances under the prime contractor's direct control. The contractor assumed liability in an agreement subsequent to the original general contract and subcontracts. While the developer and owner had a right of pre-approval as to any specific subcontractor who would perform retail work, there was no generic right to pre-approve contracts between the contractor and its subcontractors, or a specific right to pre-approve any liquidation agreement. There was no authority cited or found for requiring the contractor to have obtained permission from the developer as a condition precedent to entering into a liquidation agreement. The no damage for delay clause did not prevent the contractor from subsequently entering into the liquidation agreement. Since the elements for a liquidation agreement were met, the developer's motion should have been denied.

Page 13-19, add at end of section:

In some cases, a subcontractor may be able to recover for its delay costs caused by the government even though the prime contractor was not delayed. For example, in *E.R. Mitchell v. Danzig*, 175 F.3d 1369 (Fed. Cir. 1999), a subcontractor was allowed to recover against the owner for its unabsorbed home office overhead costs. The subcontractor incurred delay to the subcontractor's performance schedule due to the owner's correction of defective drawings, even though the owner's actions did not delay the performance of the prime contractor or the overall project completion schedule. The ruling may have no application in the case where the subcontractor's performance time is indicated on the overall project schedule but not specifically approved by the owner.

The burden of proof also varies among jurisdictions. *Interstate Contracting Corp. v. City of Dallas, Texas*, 2003 U.S. App. LEXIS 2083 (5th Cir. 2003), *citing Frank Coluccio Constr. Co.*, 779 S.W.2d at 552 (holding that the government/ owner has the burden of proving that the prime contractor has been relieved of responsibility to pay any recovery to the subcontractor); *Cam Constr. Co., Inc.*, 480 A.2d at 799 (same); *Kensington Corp.*, 253 N.W.2d at 784 (same) with *Claussen Paving Co.*, 273 S.E.2d at 164 (holding that prime contractor must prove that it is liable to the subcontractor before it can assert a pass-through claim); *Wexler Constr. Co. v. Housing Auth.*, 149 Conn. 602, 183 A.2d 262, 264-65 (Conn. 1962) (same).

In *Interstate Contracting Corp. v. City of Dallas, Texas*, 2003 U.S. App. LEXIS 2083 (5th Cir. 2003), City of Dallas, Texas and Interstate Contracting Corporation (ICC) entered into a fixed sum contract for the construction of levees around a City water treatment plant; the excavation of two areas to create storm water detention lakes; and some miscellaneous work including trash removal, surveying, and linear depth checking. In turn, ICC subcontracted with Mine Services, Inc. (MSI) for the levee construction and the excavation of the storm water detention lake. The subcontract between MSI and ICC provided, in part:

> In the event SUBCONTRACTOR has a claim for which the Owner may be responsible, the CONTRACTOR, in its sole discretion, may initiate with the Owner, at the SUBCONTRACTOR'S expense and which shall include attorney's fees, any dispute or claim procedures provided for in the Contract Documents for the use and benefit of SUBCONTRACTOR: otherwise SUBCONTRACTOR shall have full responsibility for the preparation of its claims and shall bear all expenses thereof, including attorney's fees . . . .
> CONTRACTOR shall be liable to SUBCONTRACTOR only to the extent of the amount, if any, actually awarded as a result of the disputes process: SUBCONTRACTOR shall be entitled only to the amount, if any, actually awarded as a result of the disputes process: and such amount when received by CONTRACTOR from the Owner shall satisfy and discharge CONTRACTOR from any and all liability to SUBCONTRACTOR for or on account of the acts or omissions of the Owner or its Architect or Engineer.

Hence, ICC was given the sole discretion to bring a claim against the City on behalf of MSI at MSI's expense. If such a suit was brought, MSI agreed to release ICC from further liability in exchange for whatever ICC recovered from the City.

The material excavated for the lakes was to be used, to the extent it met specifications, to construct levees. The Interior Borrow Lake (IBL) was one of the "borrow" sites the City designated as a source of fill material. Shortly after work began, MSI discovered that the materials in the IBL differed from what it expected. Due to a lack of suitable material, MSI was forced to manufacture material by mixing sand with the limited quantities of clay. The contract was silent on the issue of manufacturing fill material. Manufacturing material substantially decreased MSI's productivity and increased its costs. The parties discussed using fill from other sites that MSI believed were not designated as borrow sites under the contract. But using these sources was more expensive than the manufacturing process and, therefore, MSI continued to manufacture fill.

ICC informed the City of MSI's increased work, but the City indicated it would deny any claim contending that manufacturing fill was beyond the scope of the contract. ICC subsequently sought MSI's direct costs from the City and re-notified the City of its protest. The City also denied claims for costs regarding trash removal, linear depth checking, surveying, and "extended performance." All of the claims presented, except the trash removal, were injuries to MSI.

ICC filed its suit on behalf of MSI against the City for breach of contract, quantum meruit, breach of implied warranty, and fraudulent inducement. Prior to the commencement of the action, ICC and MSI entered into a detailed "Claims Presentation and Prosecution Agreement" concerning MSI's claims for significant project costs overruns due to the City's failure to disclose anticipated difficulties. The Agreement provided:

II. RECITALS

... E. MSI represents that its Claim is based on the conduct of the City and that it has no other claims against Interstate except MSI's claim that is the subject of this Agreement . . . .

G. Interstate and MSI agree that it is in their mutual best interests for Interstate and MSI to pursue a claim against the City of Dallas in the name of Interstate ("the Claim"). The Claim shall consist of MSI's Claim in the estimated amount of $4,062,584.00 plus a 15% markup for profit and overhead for Interstate and Interstate's own costs claim in the amount of $222,798.18 for jobsite costs and jobsite general and administrative costs associated with extended performance caused by the City's interference with performance of the Contract ("Interstate Claim"). The parties desire, therefore, to agree upon a procedure through which they will coordinate the preparation, presentation and prosecution of the Claim against the City of Dallas.

III. TERMS

... 1. MSI may pursue the Claim against the City in Interstate's name. Interstate shall cooperate fully with MSI including, but not limited to, passing on the Claim to the City and executing such documents that may be required to further the Claim to the City and executing such documents that may be required to further the Claim; and MSI shall cooperate fully with Interstate. MSI shall have the responsibility for the preparation of any claim, the presentation and prosecution of any such claim, and the conduct of any litigation . . . .

3. MSI shall diligently pursue the Claim. The right to abandon, settle, compromise or dismiss the Claim shall be shared by MSI and Interstate. Interstate and MSI shall each not settle the Claim without the others['] prior written approval . . . .

4. All costs, fees and other expenses (including expert and attorney fees) incurred by MSI in connection with the preparation, prosecution and litigation of the Claim shall be paid by MSI. MSI shall have no responsibility for any attorney fees or expenses that Interstate may elect to incur . . . .

6. From any amount paid in settlement of the Claim, Interstate and MSI shall be paid first for their respective markup (including profit and overhead). If the percentage of markup actually paid as part of any settlement or judgment is specified, the markup payable shall be calculated according to the June 21, 1995 Letter of Understanding agreement. If the markup is not specified then the settlement amount will be presumed to include a total markup of 15% and each party shall receive one-half of the markup or 7.5%. . . . The remainder of the settlement funds shall be prorated and paid between Interstate and MSI in the same percentage that each party's portion of the Claim (exclusive of markup) is to the total Claim (exclusive of markup) submitted to the City. . . .

The district court allowed ICC to bring its claims on behalf of MSI. Following an 11-day jury trial, the jury found that the City breached its contract with ICC. The jury also found the City breached an implied warranty to provide accurate and suitable plans and specifications in light of subsoil conditions at the project.

On appeal, the City argued that the district court erred in concluding that ICC could seek damages on behalf of its subcontractor MSI because there was a lack of privity of contract between the City and MSI. There was no privity of contract between MSI and the City. Under Texas law privity of contract was an essential element necessary to any recovery in an action based on contract. However, ICC argued that even though there was a lack of privity between MSI and the City, the district court was correct in permitting ICC, under Texas law, to present MSI's claim on a pass-through basis. No controlling precedent from the Supreme Court of Texas or the Texas Courts of Appeals existed to resolve the issues created by the conflicting contentions of the parties. Accordingly, in light of the absence of Texas authority on these issues and the varied interpretations of these issues by other state courts, the court of appeals certified questions to the Supreme Court of Texas regarding whether Texas law recognized pass-through claims, and if so, what were the requirements that needed to be satisfied for a contractor to assert a claim on behalf of its subcontractor.

§ 13.11   SELECTION OF REMEDIES

[A]   Termination and Rescission

Page 13-43, add after note 211 in second full paragraph:

In *Harley Paws, Inc., d/b/a Three Dog Bakery v. Mohns, Inc.*, 249 Wis. 2d 488, 639 N.W.2d 223 (2001), for example, Mohns, Inc. and Harley Paws, Inc., contracted for the remodeling of a retail store. Mohns told Harley Paws that the construction should be completed in approximately five weeks, and estimated the cost to be $52,000. Based on that information, Harley Paws scheduled its grand opening for September 26, 1998. Construction commenced in early August 1998 and continued until September 11, when disputes developed primarily involving: (1) the modification, possible delay, and additional costs involving the construction of the store's cabinetry; and (2) the rescheduling of the faux finisher, who was scheduled to do the finishing painting on September 12, but could not because Mohns had failed to complete the preliminary painting. When Harley Paws discovered defects in the drywall and learned from Mohns' President, that the store would not be completed by the grand opening date, Harley Paws fired Mohns and arranged for other contractors to complete the remodeling. Harley Paws subsequently sued Mohns for breach of contract. The court concluded that Mohns had breached the contract. In its findings of fact, the court explained that, given the need to be ready for the September 26 opening, the parties clearly understood that "time was of the essence." The court concluded "that the termination on the 11th of the contract and the hiring of replacement contractors was reasonable."

Mohns first argued that the trial court erred in finding that it was in breach of contract at the time Harley Paws terminated the contract. Mohns argued that anticipatory breach could not support the trial court's conclusion. Whether the trial court based its decision on an unarticulated theory of anticipatory breach or on a theory of actual breach was not necessarily determinative of the outcome. The facts supported the trial court's conclusion that Harley Paws breached the contract, that the breach could be viewed as an anticipatory one. The work had not progressed as scheduled and by September 11 it had become evident that the work would not be completed within the contracted time. Mohns had substantially underestimated the cost of the cabinetry and as of September 11 did not know who would construct the cabinets or when they would be installed. The contractors who replaced Mohns testified that Mohns' workmanship had been shoddy and delayed the scheduled subcontractors' work, further indicating that the job would not be completed on schedule. The new contractors worked 12 to 13 hours a day to complete the project by September 23. The court implicitly found that Mohns' words and actions constituted an anticipatory breach.

[B] Abandonment

Page 13-50, add at end of subsection:

This theory may not work for public construction contracts. For example, in *Amelco Electric v. City of Thousand Oaks*, 95 Cal. App. 4th 448, 115 Cal. Rptr. 2d 527 (S. Ct. 2002), the contractor alleged the public owner had abandoned the project in order to support its quantum meruit claim. The Supreme Court reversed, concluding that a public works contract in California could not be abandoned. The City of Thousand Oaks awarded Amelco Electric the prime contract for electrical work at the Civic Arts Plaza. Lehrer McGovern Bovis, Inc. (LMB) managed the project. Amelco expressed concern that the electrical drawings did not identify all revisions, or contain all prior revisions. Amelco requested a change order and $203,759 in additional funds to update the drawings. LMB refused. Amelco accepted this decision and signed a change order for zero dollars and zero additional time, because LMB verbally promised that, "things are going to get better." Things did not get better and Amelco performed a huge number of change orders in order to complete the work. Amelco submitted a $1.7 million total cost claim for costs allegedly resulting from the noncaptured costs of the change orders. While Amelco maintained daily records of its work activities, it was unable to produce documentation of instances in which its performance of change order was delayed or interfered with by LMB's actions, and for which it was not compensated. The person responsible for actually recording the information in the contractor's daily log testified he would not record changes. Amelco's vice-president asserted the sheer number of changes made it "impossible" to keep track of the impact any one change had on the project or on Amelco. Amelco conceded it was inefficient in performing the work, but assigned responsibility for virtually all of that inefficiency to LMB. The jury found the City had both breached and abandoned the contract, and awarded Amelco $2,134,586. The court of appeal concluded that as a matter of law a public works contract could be abandoned.

Under the abandonment doctrine, once the parties ceased to follow the contract's change order process, and the final project had become materially different from the project contracted for, the entire contract — including its notice, documentation, changes, and cost provisions — was deemed inapplicable or abandoned, and the plaintiff may recover the reasonable value for all of its work. If such a theory applied in the public works context, the notion of competitive bidding would become meaningless. Even assuming there was substantial evidence of abandonment, the parties could not abandon a public works contract, with its strict statutory requirements. If the City's numerous changes could result in the public contract being set aside in its entirety, Amelco would find itself in no different situation, and should receive no different treatment, than a contractor who has performed under a void contract.

Under the abandonment doctrine, the plaintiff need not demonstrate at what point the contract was abandoned. Amelco's project manager did not even determine Amelco had a claim on the project until after the work was completed. Under Amelco's approach, a certain number of changes may be permissible, but at some indeterminate point, the next requested change makes the number "excessive," the competitively bid contract was set aside, and the contractor recovered on a quantum meruit basis from the beginning of the project onward. Such a vague definition failed to provide any meaningful guidance as to when that line has been crossed. Public entities would not receive timely notice of claims that would allow them to make project management, budget, or procedural adjustments during the course of construction, thus creating intolerable uncertainty in the budgeting and financing of construction projects.

In addition, allowing contractors to recover in quantum meruit for the actual as opposed to the bid cost of a project encouraged contractors to bid unrealistically low with the hope of prevailing on an abandonment claim based on the numerous changes inherent in any large public works project.

California Public Contract Code § 7105 provided that a public works contract required to be awarded by competitive bid, may be terminated, amended, or modified only as provided in the contract or authorized under another provision of law. The compensation for amendments and modifications were determined by the contract. Amelco contended Public Contract Code § 7105 applied only to compensation for termination, amendment, or modification of a contract, not to damages for its abandonment. Given a public works project must generally be governed by a valid contract, abandonment could not be one of the changes "authorized under provision of law" contemplated by § 7105. Reversed and remanded for retrial on damages.

[C] Quantum Meruit

Page 13-52, add after carryover paragraph:

The general rule is that no quasi-contractual claim can arise when a contract exists between the parties concerning the same subject matter on which the quasi-contractual claim rests. When parties enter into a contract they assume certain risks with an expectation of a return. Sometimes their expectations are not realized, but they discover that under the contract they have assumed the risk of those expectations. As a result, they have no remedy under the contract for restoring their expectations. In desperation, they turn to quasi-contract for recovery. The law may not allow this. Generally, courts are hesitant to allow unjust enrichment claims unless there is evidence of fraud or bad faith, there has been a breach of contract or a mutual recission of the contract, when recission is warranted, or when the express contract does not fully address a subject matter.

Two cases illustrate the rule and the exception. In *Commissioners of Caroline County v. J. Roland Dashiell & Sons, Inc.,* 358 Md. 83, 747 A.2d 600 (2000), there was an express contract between the County and the contractor for the renovation of the Caroline County Detention Center. The recovery of money for work performed on the detention center was covered by several valid and enforceable provisions of the written contract between the parties. The contract clearly addressed the process for submitting claims, liquidated damages, and for the waiver of rights and duties as well as covering the basic guidelines for construction of the building addition. The court found the contractor's claim that the County had been unjustly enriched because of its use of the detention center was without merit. Even if the County was enriched, such enrichment was not unjust because it was in strict compliance with the terms of their contract. According to the court, both the County and contractor got what they bargained for by the terms of the contract.

In contrast, in *Abington Constructors, Inc. v. Madison Paper Industries,* 2000 U.S. App. LEXIS 4454 (1st Cir. Mar. 21, 2000), the owner requested bids on a project to reconstruct the Anson Dam waste gate and repair a power station. In order to conduct the repairs, both an "upstream" and a "downstream" cofferdam were necessary because much of the work would be done below the water level of the river. The conditions of the contract stated that a bidder could rely on "the general accuracy of the technical data" in the materials, but authorized only "limited reliance" on drawings. The bidding instructions placed responsibility on the bidder to be familiar with the site terrain. When the contractor visited the site to conduct an inspection, the river flows were too high for it to survey the river. When the owner's project manager later invited the contractor to revisit the site, the contractor declined. Later the contractor agreed to do the work for $808,500.

In its bid form, the contractor represented that it had carefully studied the subsurface conditions at the site. Although the conditions of the contract had been included in the project manual, the parties agreed to a purchase order to signal its acceptance of the contractor's bid, creating a contract. The purchase order referenced the project manual as well as the contractor's bid form in describing the work to be performed. The district court found that Abington committed a breach, although not in bad faith, by failing to conduct its own investigation.

Abington was forced to use 300 bulk bags filled with sand and 5000 smaller bags to construct the downstream cofferdam, rather than the 180 bulk bags and 250 smaller bags it had initially allocated, due to water levels and river bottom configurations that were different from specifications in the project manual. The route of the cofferdams also had to be altered due to the river bottom configuration. Abington conveyed to Madison its fears that surmounting these obstacles would create additional costs. It later memorialized its concern in a letter to Madison stating that it was compiling the costs associated with overcoming the unexpected conditions and requested that a change order be issued. Madison, however, did not respond. Over the next several months, a series of floods caused extensive delay on the project. The conditions provided that when high water flows caused delay, Abington would be granted an extension of time equal to the length of the delay. The conditions placed responsibility for any overtopping of the cofferdams due to the high water flows on the contractor. Nevertheless, prior to awarding Abington the project, Madison issued an addendum (Addendum I), stating that "in the unlikely event of a major flood, [Madison] will pay the direct replacement costs of cofferdams provided cofferdams have been completed and approved by [Madison] prior to flooding. Madison indicated that it would cover some, if not all, of the additional costs caused by the faulty specifications and high water flows. Abington relied on this statement in continuing to work on the project during subsequent high water flows even though it was entitled to delay performance under the terms of the contract. By mid-October it was working seven days a week in hopes of completing the project on schedule.

The contractor also sent a written memo entitled "Confirm Verbal Agreements," seeking a change order and reiterating Abington's position that the costs associated with repairs and dewatering of the site due to the previous flooding would be covered by Madison pursuant to Addendum I of the contract. Abington subsequently submitted documentation that it had incurred $180,000 in additional costs. The owner's project engineer then cautioned the contractor's project manager that he was not authorized to approve the amount and that new management might not be willing to pay all the additional costs. Moreover, at several subsequent construction meetings, Madison indicated either that it was reviewing the cost overruns or that they would be dealt with at the end of the job, never stating that it refused to pay. Madison's internal documents from this period show that it planned to set aside $100,000 for anticipated extra costs.

The contractor incurred $404,738 in disputed costs above budget. After assuming responsibility for over $121,000 in costs, Abington claimed $283,680 in costs from Madison and an additional 17.8 percent allowance, or $50,495, for overhead and profit, for a total of $334,175. Abington's complaint suggested a number of theories of liability including quantum meruit, unjust enrichment, mutual mistake, impracticability, and breach of contract. The district court found that although the parties had a contractual agreement, Abington was entitled to quantum meruit recovery for the additional work and costs resulting from the defects in the data in the project manual combined with high water flows which were the subject of post-contractual communications between the parties. It granted Abington an award of $334,175, the reasonable value of its services, but did not reach Abington's remaining theories of liability.

The owner appealed, contending that quantum meruit recovery was not available under Maine law when the parties have negotiated a contractual agreement and, even if it were available, the predicate elements for quantum meruit recovery are not found in this case. Where the parties have made an express contract, the court should not find a different one by "implication" concerning the same subject matter if the evidence does not justify an inference that they intended to make one. The fact that an express contract has been made does not prevent the parties from making another one tacitly, concerning the same subject matter or a different one. Further, the fact that a contract has been put into express words does not prevent the meaning and legal operation of those words from being affected by the process of "implication" from the conduct of the parties and from surrounding circumstances. The appellate court believes that Maine law permitted the contractor's claim for quantum meruit relief. If good faith efforts in the field to overcome adverse conditions and get on with the job could always be trumped by the original written contract, the arteries of commerce, particularly in construction, would harden. The contractor was entitled to pursue recovery on the basis of quantum meruit and that the evidence supported the district court's conclusion that the elements of quantum meruit existed.

[E]   Contractual Remedies

Page 13-56, add to end of first full paragraph:

Interpreting the Differing Site Condition clause that may permit recovery and other clauses in the contract that relate to below-ground interferences that may restrict recovery. Delays in relocating underground utilities are not unknown subsurface or latent physical conditions under a differing site condition clause. *Indiana Department of Transportation v. Shelly & Sands, Inc.*, 726 N.E.2d 1063 (Ind. Ct. App. 2001), the Indiana Department of Transportation agreed to administer federal funds to pay for road reconstruction for the city of Carmel. In preparation, the owner entered into a series of utility agreements to relocate utility facilities. The bid package contained estimates on when the various utilities would relocate their facilities. The owner awarded the contract to Shelly & Sands, Inc. Before the contract was awarded, the owner held a utility coordination meeting to discuss the timetables for utility relocation. Numerous conflicts in the timetable for utility relocation delayed the work. The owner extended the completion date. The contractor later submitted a claim for additional costs caused by the delay. The owner denied the claim. The contractor filed suit alleging the owner failed to timely relocate the utilities. The owner moved for summary judgment, which the trial court denied. The owner appealed.

The owner alleged that the contractor's delay claim was barred by clauses that limited the remedy for utility relocation delays to an extension of time. "Cooperation with Utilities" indicated that no additional compensation would be allowed for delays due to interference from moving utilities, but the time for completion was to be extended. "Contractor's Responsibility for Utility Property and Services" stated that the contractor assumed all risk for any delay or expense caused by public utilities, but also required the contract to be extended. The contractor contended that the language in the "Cooperation with Utilities" clause was internally inconsistent because it established a duty while at the same time relieving the owner from liability if it failed in the task. The clause did not relieve the owner of its duty under the contract. It merely shifted the risk of loss to the contractor and limited the remedy if delays occurred. Limiting the remedy for relocation delays did not render the owner's contractual obligations meaningless. The contractor also asserted that the clause concerning utility relocation was ambiguous when coupled with a differing site conditions clause because delays in utility relocation should be interpreted to be subsurface or latent physical conditions or unknown physical conditions of an unusual nature. The contractor also asserted that the contract was ambiguous because the contract allowed for contract cost adjustments based on unknown physical conditions limiting the remedy for utility relocation delays to time extensions. The utility fixtures, pipelines, and other appurtenances that needed to be relocated for the roadwork to proceed were known physical conditions. The utility fixtures were contemplated in the plans for the project and in the contract. The contract language was not ambiguous.

§ 13.12   CARDINAL CHANGES

[B]   Recovering Costs for a Cardinal Delay

Page 13-66, replace note 323:

Unpublished private contract.

§ 13.13   THE BURDEN OF PROOF

Page 13-67, add at end of carryover paragraph:

When the claim asserted by the contractor is based upon alleged government-caused delay, the contractor has the burden of proving the extent of the delay, that the delay was proximately caused by government action, and that the delay harmed the contractor. In addition, when the contract utilizes CPM scheduling, the contractor must prove that the critical path was prolonged in order to prove a delay in project completion. Some courts have stated that a contractual requirement for a schedule is not necessary of this obligation. *Morrison Knudsen Corp. v. Fireman's Fund Insurance Co.*, 175 F.3d 1221 (10th Cir. 1999). The critical path is crucial to the calculation of delay damages because only construction work on the critical path had an impact upon the time in which the project was completed. If work on the critical path was delayed, then the eventual completion date of the project was delayed. Delay involving work not on the critical path generally had no impact on the eventual completion date for the project. *Hoffman Construction Co. v. United States*, 40 Fed. Cl. 184 (1998) *citing G.M Shupe*, 5 Cl. Ct. at 728; *Kelso v. Kirk Bros. Mechanical Contractors, Inc.*, 16 F.3d 1173, 1177 (Fed. Cir. 1994); *J.A. Jones Construction Co.*, ENG BCA No.

6252, 97-1 B.C.A. (CCH) ∂28,918 at 144,168 (to be compensable, government-caused delay must interfere with the project's critical path and extend completion of the project).

Page 13-67, add to note 325:

1992

Page 13-67, add to note 328:

SIPCO Servs. & Marine, Inc. v. United States, 41 Fed. Cl. 196 (1998) (contractor had fulfilled its duty by informing NASA of patent ambiguity during the bidding process. At that point, the court held that the burden was shifted to NASA, as the drafter of the specifications, to correct the defect in the specifications. The court held that NASA's failure to solve the problem required it to pay the contractor the costs expended in excess of its bid).

CHAPTER 14
DISPUTE RESOLUTION FORUMS

§ 14.03   ARBITRATION

Page 14-11, add at end of first paragraph:

While arbitration is generally considered to be a consensual forum, in some construction contracts one party may have the right to choose between arbitration and litigation. For example, the following language may appear in a subcontract.

> The General Contractor shall have the sole and exclusive right to determine whether any dispute or claim arising out of or relating to this Subcontract shall be submitted to arbitration or to a court of law.

Similar provisions may appear in the construction contract between an owner and general contractor where the owner retains the right to decide whether to litigate or arbitrate. In either event, arbitration may not be a matter of mutual consent as one party has the unilateral right to decide whether to arbitrate.

Courts have considered whether such provisions are enforceable. For example, in *Stevens/Leinweber/Sullens, Inc. v. Holm Development and Management, Inc.,* 795 P.2d 1308 (Ariz. Ct. App. 1990), the general contractor filed suit against the owner and architect for the unpaid balance and to foreclose on its mechanic's and materialman's liens. The owner moved to compel arbitration pursuant to a provision in the construction contract. The construction contract also contained an addendum that gave the owner the option of arbitrating or litigating any disputes, and even allowed the owner to change its choice if it was timely exercised. The trial court denied the owner's motion to compel arbitration on the grounds that: (1) the arbitration provision was unenforceable because of the lack of mutuality; and (2) that the unilateral arbitration provision lacked consideration. On appeal, the owner argued that since the entire contract was supported by consideration, it was sufficient to support the arbitration option. However, the court reasoned that since the owner did not promise to do anything in consideration of the rights given to it in the arbitration provisions, there was a lack of consideration to support the arbitration option. Further, since arbitration provisions are independent and separate agreements, the owner could not "borrow" consideration from the main contract to support the arbitration provision. There was no mutuality because the owner had absolute discretion to choose arbitration or litigation.

Other courts considering unilateral arbitration provisions have similarly held that arbitration agreements must be mutually binding to be enforced. *R.W. Roberts Constr. Co. v. St. John's River Water Management Dist.*, 423 So. 2d 630 (Fla. App. 1982); *Miner v. Walden*, 422 N.W.2d 335 (1979).

There is no uniformity of case law in this area. Rather than being deemed "unilateral provisions," such arbitration agreements may be considered "discretionary" and as such are valid and enforceable. For example, in *Willis Flooring, Inc. v. Howard S. Lease Constr. Co.,* 656 P.2d 1184 (Alaska 1983), the subcontract gave the general contractor the "sole option" of requiring the disputes to be arbitrated or litigated. The subcontractor argued that the arbitration provision was a unilateral option to arbitrate, that it lacked mutuality of remedy and that it would be inequitable to coerce a party to arbitrate. The court rejected these arguments, and upheld the enforceability of the arbitration provisions, reasoning that it was neither unfair nor coercive to require the subcontractor to arbitrate. Arbitration is not so clearly more or less fair than litigation that it is unconscionable to give one party the right of forum selection. *Id.* at 1185-86.

Page 14-13, add after second full paragraph:

Another form of arbitration that may have application in construction is commonly known as "baseball arbitration." It is a form of binding dispute resolution where the arbitrators' award is limited to the choice of one of the two alternative offers made by the parties—an either/or resolution. A formal arbitration clause may include the following: "The parties shall exchange with one another and submit to the arbitrator(s) their last, best offer to the other. The arbitrator(s) shall select only one or the other of such two offers that are submitted and shall award such selection." Rumbaugh & Powell, *Baseball Arbitration: Part Two,* 23 Disp. Resol. Times 18 (Oct.–Dec. 2000).

Baseball arbitration provides a mechanism or incentive for the parties to resolve the dispute in a timely manner that gives them more control over the outcome of the process and the form of the award. Good faith attempts to be reasonable are often made by the parties to baseball arbitration, or at least the parties will attempt to avoid the appearance of being unreasonable for fear that their offer will not be selected by the arbitrator.

Baseball arbitration has the potential for being a good way to solve many types of disputes in the construction industry and to streamline the resolution of disputes. The value in baseball arbitration is that the parties may be motivated to resolve the dispute themselves when no trendsetting legal issues are at stake and business decisions can be made. For example, when the pricing of sole-source items is in dispute, it may give incentive to the seller to provide pricing information and negotiate in good faith. If the timely resolution of a dispute is crucial to the parties, an "either/or" decision may be made based upon expedited hearings. Pricing disputes related to extras, change orders, credits, and payments may be good areas for application of baseball arbitration. The resolution of multiple-item punch lists and substantial completion disputes could be done among the parties if they knew there would be an either/or decision in baseball arbitration. *Id.* However, some parties may resist the idea of such a simplistic decision-making process, which gives the appearance of being arbitrary.

§ 14.08   DISPUTES REVIEW BOARDS

Page 14-33, add after note 96:

The Disputes Review Board (DRB) members may visit the project site to keep abreast of the construction activities and potential problems. When a dispute arises between the parties, a hearing may be requested by the parties for the DRB panel to consider the issues. The results of the hearing may be a DRB panel recommendation that includes an explanation or reasons for the recommendations. The DRB panel results may be oral or written. Oral recommendations allow the parties greater flexibility in implementing the resolution of a problem, in addition to the benefit of a third-party independent review. Many DRB procedures require a written, advisory decision or report from the DRB panel. Typically, DRB written decisions are not binding on the parties, but are often accepted by the parties to avoid an escalation of the problem or a loss of credibility or trust between the parties to the construction contract. In certain circumstance, the DRB panel's recommendations may be admissible in court or other forums for certain limited purposes. The extent of the admissibility and other uses of the DRB panel recommendations should be addressed in the construction contract specifications or separate agreement dealing with the DRB process. *Expert DRB Panel and Administration,* 6 Punchlist 1 (Nov. 2000–Jan. 2001).

CHAPTER 15
SURETIES AND DELAY CLAIMS

§ 15.02   PAYMENT BONDS

Page 15-5, add to note 15:

See Recovering Delay Damages Against Payment Bonds—Part I, 21 Constr. Claims Monthly 1 (May 1999); *Recovering Delay Damages Against Payment Bonds—Part II,* 21 Constr. Claims Monthly 1 (June 1999).

§ 15.03   PERFORMANCE BONDS

Page 15-11, add after carryover paragraph:

However, just as a modification without notice to the surety may discharge the surety's obligations under the bond, an owner that demands the surety accelerate after rejecting the surety's offer to complete and pay liquidated damages may breach the performance bond. For example, in *St. Paul Fire & Marine Insurance Co. v. City of Green River,* 2001 U.S. App. LEXIS 6269, 6 Fed. Appx. 828 (10th Cir. 2001), the Wyoming Joint Powers Water Board constructed a 32-million-gallon-per-day water treatment plant. St. Paul Fire and Marine issued a performance bond to guarantee the contractor's performance. The construction agreement required substantial completion of the project by December 1, 1998 and included a time is of the essence clause with a liquidated damages penalty for time after the stated December 1 completion date. The contractor fell behind in construction of the plant and the board issued a notice of termination for default. This triggered the surety's obligations under the performance bond. The surety had several options in the event of contractor default, and chose to complete the project by September 24, 1999, paying the daily penalty after December 1, 1998. The board, however, informed the surety that it had stepped into the shoes of the contractor for all purposes and thus was bound by the time is of the essence clause and the December 1, 1998 completion date. The board rejected the surety's proposed performance and declared the surety to be in breach. The surety sued to be discharged from further performance obligations on the ground that the board had breached the terms of the performance bond. Both parties sought summary judgment. The trial court granted summary judgment to the city. The surety appealed.

Although the surety essentially stepped into the shoes of the contractor upon the latter's default, it did not follow that the surety was bound by the original completion date. The board would continue to be entitled to $2,500 per day liquidated damages, but the surety under the bond need only proceed with reasonable promptness. The appellate court concluded that because the surety selected one of the bond options available to it and was ready to proceed to completion, the board's rejection of its proposed performance breached the agreement. The surety's offer to substantially complete the project, by a date that the board conceded would have been acceptable, would have occasioned much greater expense. It was not unreasonable for the surety to seek compensation from the board for the cost of accelerating performance beyond the reasonable promptness standard the bond specified.

Page 15-11, add after note 55 in first full paragraph:

Liquidated damages clauses may serve to cap the takeover surety's liability for delay damages, shielding the surety against exposure for the owner's claims for consequential delay damages. Because the takeover surety stands in the place of the defaulted contractor, it assumes the rights and liabilities under the construction contract such as the liquidated damages provisions. *United States Fidelity and Guaranty Co. v. West Rock Development Corp.*, 50 F. Supp. 2d 127 (D. Conn. 1999).

Page 15-12, replace note 62 with:

Id. at 112.

Page 15-15, add after carryover paragraph:

In *Cates Construction, Inc. v. Talbot Partners,* 21 Cal. 4th 28, 980 P.2d 407, 86 Cal. Rptr. 2d 855 (1999), Talbot Partners hired Cates Construction, Inc. to build a condominium project in Malibu. The construction contract called for Cates to complete the project in eight months. The construction contract also required Cates to furnish a performance bond. Transamerica Insurance Company issued the surety bond in favor of Talbot as obligee. A fund control agreement required Cates to submit monthly applications to Talbot for reimbursement of costs incurred. The 23rd payment request was not paid because both Talbot's and Cates's records showed that Talbot had already paid several hundred thousand dollars more than the cost of work. Six months after the contract should have been completed, Talbot advised Transamerica that Cates intended to default and that Talbot already had paid everything it owed under the contract. Talbot demanded that Transamerica perform under the bond. Cates later abandoned the project. At the time of the abandonment, construction was not complete and some of the work was defective and required repair. Transamerica informed Talbot that Talbot had breached the contract by failing to make payments. Transamerica refused to intercede or arrange for performance of the contract, claiming a legitimate dispute existed between Cates and Talbot.

The court considered whether an obligee may of a construction performance bond recover in tort for a surety's breach of the covenant of good faith and fair dealing. The court concluded that the exceptional approach thus far reserved for breaches in an insurance policy should not be extended to breaches of a surety bond given to assure performance on a construction contract. Talbot argued that a performance bond was a form of insurance and that breaches in the performance bond could justify the same extraordinary remedies that are available in insurance policy cases. Transamerica argued that performance bonds were fundamentally different from insurance policies and failed to warrant similar treatment. The court held that a construction performance bond was neither an insurance policy nor a contract of adhesion. Obligees have ample power to protect their interests through negotiation, and sureties were deterred from acting unreasonably by the threat of stiff statutory and administrative sanctions and penalties, including license suspension and revocation. The court ruled that in the absence of an independent tort, punitive damages may not be awarded for breach of contract even where the defendant's conduct in breaching the contract was willful, fraudulent, or malicious. Since Talbot may not recover in tort for Transamerica's breach of the implied covenant of good faith and fair dealing, the award of punitive damages was reversed in its entirety.

Page 15-15, add after first full paragraph:

There are at least two lines of reasoning to bind the performance bond surety to the arbitration provisions in the contract signed by the surety's principal. The first rationale is that the subcontract and the arbitration clause are incorporated by reference into the performance bond. Given the proper factual circumstances, this position is accepted by many federal jurisdictions. *United States Fidelity & Guaranty Co. v. West Point Construction Co.,* 837 F.2d 1507 (11th Cir. 1988); *Exchange Mutual Insurance Co. v. Haskell Co.,* 742 F.2d 274 (6th Cir. 1984); *Compania Espanola de Petroleas, S.A. v. Nereus Shipping, U.S.A.,* 527 F.2d 966 (2d Cir. 1975), *cert. denied,* 426 U.S. 936 (1976). A different rationale may be employed when the surety steps in to complete the contract after its principal defaults. The obligee may then argue that the surety is bound by all of the terms of the contract it assumed, including the arbitration provisions. This position was accepted by courts in Pennsylvania, in *Buck Run Baptist Church v. Cumberland Surety Insurance Co.,* 355 F. Supp. 913 (E.D. Pa. 1973); and in Kentucky, in *U.S. Fidelity & Guaranty Co. v. Bangor Area Joint School Authority,* 983 S.W.2d 501 (Ky. 1998).

§ 15.04 SURETY'S RECOVERY OF DELAY DAMAGES

Page 15-18, add after note 100 in first carryover paragraph:

Other elements may also be necessary to support the surety's claims. For example, a surety is not entitled to relief for pre-takeover agreement claims if it is not a party to a contract prior to the takeover agreement. In *Fireman's Fund Ins. Co. v. England,* 313 F.3d 1344 (Fed. Cir. 2002), the United States Navy contracted with

Summit General Contracting Corp. to construct a government building. Fireman's Fund Insurance Company provided performance and payment bonds. The contractor and the surety executed a General Indemnity Agreement. The government terminated the contract for default after the contractor failed to complete the contract by the scheduled date. The government and the surety entered into a takeover agreement under which the surety agreed to complete the contract. The contractor was not a party to that contract, which did not mention the General Indemnity Agreement or its assignment of claims to the surety. The surety submitted a claim to the contracting officer seeking an equitable adjustment and/or rescission of assessed liquidated damages. Its claims related to delays in performance that the government allegedly caused, both before and after the takeover agreement. The contracting officer denied all the claims, and the surety appealed to the Board of Contract Appeals. The board dismissed the claims that arose before the takeover agreement. The board held that the surety was not a "contractor" under the Contract Disputes Act. The board also ruled that the contractor's assignment of its claims to the surety was barred by the Anti-Assignment Act. The board also rejected the surety's claim of equitable subrogation, determining the doctrine was inapplicable. The surety appealed.

On appeal, the government contended that the surety was not entitled to seek relief for pre-takeover claims under the Act since the surety was not a contractor prior to the takeover, and the contractor's assignment of its claims to the surety was invalid under the anti-assignment statutes. The surety asserted that, under the doctrine of equitable subrogation, the surety succeeded to the contractual rights of its contractor. According to the appellate court, before the assignment was made, no claims against the government arising from a default in the construction contract had arisen. The assignment of the claims in the General Indemnity Agreement was invalid. Neither equitable subrogation nor the Act provided the surety with any contractual rights prior to the takeover agreement. The statutes precluding assignment of any interest in a contract with the government rendered the contractor's assignment to the surety invalid, and the surety was not a financing institution, which was exempt from the statutory prohibitions. Also, prior to the takeover agreement, the surety was not a contractor that could pursue claims under the Act. While equitable subrogation otherwise provided an available remedy, the doctrine could not be used to expand jurisdiction under the Act. For the board to have jurisdiction under the Act, the claim must be brought by "a contractor," which was defined as "a party to a government contract," and be one "relating to a contract." The surety was not a party to any contract with the government prior to the takeover agreement it had with the government, and its pre-takeover claims did not arise under such a contract. Although the surety did enter into a takeover agreement, its claims all related to its pre-takeover agreement activities.

CHAPTER 16

AVOIDING AND MINIMIZING CLAIMS

§ 16.06   THE CONTRACT

Page 16-22, add at end of section:

Contract conditions also influence claims. Statistics show that construction is the riskiest of human work activities. The risks are generally allocated to the contracting parties in the construction project in accordance with standard terms of contract contained in standard contract forms. Experience shows that a significant number of disputes in construction arise from the application and interpretation of the special standard conditions of contract used. It must, therefore, be realized that where parties choose to super-impose a set of conditions into their contract, these conditions take effect as an agreed legal code in addition to the applicable law of their contract. Therefore, in construction there is an additional area of law to be mastered, which is continuously evolving and being refined to meet the particular type of project envisaged by the owner or promoter and his advisory team. N. Bunni, *Construction Disputes on the Eve of the New Millennium,* 65 Arbitration 308, at 310 (No. 4, Nov. 1999).

While it is true that construction disputes tend to turn on questions of fact, they do frequently give rise to two different types of law issues. The first is related to issues of general law, such as negligence and the rights and obligations of the contracting parties and others. More important, however is the second type of legal issue, which is more frequent and which arises out of the standard conditions of contract used on the project. These conditions have developed into specialized areas of the law and have crossed national frontiers to form an international legal code for construction activities. They have been very successful in coping with any conflict of laws which may have existed between the various legal systems involved. Bunni, at 312.

TABLE OF CASES

References are to sections.

INDEX TO SUPPLEMENT

References are to sections.

REVISED INDEX
TO MAIN VOLUME

References are to chapters (Ch.) and sections.

D

Daily logs, proof of delay and, 8.08
Damages, Ch. 12
    acceleration claims, 6.07
    accuracy of claim, importance of, 12.01
    attorney fees. *See* Attorney fees
    bond premiums, 12.17
    calculation, theories, 12.04
    cardinal changes, resulting from,
        13.12[B]
    changes clauses, limitations, 3.02[F]
    characterizing damages, 12.03
    checklists, 1.05[D], 12.21
    compensable delay and, 1.01[B]
    compensation as synonymous with, 12.03
    concurrent delay and, 1.01[D]
    consequential damages
        owners' damages, 12.19[B]
        recovery precluded, 12.18
    critical delay and, 1.01[C]
    efficiency, loss of, 5.04
    Eichleay formula, 12.06[A]
        change order overhead, 12.06[E]
    emotional distress, recovery for pre-
        cluded, 12.19[B]
    escalation. *See* Escalation
    excusable delay, not allowed, 1.01[A]
    extended general conditions, recovery
        for, 12.05
    historical development, 12.02
    Hudson formula, 12.06[D]
    idle equipment costs. *See* Idle equip-
        ment costs
    importance of proving damages, 12.01
    insurance premiums, 12.17
    interest. *See* Interest
    jury verdict method, 12.04[A]
        loss of productivity claims, 5.07
    liquidated damages. *See* Liquidated
        damages
    mental anguish, recovery for pre-
        cluded, 12.19[B]
    mitigation, duty of, 12.20
    modified total cost method,
        12.04[B][3]
        loss of productivity claims, 5.07
    nonrecoverable damages, 12.18
    overhead costs. *See* Overhead costs
    overview, 12.01
    owners' damages. *See* Owners
    payment bonds, liability of sureties,
        15.02
    performance bonds, liability of
        sureties, 15.03
    preparation of claims, costs of, 12.16
    productivity, loss of. *See* Productivity,
        loss of
    profits, loss of. *See* Profits, loss of

prospective pricing, 12.04
    punitive damages, 12.11
    quantum meruit. *See* Quantum meruit
    required elements, 1.02
    retroactive pricing, 12.04
    speculative damages, recovery pre-
        cluded, 12.18
    substantial completion, upon, 2.04[B]
    sureties, recovery, 15.04
    total cost method. *See* Total cost
        method
Davis-Bacon Act, submission of claims
        prior to final payment under, 9.02
Deceit. *See* Fraud
Default
    performance bonds, recovery on,
        requirements, 15.03
    termination of contract for, 2.14[A]
Defective design
    cardinal change, causing, 13.12[A]
    designer responsibility, 3.03[A]
    owner responsibility, 3.02[D]
Definitions, Ch. 1
    acceleration, 1.04, 6.01
    cardinal change, 13.12[A]
    compensable delay, 1.01[B]
    concurrent delay, 1.01[D]
    constructive acceleration, 6.02, 6.05
    convenient unit price, 5.02
    critical delay, 1.01[C]
    delay, 1.01
    directed acceleration, 6.02
    disruption, 1.03
    escalation, 12.09
    excusable delay, 1.01[A]
    learning curve, 5.02
    lost efficiency, 5.02
    mortatory interest, 12.10
    negligence, 13.07
    noncompensable delay, 1.01[B]
    noncritical delay, 1.01[C]
    nonexcusable delay, 1.01[A]
    prejudgment interest, 12.10
    substantial completion, 2.04[A]
Design
    avoiding delay, 16.04
        constructability assessments, 16.04[E]
        coordination, 16.04[B]
        predesign stage, 16.04[A]
        review, 16.04[B]
    constructability assessments, avoiding
        delay, 16.04[E]
    coordination, avoiding delay,
        16.04[B]
    defective
        cardinal change, causing, 13.12[A]
        designer responsibility, 3.03[A]
        owner responsibility, 3.02[D]
    drawings. *See* Drawings

F

False Claims Act, federal contracts, false
   claims under, 9.06[A]
FAR. *See* Federal Acquisition Regulations
Fast track construction, 7.03
   potential for delay, 7.03[A]
Federal Acquisition Regulations (FAR)
   bid protests, time for, 2.03[A][1]
   contracts, obligation to accelerate,
     6.04
   interest, recovery under, 12.10[A]
   overhead costs, unallowable costs,
     12.06[G][1]
   preparation of claims, costs of as
     damages, 12.16
Federal Acquisition Streamlining Act of
   1994, federal contracts, claims
   under, 9.06[A]
Federal Arbitration Act (FAA), vacating
   awards under, 14.03[C]
Federal contracts, processing claims,
   9.06[A]
Federation International des Ingenieurs-
   Conseils (FIDIC)
   contracts
     delay standards, 1.01[A]
     obligation to accelerate, 6.04
   termination of contract, 4.08
Flow-down clauses, 2.16[A]
Force majeure clauses, 1.01[A]
Foreseeability
   cardinal changes, 13.12[A]
   differing site conditions. *See* Differing
     site conditions clauses
   excusable delay and, 1.01[A]
Forum Committee on the Construction
   Industry
   arbitration of delay claims, 14.03
   mediation, statistics, 14.05
   task force on alternative rules, 14.03[B]
Fraud
   elements of, 13.08
   liability based on, 13.08
   loss of productivity, as basis of liabil-
     ity for, 5.06[A]
   no damages for delay clauses, excep-
     tion to, 2.16[E]
Funds, change orders, additional funds
   for, 9.04

G

General contractors
   completing contractors, liability of
     sureties to, 15.05
   delay caused by. *See* Contractor-
     caused delay
   scheduling, powers, 2.09

   selection, avoiding delay, 16.05[A]
General Services Administration (GSA),
   use of mini-trials, 14.07
Geological data, proof of delay and, 8.08
Geological studies, avoiding delay,
   16.04[A]
Global impact method, 11.07[E]
Good shepherd rule, 13.02[F]
GSA (General Services Administration),
   use of mini-trials, 14.07
Guarantees. *See* Warranties

H

Hazardous materials, abatement studies,
   avoiding delay, 16.04[A]
Hearings, arbitration, 14.03[B]
Hindrance. *See* Interference
Historical data, loss of productivity
   claims, as evidence in, 5.06[F]
Historical development, damages, 12.02
Home office overhead costs. *See* Over-
   head costs
Hudson formula, 12.06[D]

I

ICE (Institution of Civil Engineers), obligation to accelerate contracts, 6.04
Idle equipment costs, 12.07
   challenges to rates, 12.07[C]
   nonproductive equipment, 12.07[B]
   published equipment rates, use of,
     12.07[A]
Implied promises, breach of contract
   claims, 13.03
   contractual remedies contrasted,
     13.11[E]
Implied warranties
   adequacy of specifications, 3.02[D]
   liability for breach of, 13.05
     contractual remedies contrasted,
       13.11[E]
Incentive/disincentive approach, reducing performance period by,2.03
Indemnity
   limitation of liability, 13.06
   liquidated damages, recovery of, 2.15[C]
   performance bonds, requirements,
     15.03
Information technology, proof of delay
   and, 8.08
Injunctions, 13.11[D]
Inspections
   designer-caused delay and, 3.03[D]
   differing site conditions, for, 2.12[C]
   owner responsibility for, 3.02[B]

Institution of Civil Engineers (ICE),
    obligation to accelerate contracts,
    6.04
Insurance premiums as damages, 12.17
Interest
    business costs, as, 12.10[A]
    capital, on, 12.10[B]
    damages, as, 12.10
    mortatory interest, 12.10
    prejudgment interest. *See* Prejudgment
        interest
Interference
    implied promise against, 13.03
    no damages for delay clauses, excep-
        tion to, 2.16[E]
    owner-caused delay and, 3.02[G]
Interim completion dates, 2.06

J

Job cost accounting, recognition of delay,
    use in, 8.03[B]
Job meetings, avoiding delay, 16.09[B]
Joinder of parties, arbitration,
    14.03[A]
Joint ventures, federal contracts, process-
    ing claims, 9.06[A]
Judges, litigation before, 14.02[B]
Juries, litigation before, 14.02[B]
Jurisdiction
    Court of Federal Claims, claims under
        federal contracts, 9.06[A]
    payment bonds, recovery on, 15.02
Jury verdict method, 12.04[A]
    loss of productivity claims, damages,
        5.07

L

Labor, loss of efficiency, increased labor
    forces as cause of, 5.05[A]
Labor costs
    acceleration claims
        additional costs, 6.01[B]
        recovery of, 6.07
    changes, effect of, 2.11
    escalation, 12.09[A]
    payment bonds, recovery on, 15.02
Labor disputes, excusable delay and,
    3.06[C]
Lane rental method, reducing perfor-
    mance period by, 2.03
Learning curve
    defined, 5.02
    productivity, affecting, 12.08
Liability, Ch. 13

anticipatory repudiation, for, 13.04
breach of contract. *See* Breach of
    contract
checklists, 3.01[A]
concurrent delay, apportionment,
    1.01[D]
express warranties, breach of, 13.05
fraud, based on, 13.08
implied warranties, breach of, 13.05
indemnity, limitation of liability,
    13.06
misrepresentation, based on, 13.08
negligence. *See* Negligence
overview, 13.01
selection of remedies, 13.11
statutory violations, 13.10
strict liability in tort, 13.09
Licenses, owner responsibility for,
    3.02[B]
Linear scheduling method, 11.03
Liquidated damages
    abandonment of project, when al-
        lowed, 2.15[B]
    adjustments, 2.15
    allocation of liability, 13.11[E]
    amounts, establishing, 2.15[E]
    apportionment of delay, 2.15[A]
    assessment, 2.15[C], 2.15[E], 8.11
    change orders waiving, 2.15[D]
    checklists, 1.05[C]
    concurrent delay, apportionment,
        1.01[D]
    contractual clauses, 2.15
    contractual provisions, 13.11[E]
    disincentives, enforceability, 2.15
    excusable delay, not allowed, 1.01[A]
    indemnity, recovery under, 2.15[C]
    nonconforming work and, 3.04[D]
    nonexcusable delay, allowed, 1.01[A]
    penalties, when constituting, 2.15,
        13.11[E]
    performance bonds, recovery on,
        15.03, 15.03[A]
    required elements, 1.02
    retainage, 2.15[C], 8.11
    subcontractor-caused delay and, 3.05
    subcontractors, assessed against,
        2.15[C]
    substantial completion, effect of,
        2.04[B], 2.15[C]
    termination of contract, when allowed,
        2.15[B]
    terms, establishing, 2.15[E]
    waiver, 2.15[D], 12.19[B], 13.11[E]
Litigation, 14.02
    appeals, 14.02[D]
    burden of proof, 14.02[C]
    complaints, 14.02

202

U

V

W

Z